Women & Antitrust
Voices from the Field

Curation & Foreword
Kristina Nordlander

Editors
Nicolas Charbit
Sonia Ahmad

Copyright © 2020 by Institute of Competition Law
106 West 32nd Street, Suite 144, New York, NY 10001, USA
www.concurrences.com
books@concurrences.com

First Printing, November 2020
978-1-939007-87-2 (paperback)
LCCN: 2020933462

Cover: Yves Buliard, www.yvesbuliard.fr
Book design and layout implementation: NordCompo

Concurrences Books

Liber Amicorum

Laurence Idot – Liber Amicorum
Christophe Lemaire, Francesco Martucci (ed.), 2022

Eleanor Fox – Liber Amicorum
Nicolas Charbit, Sonia Ahmad (ed.), 2021

Herbert Hovenkamp – Liber Amicorum
Nicolas Charbit, Sonia Ahmad (ed.), 2021

Albert Foer – A Consumer Voice in the Antitrust Arena
Nicolas Charbit, Sonia Ahmad (ed.), 2020

Richard Whish – Taking Competition Law Outside the Box
Nicolas Charbit, Sonia Ahmad (ed.), 2020

Frédéric Jenny – Standing Up for Convergence and Relevance in Antitrust, Vol. I & II
Nicolas Charbit, Sonia Ahmad (ed.), 2019 & 2021

Wang Xiaoye – The Pioneer of Competition Law in China
Adrian Emch, Wendy Ng (ed.), 2019

Douglas H. Ginsburg – An Antitrust Professor on the Bench, Vol. I & II
Nicolas Charbit, et al. (eds), 2018 & 2020

Ian S. Forrester – A Scot Without Borders, Vol. I & II
Assimakis Komninos et al. (ed.), 2015

William E. Kovacic – An Antitrust Tribute, Vol. I & II
Nicolas Charbit et al. (ed.), 2013 & 2014

Practical Books

Competition Law Dictionary
Deborah Healey, William Kovacic, Pablo Trevisan, Richard Whish (ed.) 2021

Competition Law & Environmental Sustainability
Simon Holmes, Dirk Middelschulte, Martijn Snoep (ed.), 2021

Perspectives on Antitrust Compliance
Anne Riley, Andreas Stephan, Anny Tubbs (ed.), 2021

Information Exchange and Related Risks – A Practical Guide
Eric Meiring, Marcio Dias Soares (ed.), 2021

State Aid & National Enforcement
Jacques Derenne, Denis Jouve, Christophe Lemaire, Francesco Martucci (ed.), 2021

Merger Control in Latin America – A Jurisdictional Guide
Paulo Burnier da Silveira & Pamela Sittenfeld (ed.), 2020

Competition Inspections under EU Law
Nathalie Jalabert-Doury, 2020

Competition Digest – A Synthesis of EU, US and National Leading Cases, 4th ed.
Frédéric Jenny (ed.), 2020

Gun Jumping in Merger Control – A Jurisdictional Guide
Catriona Hatton, Yves Comtois, Andrea Hamilton (ed.), 2019

Choice – A New Standard for Competition Analysis?
Paul Nihoul et al., 2016

PhD Theses

Essays in Industrial Organization: Competition and Regulation in Network Industries
Jean-Marc Zogheib, 2021

The Role of Media Pluralism in the Enforcement of EU Competition Law
Konstantina Bania, 2019

Buyer Power in EU Competition Law
Ignacio Herrera Anchustegui, 2017

General Interest

Women & Antitrust – Voices from the Field, Vol. I & II
Evelina Kurgonaite & Kristina Nordlander (ed.), 2020

Conference Proceedings

Antitrust in Emerging and Developing Countries, Vol I & II
Eleanor Fox, Harry First (ed.), 2015 & 2016

Global Antitrust Law – Current Issues in Antitrust Law and Economics
Douglas Ginsburg, Joshua Wright (ed.), 2015

Competition Law on the Global Stage: David Gerber's Global Competition Law in Perspective
David Gerber, 2014

e-Book versions available for
Concurrences+ subscribers

Foreword

KRISTINA NORDLANDER

The vibrant antitrust community reflected in these pages makes me proud. Readers will find reflections and conversations among many of the leading lights in the field – women who have headed major enforcement agencies, advocated on behalf of large multinationals, led policy development among national competition authorities, coordinated complex multi-jurisdictional cases, headed large in-house legal teams and compliance programs, drafted and developed key guidance for the assessment of mergers and cooperation among competitors, and much more. Our different roles as in-house counsel, enforcers, private practitioners, academics, judges, and so on are reflected in this volume in a rich set of interviews and profiles.

What attracted these women to antitrust? How did they navigate their paths to the leading and game-changing roles they have performed? What advice do they have for younger professionals just starting careers in antitrust? You will find perspectives from Europe, the United States, Asia, and Latin America. In many cases, our interviewers and interviewees have coordinated enforcement and policy or worked across multiple jurisdictions. The learnings, reflections, and wisdoms shared here will be of interest to all lawyers – both women and men – in our global antitrust community.

The attractions of an antitrust practice are many – it is a creative field of law and policy where good lawyering can really make a difference; where law meets economics, advocacy, politics, and ever-changing market factors. Never a dull moment. Always a challenge.

Women & Antitrust is a timely and important topic. It is certainly a topic that has shaped my own career in both good ways and bad. The many talented and supportive male mentors that have allowed me to learn and grow and handle big cases with important clients have shaped my career in a wonderful way. I count myself lucky to have worked with and learned from many of the best in the field. That said, I have never in my entire career worked directly with a female antitrust law firm partner. The lack of a female role model, of someone to support me and share experiences of juggling work in the competition team with motherhood, was striking.

To contribute to creating the network I felt was needed, I started the Women's Competition Network (WCN) in 2008. The aim was and continues to be to connect and build a community of senior partner-level women in competition roles in law firms, companies, regulators, consultancies, courts, enforcement agencies, media, and so on. Pre-COVID-19, we had held 45 in-person networking events featuring as speakers top EU and US enforcers, in-house counsel, and judges, among others. The WCN has given me the enormous pleasure of getting to know most of the amazingly talented women featured in this volume. Readers will no doubt agree that the different perspectives on our practice reflected in these pages are enriching. I hope this book will help profile female talent in our field and serve as inspiration and encouragement to younger generations. There is no doubt that the combination of women and antitrust is a fact and a force to be reckoned with.

Being a European and a Scandinavian, I have to give special mention to European Union Commissioner Margrethe Vestager – no one (male or female) has done more to put antitrust enforcement on the global map and in the headlines. There can be no doubt that being a woman and mother presents no impediment to her brilliant achievements. Her guiding mantra of "fairness" has perhaps brought a more female touch to antitrust enforcement, but without compromising its strength and focus.

I am proud to present the reflections and voices of this vibrant community of professionals, and I am sure you will join me in thanking all our amazing contributors.

Enjoy your reading!

Contributors

Rima Alaily
Microsoft
Redmond

Hanna Anttilainen
DG COMP, European
Commission
Brussels

Inge Bernaerts
DG COMP, European
Commission
Brussels

Sarah Biontino
Biontino Europe
Brussels

Sarah Blazek
Noerr
Munich

Kelig Bloret-Dupuis
Essilor
Paris

Rachel Brandenburger
Hogan Lovells /
University of Oxford
New York

Anne-Sophie Choné-Grimaldi
University Paris Nanterre
Nanterre

Leonor Cordovil
Grinberg Cordovil Advogados
São Paulo

Lilla Csorgo
Charles River Associates
Sydney

Leonor Davila
Intel
Santa Clara

Angélique de Brousse
Johnson & Johnson
Brussels

Tal Eyal-Boger
Fischer Behar Chen Well
Orion & Co
Tel Aviv

Deborah Feinstein
Arnold & Porter
Washington, DC

Kathleen Foote
California Department
of Justice
San Francisco

Eleanor Fox
New York University
New York

Michal Gal
University of Haifa
Haifa

Deborah Garza
Covington & Burling
Washington, DC

Michal Halperin
Israel Competition Authority
Jerusalem

Catriona Hatton
Baker Botts
Brussels

Grania Holzwarth
Deutsche Telekom
Brussels

Xiaojin (Jenny) Huang
Tencent
Beijing

Laurence Idot
University Paris II
Panthéon-Assas
Paris

Bojana Ignjatovic
RBB Economics
Brussels / London

Elaine Johnston
Allen & Overy
New York

Nicole Kar
Linklaters
London

Karen Kazmerzak
Sidley Austin
Washington, DC

Lina Khan
Columbia University
New York

Birgit Krueger
German Competition Authority
Bonn

Gail Levine
Federal Trade Commission
Washington, DC

Lindsay Lutz
Intel
Santa Clara

Josephine Mackintosh
Competition and Markets
Authority
London

Deborah Majoras
Procter & Gamble
Cincinnati

Janet McDavid
Hogan Lovells
Washington, DC

Gabriella Muscolo
Italian Competition Authority
Rome

Edurne Navarro
Uría Menéndez
Brussels / Madrid

Nicola Northway

Maureen Ohlhausen
Baker Botts
Washington, DC

Sofia Oliveira Pais
Catholic University of Portugal
Porto

Johanne Peyre
Pearson
New York

Lisa Phelan
Morrison & Foerster
Washington, DC

Elizabeth Prewitt
Latham & Watkins
New York

Maria Raptis
Skadden, Arps, Slate,
Meagher & Flom
New York

Amanda Reeves
Latham & Watkins
Washington, DC

Elisabetta Righini
Latham & Watkins
Brussels

Anne Riley
Independent Antitrust
Compliance Consultant
Shropshire

Fiona Schaeffer
Milbank
New York

Lauren Stiroh
NERA Economic Consulting
New York

Mariana Tavares de Araujo
Levy & Salomão
Rio de Janeiro

**María Luisa (Marisa) Tierno
Centella**
DG COMP, European
Commission
Brussels

Deirdre Trapp
Freshfields Bruckhaus Deringer
London

Emma Trogen
Cosmetics Europe
Brussels

Ingrid Vandenborre
Skadden, Arps, Slate,
Meagher & Flom
Brussels

Christine Varney
Cravath, Swaine & Moore
New York

Anna Vernet
DG COMP, European
Commission
Brussels

Suzanne Wachsstock
Walmart
Washington, DC

Elizabeth Xiao-Ru Wang
Compass Lexecon
Boston / Beijing

Diane Wood
US Court of Appeals
for the Seventh Circuit
Chicago

Stéphanie Yon-Courtin
European Parliament
Strasbourg

Angela Huyue Zhang
The University of Hong Kong
Hong Kong

Franziska Zibold
Cruz Vilaça Advogados
Lisbon

Table of Contents

Part I – Enforcers & Academics

Part II – In-House Counsel & Consultants

Part III – Lawyers

Part I
Enforcers
& Academics

Inge Bernaerts[*]

DG COMP, European Commission

Nicole Kar

Inge Bernaerts is director for strategy and policy in the European Commission Directorate-General for Competition. Before that, she held management positions in the Directorate-General for Energy and was head of cabinet to Marianne Thyssen, commissioner for employment and social affairs in the Juncker Commission. Between 1996 and 2010, Inge practiced competition law, first at the Brussels bar and later as case handler in antitrust and state aid and as assistant to the Directorate-General for Competition. Inge holds a law degree from the Katholieke Universiteit Leuven, where she also lectured European law seminars, and a postgraduate degree in European law from the Universität Saarbrücken. She is married and has two sons.

Nicole Kar is a partner of Linklaters LLP and heads the London competition practice. Nicole has led on over 40 significant merger control investigations before the European and UK authorities and regularly appears before international agencies and courts. Alongside her busy merger control practice, she is a cartel specialist, advising on global investigations by competition, financial services and other regulators and associated litigation. Nicole is co-head of Linklaters' Trade Law Practice; and is a specialist adviser to the Foreign Affairs Committee of the UK Parliament. Nicole is married and has a daughter and son.

---

* The information and views set out in this contribution are those of the author and do not necessarily reflect the official opinion of the European Commission.

Inge, you have been at the European Commission since 2003 and have witnessed some big changes in competition policy, from the introduction of the Modernisation Regulation to the current EU Merger Regulation. Looking back, what stands out for you as the most important moments in EU competition law and policy since you've been at the Commission?

I don't think that we have seen any single change in EU competition policy of that order of magnitude since the introduction of merger control 30 years ago and the modernisation of antitrust enforcement in 2003. But that does not mean that competition policy has stood still. From my perspective, it has been in permanent evolution, with boundaries tested and reset through cases and court judgments. In that sense, the evolution of EU competition policy has been closer to the Anglo-Saxon common law tradition, and not so much driven by legislative change, with the exception of the introduction of private actions for antitrust damages in 2014.

I started my career in the Commission in the antitrust unit of the telecommunications directorate. It was the aftermath of the major liberalisation packages in the 1990s, which had opened Europe's network industries, notably the energy and telecommunications sectors, to competition. One of the challenges was to find the right balance and complement between *ex ante* sector-specific regulation and competition enforcement. We tried to address margin squeeze and even exploitative pricing behaviour by dominant incumbents through antitrust enforcement, but concluded that those were more effectively and more efficiently addressed through regulation. That interplay between competition enforcement and regulation in EU network industries has been very fruitful, I believe, with demonstrable benefits for consumers. The issue is still very relevant today, notably when it comes to giant gatekeeper platforms in the digital economy.

In addition to cases setting new boundaries and the productive interplay between competition policy and regulation in the liberalisation of network industries, the Commission has expanded its investigative and procedural tools. It conducted four sector inquiries and I remember vividly the preparation of the first, which concerned the pharmaceutical sector. It was a large operation to manage but it was successful and led to several enforcement cases. In cartels, the settlement procedure has speeded up procedures, the possibility to search private homes has been created and the Commission has acted forcefully against violations of procedural rules, such as breaches of seals.

What has changed a lot, compared with 2003, is that the family of competition law enforcement bodies in the EU and around the globe has grown and become closer. The vast majority of EU antitrust cases today are handled by national competition authorities in Member States and the European Competition Network (ECN) operates as a true network with intense contacts in multiple directions on a daily basis. And, globally, the International Competition Network (ICN) has grown strong, not only in competition law advocacy but also in operational cooperation.

You have recently returned to competition law after almost 10 years in other fields (energy and employment/social policy). What drew you back to the competition policy area and what do you bring back from your energy and employment/social policy roles?

After graduating from Leuven University, I trained and for almost 15 years practiced as a competition lawyer at both sides of the bar. That early experience in my professional life is something that marked me profoundly as a professional. I noticed that when I was dealing with energy matters, and even with social and employment matters in the past 10 years, I'd often fall back on a number of very basic reflexes that I was taught as a competition lawyer: always establish the facts first, look for what the market can deliver on its own and where the market fails and corrective action through public intervention is needed, value the contradictory debate as a means to establish the truth. And in the grand scheme of things, irrespective of their very different objectives, competition policy and employment and social policy pursue fairness.

After 10 years in energy and social policy, returning to competition law feels like coming home, a feeling strengthened by the warm welcome back that I was given in DG COMP and in the broader competition community. That being said, it feels, I guess, like someone who has been on a trip around the world feels when coming home: you have experienced a lot, seen a lot of new things, made a lot of new friends, and you want to tell your family all about it. But your family members' lives have in the meantime been very different from yours, they had to deal with all the family problems and keep the house in order while you were enjoying your trip. I am very conscious of that.

At the same time, I am convinced that my learnings from those other fields can add value, in particular at this juncture in the history of EU competition law where the role of competition policy in the broader context of EU policy and in society is up for debate. I am not afraid of such debates, but see them as an opportunity. I remember the first meeting I had as head of cabinet of Marianne Thyssen, commissioner for employment, social affairs, skills and labour Mobility in the Juncker Commission, with the European Trade Union Federation. ETUC's leadership told us in no subtle words that workers had lost trust in the European Union, that they felt the EU only served the interest of companies and banks on the back of workers. Five years later, after many hours of listening and discussing, an update of the EU social rulebook and a Social Pillar of European Rights proclaimed at the first social summit held by EU heads of state and government in 20 years, the mood had changed radically.

It is a sign of our times that policies – at EU, national and local level – are more closely scrutinised and more intensely challenged than ever before. It is not necessarily something to be frustrated or discouraged about. I do regret that those debates are not always based on evidence – that too is a sign of our times, I am afraid, and something competition enforcers are not always used to. I see it as an opportunity for competition enforcers to rethink, engage, where appropriate adjust and, importantly, build a much broader support base for competition policy in our societies. No offence to the highly qualified and no doubt expert readers of this publication, but I profoundly believe that we must take competition policy out of its bubble and discuss it much more widely in civil society, with the business community of course, but also with youth, trade unions, environmental NGOs, etc.

In the energy field, I discovered that the EU has irreversibly made the turn towards a zero-carbon society. Not only the EU in the sense of its institutions, but also industry and consumers, and that makes me hopeful in the face of the huge and pressing climate change challenge. In my new job, I want to take forward the discussion on how competition policy can support that transition. It is not the goal nor task of competition policy to lead the fight against climate change. Other instruments, notably legislation, regulation and taxation are much better suited. But that does not mean that competition policy has no role to play.

I have been struck by the ways in which labour market issues, for example, issues around monopsony power in labour markets, no-poach agreements and collective bargaining by gig economy workers, have really come to the fore in competition policy in recent times after perhaps decades of little real interaction between labour laws and rights and competition law. Do you have a view on why this is and whether there is more to come in terms of this interaction?

The world of work has changed a lot over the last 20 years. One of the trends is an increase in the number of self-employed people and a bigger variation in the economic situation they are in. In the 20th century, the self-employed were either entrepreneurs or liberal professionals: e.g. lawyers, doctors, architects. And there is consistent case law qualifying price coordination between the self-employed or by their associations as anticompetitive price-fixing agreements.

Today we see, in addition to those traditional groups, a different type of self-employed, often – but not only – in the platform economy. And often these self-employed – delivery service providers, cleaners, carers, musicians or translators – work under less favourable payment and social protection conditions than their colleagues with an employment contract, who are often protected by collective labour agreements. To people in these jobs it may sound strange that we qualify them as "undertakings" and their collective actions for fair working conditions as "price-fixing agreements". We should be careful that our rules and enforcement priorities are in tune with the evolving socioeconomic reality and do not unnecessarily stand in the way of a socially desirable correction of the market.

The Commission has recently carried out a public consultation into the question of how collective bargaining between self-employed people in vulnerable positions should be dealt with under competition law. We received around 1,300 replies, which we will take into account when deciding on further action.

In the energy field, in particular, there is a real European policy drive for environmental sustainability. What is your perspective on whether competition policy is an obstacle to achieving industry-wide sustainability objectives and is there more the European Commission can or should do to enable companies to collaborate with confidence?

Competition is an enabler of change. It ensures that capital is allocated efficiently, stimulates innovation and prevents costs being passed on to consumers without exploiting efficiency gains first. To reach the EU's goal of making Europe the first carbon-neutral continent in the world by 2050 at the latest, putting competition rules aside or turning a blind eye on enforcement is therefore out of question.

But in our enforcement of those competition rules we must get it right, which means that we must avoid over-enforcement and under-enforcement.

That is something we must, of course, do in all sectors, but since climate change represents an existential challenge it is in this field also a societal imperative.

There is no doubt that the transition to a carbon-neutral economy will require massive investment: private investment – which is taking place at large scale – but also public investment where markets fail. State aid control has in recent decades been instrumental in limiting the distortive effect of state subsidies, for example in offshore wind farms. Conditions, such as tendering requirements, have limited the crowding-out of private investment and have, alongside technological developments, significantly pushed down the cost to taxpayers. That disciplining effect of state aid control will continue to be important as the EU and Member States will, in the next few years, roll out their post-COVID-19 recovery plans, for which the EU's ambition is that they should contribute to the twin digital and green transition. It will be important to provide as much legal certainty upfront, for the market and for public authorities, and that is why we are working as fast as we can on the revision of our Environmental and Energy Aid Guidelines and our General Block Exemption Regulation.

Legal certainty is important also when it comes to antitrust aspects of sustainability agreements. It is true that the abolition in 2003–2004 of the possibility of notifying restrictive agreements to the Commission, with a view to obtaining an individual exemption decision, has inevitably diminished legal certainty and put the onus of assessing the compatibility of agreements and concerted practices with companies and their advisers. For novel kinds of agreements, requiring delicate balancing exercises, this may not always be straightforward and the precedent value of individual exemption decisions prior to 2004 was undoubtedly helpful in this regard. I remember, for example, a series of decisions regarding waste management agreements.

The Commission has addressed this by publishing informal guidance papers on specific topics, in addition to the horizontal and vertical block exemptions and guidance notices. On waste management agreements, for example, it published a guidance paper in 2005. We are open to considering whether additional guidance is needed and what format is best suited for it, including guidance letters and decisions finding that article 101 TFEU is not applicable in individual cases if the right cases are presented.

It is important to note that the issue of sustainability agreements emerges frequently in markets that are national in nature, and national competition authorities in Member States have experienced this in their case practice. It has recently led the Dutch and Greek competition authorities to relaunch a very welcome public debate on the matter, and we are actively engaging through the ECN.

This being said, the role of competition policy in "greening" the economy must be seen in perspective and must not be over-interpreted. Competition policy cannot and should not replace or fill the gaps left by environmental and climate policy. Climate targets and environmental norms should be set through legislation and regulation, not through competition policy. But competition policy must play its role in ensuring that markets remain open and competitive when undertakings adjust their business plans and public authorities intervene through subsidies to achieve the new standards and norms that legislators and regulators have set.

Could you give us some insights into your policy role: what does a typical day involve for you?

My role is to provide a steer to the Strategy and Policy Directorate of DG COMP and to oversee its day-to-day management. My directorate consists of five units. For each of the three instruments of EU competition policy – antitrust, mergers and state aid – a unit coordinates policy development and provides case support to the case teams in the sectoral directorates. In addition, there is a unit that manages the interaction with the ECN and coordinates contact with the national judiciaries in Member

States. Our international unit manages our external relations and interactions with the ICN. The latter is also involved in the competition policy aspects of the Brexit negotiations.

The European Commission works in policy cycles of five years and the headline objectives for the current mandate are laid down in the political agenda on the basis of which Commission President von der Leyen was elected in 2019, and in her mission letter to Executive Vice-President Vestager, who is in charge of the competition portfolio. You see from those documents that we have a policy-heavy competition agenda for the coming years, with a focus on bringing the existing framework of notices, guidelines and block exemption regulations up to date across all three instruments. In addition, we are currently consulting on two potential new competition instruments to be created: an instrument to assess and address distortive effects of third country subsidies on competition in the internal market, and an instrument to assess and address structural market failures that articles 101 and 102 TFEU do not allow to be tackled effectively, notably in digital markets.

Three weeks into the job it is a bit early to say what a typical day looks like, and the extraordinary working circumstances that the COVID-19 pandemic continue to force upon us are disturbing normality, with most physical meetings still banned and most staff, including me, teleworking almost full time from home. But what I can say already is that working days are long, intense and varied.

I typically start the day with a short call with my assistants, where we go through the diary management and make sure that the information flow and "production machinery" in the directorate runs smoothly. During the day, I typically have one or more meetings with the management team in my directorate or with teams working on specific issues. Once a week, we meet with the entire senior management of DG COMP. Another important moment is the weekly meeting with Executive Vice

President Vestager, where she gives a steer on the cases and policy files presented to her. As director of policy and strategy, I have a seat in those weekly meetings alongside the chief economist and the Commission Legal Service, and of course our director general, Olivier Guersent, and the deputy directors general.

Engaging with external stakeholders through meetings and conferences, on competition policy in general and the specific policy initiatives under preparation, is an important part of my job. And, as said before, I will try as much as I can to broaden that debate also beyond the traditional competition community.

Finally, there are inter-institutional meetings to attend. Tomorrow, I have a full-day meeting scheduled with the European Court of Auditors, where we will be given an opportunity to comment on the Court's draft audit report into the effectiveness of EU antitrust and merger policy in recent years.

If I could ask you to crystal ball – gaze for a moment: what do you see as being the policy priorities for DG COMP beyond the COVID crisis and the current crop of big tech cases?

The COVID pandemic reminds us brutally that crystal ball – gazing is a difficult and dangerous exercise! As was the case with the financial crisis in 2007–2008, no one saw it coming even if there were warning signals in the distance.

One lesson learned is always to be ready for the unexpected. In both crises, competition rules have been proven to have a lot of in-built flexibility to cope with crises, and the Commission as an institution has proven its agility to act decisively and fast, making use of that flexibility.

The core task of the Commissioner for Competition and of DG COMP is to enforce the competition rules, in all sectors and across the three instruments: antitrust, mergers and state aid. When setting enforcement priorities, I think it is important that we align those well with the broader policy priorities of the Commission. That is not too difficult as "an economy that works for people" is one of the six priorities of this Commission and that is essentially what competition enforcement is about too. A European green deal and a Europe fit for the digital age are two further cross-cutting objectives with a link to competition policy.

As enforcers of EU competition rules, we need to keep our eyes wide open for anticompetitive practices and restrictions of competition that could be particularly harmful not only for consumers, but also for achieving those broader objectives. When assessing industrial mergers, for example, I think that we should pay close attention to raw materials and intermediate products that are key for the green and digital transitions. Of course it should not influence our substantive assessment – whether there is a risk of a significant impediment of effective competition in those markets – but we should be aware of the importance of preserving effective competition in those markets, not only for consumers but for our broader strategic objectives.

And in the context of the post-COVID economic crisis, we should keep our eyes open for crisis cartels, which would harm consumers, stand in the way of restructuring and drag economic recovery for longer than needed.

On the policy side, our priorities will be to update the existing framework of notices, guidelines and block exemption regulations. Here, we will also have the twin digital and green transition in the back of our minds. The review of the Vertical Block Exemption Regulation and Notice in antitrust touches upon distribution agreements in the context of e-commerce and the review of the Horizontal Block Exemption Regulation and Notice may look into sustainability agreements. We are also looking into the question of whether measures are needed to clarify the rules on collective bargaining by self-employment. It is not unrelated to COVID, as COVID-related measures have hit particularly hard some sectors where that issue is acute, such as the cultural sector. And finally, we'll give priority to completing our toolbox, following-up on the White Paper on third country subsidies published in June 2020 and on our consultation on a new competition tool to tackle structural market weaknesses that cannot be tackled effectively under articles 101 and 102 TFEU.

What do you think are the biggest challenges for competition policy in Europe and globally?

The biggest challenge I see is that the socioeconomic fallout of the COVID-19 pandemic in the EU and elsewhere in the world will add to pre-existing pressures on free trade and undistorted competition stemming from the radically changed geopolitical landscape. Moreover, public bodies will, in western economies, unavoidably take a bigger role in the economy after COVID, at least temporarily, as they did after the Great Depression and the Second World War, although they will hopefully avoid some of the mistakes made then. That may exacerbate pre-existing tensions between competition policy and other policy objectives.

I firmly believe that it would be a dramatic mistake to put competition rules aside or tone them down, as we will need the pulling strength of competition and cross-border trade now more than ever to drive the recovery and the twin digital and green transition. And we will need a stable business and investment climate, for which an objective, independent and predictable enforcement of competition rules, within a clear legal framework and based on economic analysis, is key.

For those reasons, I see it as a priority for competition policy in Europe and globally – and as a personal objective for me in my job as strategy and policy director in DG Competition – to advocate relentlessly for the value of competition and of competition enforcement. We need to listen and engage, be open to adjusting our rules and policies where needed and show that we are aware of the context in which we operate. And, as indicated earlier, we need to debate among ourselves, but we also need to get out of our bubble and engage with society at large.

Aside from the other tumultuous events of 2020, this year seems to represent a watershed in terms of proposed new competition tools: a new markets tool and unprecedented, in terms of international analogues, anti-subsidy tools. These are the most significant proposed new instruments in around 30 years, since the Merger Regulation was introduced in Europe. What has changed in your view to mean that existing, expansive European competition law instruments are not fit for purpose?

One could also ask why it took so long. How it came that for such a long period of time there were no fundamental changes to EU competition law.

When reading the treaty provisions on competition policy, it is incredible how age-proof they are. Our founding fathers and their advisers have been incredibly forward-looking. But the treaty provisions in themselves are insufficient to deal with the full complexity of competition policy, and that is where the role of secondary legislation comes in.

It is true that the Commission has not put many legislative proposals on the table in the last 20 years, although there have been some, notably on private damages actions, for which a legal basis in EU law was created in 2014.

Why we are now actively considering the two legislative proposals you mention, in my view, is for two reasons that came together at this particular juncture. The first is that the Commission has tried, in its case practice, to use existing instruments to tackle competition problems, but it has run into the limits of those instruments. This is true for third country subsidies which the Commission has occasionally come under pressure to address in the context of merger control, while the issue turned out to be not only legally impossible but also practically ineffective to address under this instrument. And it is true for a number of structural market problems, in digital markets and elsewhere, that articles 101 and 102 TFEU do not allow effective address of, for example, monopolisation strategies by non-dominant market players.

The second reason is the intensity and speed of underlying transformations that make those issues now much more pressing than in the past. The fact that the treaty prohibits distortive state subsidies by EU Member States, while not those by third countries, has been a problem for longer, but the scale of the problem has become much bigger, not least due to the growth and expansionist position of China and other countries. Similarly, the growing size and position of a limited number of major digital players, their importance in society, the position they take in digital ecosystems without necessarily being dominant in every single market and the specific features of those markets, make it much more pressing to consider new enforcement instruments.

That is why we are now looking into those issues to see whether legislative initiatives are warranted to complete our toolbox. The public consultations are coming to a close at the time of writing, and we will assess further steps on that basis.

Reflections and Advice to Antitrust Practitioners

What advice would you give to women starting their careers as antitrust practitioners and what is the most valuable piece of advice you have received?

To learn as much as you can from every job you do, from every case you handle, from your successes and even more so from your failures. I have been lucky throughout my career to work with inspiring and highly competent people, bosses, colleagues, clients and adversaries. I have stolen from them with my ears and my eyes and pushed myself to get better with every case or policy file that I handled, in every job that I took on. And if you have the feeling that you stop learning, probably it is time for a new challenge – in the job you are in or in a different one.

A valuable piece of advice I received when I was a senior associate in a large international law firm – but it served me well also at the Commission – is that you are the only one who can guard your own work – life balance. It is a piece of advice, by the way, that is valid equally for men and women. You have to decide for yourself what makes you a happy and fulfilled person. That balance inevitably will get distorted from time to time (generally at the expense of your private life) but if it lasts too long or happens too frequently, consider how you can get it levelled again. It can be by outsourcing some tasks, by cutting down on side activities that you actually do not like as much as you thought, or by adjusting your professional ambitions, at least temporarily. The latter, in my experience, is not irreversible. That is one of the advantages of today's world of work: linear careers are no longer the only model.

Looking back on your career to date, what are the most important lessons you have learned?

Stay curious. There is so much to learn and so many new experiences to discover in every case, every encounter, every job.

And try to make the best out of every job you do. It is being noticed, even if you do not always receive direct feedback or reward. Cream does rise to the top, albeit not always immediately.

It is normal to encounter frustrations and set-backs. Life is not always fair, and that is true for life in the workplace too. Do not let those frustrations take over, but see what they tell you about yourself, analyse what went wrong and try again next time. What doesn't kill you makes you stronger.

And last but not least: stay humble. Making a career is partly a matter of talent and will, but partly a matter also of luck. It is nothing that makes you a better person than someone else. So reach for the stars, but keep your feet on the ground!

Kathleen Foote
California Department of Justice
Karen Kazmerzak

Kathleen Foote joined the California attorney general's antitrust unit in 1988, and has been its antitrust chief since 2001. She is a past chair of the multistate antitrust task force of the National Association of Attorneys General (2012–2015). She received the American Antitrust Institute's Alfred E Kahn Award for Antitrust Achievement, and was named "2013 Antitrust Lawyer of the Year" by the California State Bar's Antitrust and Unfair Competition Law Section. Before joining the attorney general's office, Ms Foote was associate dean at University of San Francisco School of Law (1981–1987) and an associate attorney with McCutchen, Doyle, Brown & Enersen (now Morgan Lewis) (1975–1978). Ms Foote is a graduate of Harvard University and the University of San Francisco School of Law.

Karen Kazmerzak, a Sidley Austin partner and former Federal Trade Commission attorney, works closely with clients to develop the best global strategy for clients' advocacy on multi-jurisdictional deals. She has a broad practice advising clients on antitrust issues in licensing, distribution, pricing and competitor collaborations. Hailed as "very knowledgeable and easy to talk to", her clients appreciate her strong legal acumen combined with her ability to address the business issues in an array of industries.

You have a wealth of experience from your time in the California Department of Justice (DOJ). During your 30-year tenure, what trends, if any, have you noticed in California's enforcement of the antitrust laws relative to other states or the federal agencies?

Three weeks after I arrived at the California Attorney General's Office in 1988, the first true multi-state antitrust case was filed. *California v Hartford Fire Insurance* began with eight plaintiff states but soon grew to 20. It led to a US Supreme Court decision that foreign companies acting in foreign countries could nevertheless be held liable for violations of the Sherman Act if they conspired to – and did – restrain trade within the United States.[1] At around the same time, two other California cases were making their way toward the Supreme Court: *California v ARC America*[2] and *California v American Stores*.[3] The first one upheld a state antitrust law allowing recovery of treble damages by indirect purchasers, notwithstanding contrary jurisprudence under the Sherman Act. The second established that a state may pursue divestiture as a merger remedy under section 16 of the Clayton Act independently of the federal enforcers. While those cases were all California-led, they set the stage for major growth in antitrust enforcement by many state attorneys general that has played out over my entire tenure.

California signed a brief with 30 other states as amici curiae in support of Pepper in *Apple v Pepper* and joined the multi-state suit challenging the *T-Mobile/Sprint* merger, but did not participate in *Ohio v Amex*. What are the key criteria California uses for deciding which path to take when other states are involved?

A disclaimer is in order here. In giving this interview I am expressing my own views, and not necessarily those of the attorney general.

---

1   Hartford Fire Insurance Co. v. California, 509 U.S. 764 (1993).

2   California *et al.* v. ARC America Corp. *et al., 490 U.S. 93 (1989).*

3   California v. American Stores *Co., 495 U.S. 271 (1990).*

Decisions to join multi-state cases, including those conducted jointly with federal enforcers, are made by the attorney general personally. I don't generally suggest joining a case, though, unless we can bring something special to the table. That usually would be: (a) focus on impacts in local markets; (b) connection to public sector purchasing or regulatory interest; (c) special harm to California consumers; or (d) input where California businesses are involved. Good examples of this on the merger side have included hospitals, supermarkets, waste haulers, oil companies – and, of course, mobile phone carriers. On the conduct side, examples have included no-poach agreements by tech companies, bid-rigging of municipal bond derivatives, and pay-for-delay agreements among pharmaceutical companies.

Similarly, California's multi-state suit challenging the *T-Mobile/Sprint* merger and its challenge to Valero's proposed acquisition of Bay Area terminals owned by Plains All American Pipeline in 2017 demonstrate that California is willing to proceed without the support of a federal agency. Are there any unique challenges to bringing an action without federal agency support?

The federal agencies have a depth of expertise and a history of professionalism in carrying out their enforcement duties that we are used to relying on during joint investigations, and miss when they are absent. But antitrust cases are fact driven, and every so often a different view of the facts may lead to different enforcement decisions, even when our interpretation of the law is largely the same. Those rare differences are especially visible in the merger context, because Hart-Scott-Rodino is understood to drive the federal investigation as well as its timetable, so our filing decisions coincide. The principal downside of going it alone is quite simply the cost – in both dollars and workload for our small staff. It is also true that the merging parties, in our experience, are not shy about urging the court to view the federal agency's choice as having greater validity than the state's decision to bring suit, the 1990 *American Stores* decision notwithstanding.

California has analysed resale price maintenance and franchisee no-poach agreements as per se unlawful under the Cartwright Act, despite more lenient treatment under the federal system. What were the key factors in deciding to deviate from a rule-of-reason analysis in these instances?

The Cartwright Act contains much more detail than the Sherman Act in spelling out what is unlawful. It is explicit in declaring unlawful any agreements to set prices. To illustrate further, the California Supreme Court has held that prices must be determined by the "interplay of the economic forces of supply and demand" and that "these rules apply whether the price-fixing scheme is horizontal or vertical; that is, whether the price is fixed among competitors... or businesses at different economic levels..."[4] And further, that the overriding purpose of the Cartwright Act is deterrence.[5] Adjacent to the Cartwright Act in our statutes is also the rule that "every contract by which anyone is restrained from engaging in a lawful profession, trade, or business of any kind is to that extent void".[6] That policy statement, traditionally enforced against non-compete agreements in employee contracts, has also been extended to small businesses by some state appellate courts.[7] This level of detail is fairly compelling, and has led California courts to pay close attention to legislative intent in interpretation. For enforcers, this means we will be reluctant to suggest applying a rule-of-reason approach to anything clearly stated to be a violation of these laws, unless we are prepared to argue that the legislature itself should be overruled.

---

4   Mailand v. Burckle (1978) 20 Cal. 3d 367, 377.

5   Clayworth v. Pfizer (2010) 49 Cal. 4th 758.

6   Bus. & Prof. Code Section 16600

7   The question of section 16600's extension to businesses was recently certified to the California Supreme Court by the 9th Circuit.

Certain states, including California, have deviated from federal law on the treatment of indirect purchasers, franchisee no-poach agreements and vertical price restraints. Do you think there is any benefit to this divergence? What would facilitate convergence?

Convergence is a worthy goal when conditions are comparable, but they are not always comparable. And by conditions, I refer to the law itself as well as to the overall economic climate. It is important to recognise that the Cartwright Act is not based on the Sherman Act, and that "interpretation of the Sherman Act is not directly probative of the intent of the drafters of the Cartwright Act".[8] Numerous studies contrasting Silicon Valley with other tech-heavy zones have attributed its robustness to the fact that California's economy has been especially labour-friendly and innovation-friendly for many decades.[9] I don't see that changing. At the same time, apart from the areas of interpretation of the Cartwright Act that you mention, there is a high degree of convergence with federal judicial precedents. Greater convergence might also develop through legislative interest at both state and federal levels in addressing new problems in certain markets.

Members of US Congress, reporters and others have called for revising the US antitrust laws, including revisions that may make it easier to break up some of California's largest tech companies. Has there been a similar movement to update California's antitrust laws? Is there anything you would change about them if you could?

Over the last two decades there have been at least three attempts to add a monopolisation clause to the Cartwright Act, all of them supported by whoever was the attorney general at the time, but all ultimately unsuccessful. Although California's Unfair Competition Law does in

---

8   California ex rel. Van de Kamp v. Texaco, Inc., 46 Cal. 3d 1147 (1988).

9   See, for example, Alan Hyde, *Working In Silicon Valley: Economic And Legal Analysis Of A High-Technology Labor Market* (Routledge 2003) 15–16.

some cases provide a remedy for single firm conduct, a Cartwright equivalent of Sherman section 2 would likely be a more serviceable means of reaching the kinds of abuses alleged against big tech companies from the standpoint of enforcers. Keep in mind also that the California legislature recently enacted an ambitious data privacy law that make it the closest corollary to the EU standard that currently exists in the US. Its enforcement by the attorney general is not through our antitrust unit; nevertheless, it will undoubtedly serve indirectly to remedy some of the issues of antitrust concern that surround the use of data by big tech companies.

There has been significant debate about the appropriate welfare standard for antitrust enforcement. Is there a similar debate occurring at state level?

I am personally deeply interested in this debate as are many state level enforcers, I imagine. To the extent we bring cases under the federal law, a shift in the standard would affect our practice directly. But to the extent we enforce state law, it would have less impact because of the importance of legislative language and legislative intent in Cartwright Act interpretation. Even new legislative proposals that might favour a more public-interest-leaning antitrust enforcement approach would likely founder on the legislature's reluctance to delegate away from itself such broad powers. That said, the California Supreme Court in *Clayworth* embraced deterrence as the overriding legislative intent behind the Cartwright Act and pointed out that under-enforcement in order to avoid the risk of false positives is not an option. This contrasts sharply with the concern over false positives that is arguably the most criticised aspect of the consumer welfare standard as articulated by the US Supreme Court.

You have litigated a number of high-profile matters since joining the California DOJ in 1988, including Hartford Fire Insurance Company, Microsoft, the TFT-LCD and DRAM Indirect Purchaser multi-state cases,

Wells Fargo/First Interstate Bancorporation, and various supermarket mergers. Of those matters, which do you think has had the most impact on consumer welfare and why?

The *T-Mobile/Sprint* merger case, which we pursued with New York and other states, is the one I would have nominated as having the greatest impact on consumer welfare – assuming we are successful. The two companies competed aggressively on price as well as non-price features, and their competition directly benefitted millions of lower-income consumers in national as well as local markets. The effects of losing that competition will be profound in the long run, although we were able to negotiate post-trial settlement terms that will obviate some impacts for several years. The litigation itself remains important for its affirmation of the relevance of local market impacts to merger analysis, and its illustration of the strongly consumer protection-driven approach to antitrust enforcement that is generally the hallmark of actions by state attorneys general.

Remedies can be difficult to get right and both federal antitrust agencies have recently made recent statements to that effect. In 2018, the DOJ withdrew its 2011 *Policy Guide to Merger Remedies* and signalled a shift away from endorsing conduct remedies to address concerns in vertical mergers. The Federal Trade Commission (FTC) published a merger remedies study last year that caused them to shift away from post-order divestitures and to take a closer look at divestitures of pipeline products in pharmaceutical markets. How do you know when you have structured an adequate remedy?

Fashioning behavioural remedies and structuring divestiture packages in already concentrated markets are thankless tasks that have failed to maintain or restore competition in many cases, so I heartily endorse efforts to rethink them. Yet the practical and legal challenges of prevailing in merger litigation will inevitably mean continued use of these methods by both federal and state enforcers in many cases. Trial and error has led to improvements in implementing and overseeing the required remedial terms. Their adequacy will continue to involve guesswork, but retrospective studies have proven illuminating and I devoutly hope there will be more of them done by both the agencies themselves and the academic community.

In addition to your position as senior assistant attorney general (antitrust), you have also chaired the multistate Antitrust Task Force of the National Association of Attorneys General and serve on the Advisory Board of the American Antitrust Institute (AAI). What have been the key achievements at each of these organisations during your tenure?

Both organisations make important contributions to antitrust enforcement through the active participation of their members, and I claim no credit for their good work. AAI's seminar discussions, policy papers and amicus briefs are an important source of information and insight. As chair of the Task Force it was my pleasure to showcase the rise of antitrust enforcement by state attorneys general and to welcome new and talented staff attorneys into multi-state working groups. The most dramatic development during my Task Force tenure was the *North Carolina Dental* decision in 2015, which caused almost every state government to review and rethink its delegation and oversight of regulatory authority to its state professional boards. My own background as a one-time mayor of a small community proved to be helpful in the ensuing conversation – still ongoing – about how to reconcile the potential antitrust liability of such boards with valid state health and safety interests and with the ordinary state administrative laws that govern them.

What are California's current antitrust enforcement priorities? For example, are there certain industries that receive more scrutiny or mergers versus conduct? What have been the biggest shifts in priorities since you started with the California DOJ? What do you envision the priorities will be in the coming years?

For as long as I can remember, health care and gasoline prices have been top priorities for my office, and for many other states as well. As the technology industry has risen in size and importance it has joined the list, beginning with the *Microsoft* case. Agriculture is another area that has come up less frequently, but one that I believe is extremely important to monitor because of its importance to California's economy.

Do you have any practice tips for parties appearing before the California DOJ?

Probably the most important advice is for parties to be aware that our attorney general is committed to vigorous antitrust enforcement, and will take action when the facts warrant it. In the merger context, parties will save themselves time and trouble by embracing a coordinated state – federal investigation process pursuant to the state – federal merger protocol found on the websites of NAAG, the FTC and the US DOJ.

Eleanor Fox
New York University

Michal Gal

Eleanor Fox is the Walter J Derenberg Professor of Trade Regulation at New York University School of Law. She teaches and writes in antitrust law, competition policy, globalisation and developing countries, and is known for her theory of inclusiveness and its role in advancing efficiency and competitiveness in developing countries. She was a partner in the New York law firm Simpson Thacher & Bartlett. She served as a member of President Carter's antitrust commission and President Clinton's international competition committee. Fox received an honorary doctorate from University of Paris-Dauphine in 2009. She was awarded lifetime achievement or inaugural awards from Global Competition Review, ASCOLA, and the Antitrust Section of Association of American Law Schools. Her most recent book is Making Markets Work for Africa, with Mor Bakhoum.

Michal Gal (LLB, LLM, SJD) is Professor and Director of the Center for Law and Technology at the Faculty of Law, University of Haifa, Israel, and the elected president of ASCOLA, the international organization of competition law scholars. Professor Gal is the author of several books, including Competition Policy for Small Market Economies (Harvard University Press 2003). She published numerous articles in leading journals and won prizes for her research and teaching. Her articles have won the Antitrust Writing Awards and other prizes numerous times. Professor Gal has served as a consultant to several international organisations (including OECD, UNCTAD and the ICN).

You started your career as an antitrust lawyer in 1962. Antitrust used to be a man's world. Yet you broke many glass ceilings that existed for women, including becoming the first female partner in a major New York firm. Can you share with us some of your experiences and takeaways from this period in your life?

Let me start with law school. I went to New York University School of Law, entering in 1958. Many law schools did not all admit women then, on grounds that women would take the place of male students and male students were serious about becoming lawyers. I was grateful that NYU Law School admitted women. For students in the first year, NYU had two sections of about 100 students each. There was one other woman in my section. One of my professors did not call on women, but he made an exception. One day a semester he would have "Ladies Day". On Ladies Day he would call on me and my female classmate. Everyone thought it was a big joke and laughed. So I laughed too.

For my second summer I looked for a law job. At that time you just walked into a firm and left your résumé at the front desk, and someone would come to interview you (at least if you had an excellent academic record and were on law review, and I did and was). Being in New York, I went to the Wall Street law firms. Everywhere I went they said that they were not hiring women. Some said, we tried it once and it did not work out. She got married (or pregnant) and left. I heard that the US Attorney's Office in the Southern District of New York would hire women in the Civil Division (not in the Criminal Division, because women were not fit to deal with blood or murder). I went for an interview and was hired. I had a great summer and I was grateful.

In 1961 when I graduated from law school, I was pregnant with my first child. For the summer and fall, I worked for professors at the law school. My son Doug was born in November. In January I was ready to look for a job. I knew that most firms were not hiring women. Simpson Thacher and Bartlett offered me a job to do a document search to answer a document request in a large antitrust case. I was grateful and I accepted. The firm liked my work. It hired me as an associate, and, eight years later, in January 1970, I became their first female partner. I believe I was the first female partner in the top 10 or so Wall Street law firms as measured by size of firm. I was in the litigation department. Antitrust was placed in the litigation department. There was a merger wave, and I advised on scores of mergers, handicapping them for investment banking firms such as Lehman Brothers. Also, I handled major monopoly litigation for plaintiff corporations. For mergers, much of the litigation was under the antitrust and securities laws to fend off takeovers. We often went to court for preliminary injunctions, which often were granted.

Was there a glass ceiling? The expression had not even been invented. But that was the theme of the novel I wrote as I was leaving the firm. The novel is entitled *WL, Esquire*. WL stood for Wendy Lieberman, the main character. Also for Women's Liberation. Esquire means gentleman. Until about the mid-1970s, lawyers were addressed, on letters and formal writing, with the honorific "Esq." following their names. Wendy Lieberman, Esq. could not rise in her profession without being a gentleman. So she was one of the boys, and she rose. But she could never rise to the top, because she was, after all, not a gentleman.

Despite your meteoric success in practice, you decided to become an academic. Can you share with us the reasons for this choice? Also – why did you choose competition law as your specialism and would you make the same choice today?

The women's movement began and blossomed in the 1960s. By the early 1970s I began to understand a lot of things. I had always assumed that the place of women was a given; things were the way they were.

If there was a Ladies Day in class and everyone laughed, maybe I should laugh too. The converse was much worse. Not laughing meant accepting humiliation. But by the early 1970s I began to take a broader view, including on what I wanted to do in life and whom I wanted to help. I always wanted to be a writer and scholar. I wanted also to be a teacher. And I wanted an environment where I could choose my own agenda for thinking and writing.

For my area of specialty, I did not *choose* antitrust; it chose me. But it was a happy choice that fit me. It has been fascinating for me to see antitrust policy move from a major tool to constrain the power of business, to microeconomics and freeing up business in the name of efficiency, and now, at least in the rhetoric and debate, a symbiosis.

You were one of the first Americans to study European Union competition law. In fact, when you started writing about the subject, there was not much interest in the US about competition law enforcement outside the US. What was the trigger for this decision, and what are the most important insights you gained from such a study?

The European Community began seriously enforcing its competition law in the mid-1960s and 1970s. At about the time that I moved from Simpson Thacher to NYU (1976), officials of the European Community began to ask me to lecture there so that they could better understand US law. Barry Hawk, who was then a professor at Fordham, took his sabbatical at the European Commission and convinced me that on my first sabbatical I must go to Brussels, which I did. A few years later US colleagues who were experts in European law asked me to join their casebook, which I did. From the start, European law fascinated me. Just at a time when US law was being magnetically drawn to the Chicago school, I saw European competition law blossom in the context of the European treaties, with no semblance of Chicago school presumptions, and with a major mission to create community.

There seems to be an apparent divergence between the way EU and US authorities currently treat the large digital platforms, although recently it seems to have narrowed. In light of your long-standing study of EU and US competition laws, what do you think stands at the basis of such divergence, can it be overcome, and do you foresee that it will increase or decrease?

US and EU competition laws are from different roots. They have a huge amount of convergence. But on monopolisation/abuse of dominance, some differences seem essential. US law assumes that single-firm conduct is efficient and that freedom of even dominant firms to act is the right prescription for inducing competitive and inventive behaviour. Firms have almost no antitrust duties to deal, and certainly no duties to deal fairly. EU competition law is greatly influenced by its place in the European treaties, which create open markets and limit discrimination and privilege. Under EU law, dominant firms have the duty not to foreclose competition on the merits. Both dominance and its abuse are easier to prove. The large digital platforms, their conduct, and the attempt to make them accountable may fall precisely in the divide.

In both jurisdictions, as well as in other parts of the world, we hear increasing numbers of voices calling for the break-up of the large technology giants, given their significant market power. There is even a branding of such voices, including as neo-Brandeisians and hipsters. What is your take on such views?

I do not use the word hipster. It was invented to belittle a point of view.

We do not hear much call for break-up outside of the United States, except to the extent of calling attention to anticompetitive mergers that should have gotten a closer look on day one.

Within the United States, the neo-Brandeisians have helpfully called attention to the great power of the big data platforms and to the general problem of increasing concentration and inequality. They want to return to roots, when US antitrust did not isolate antitrust from political economy. The neo-Brandeisians have given voice to a debate that had to happen. They touch concerns of the people. While they are criticised for importing non-competition values into the debate on antitrust, in fact, if you look at it closely, at least 95% of their critiques and proposals map entirely on to the question of how to improve competition in America. They would improve competition with more inclusiveness and less indulgence for incumbent firms. They would topple the traditional high burdens for proving monopoly power, which, according to conservative analysts, would require proof of power to reduce output in a market. They would topple the requirement that no conduct of a monopolist is anticompetitive unless it increases the power to reduce output in the same or an adjacent market. Their approach would make it possible to call big data platforms to account.

Whether break-up is the right solution is a different question. But it is the call for break-up that has galvanised the debate.

Your expertise reaches well beyond these two jurisdictions. In fact, much of your work focuses on international and comparative competition law. You have also taken an active part in some of the US endeavours to determine, inter alia, the relationship between trade and competition law, and in particular the role that the World Trade Organization (WTO) should play in competition law enforcement. Could you describe some of your experiences in the field? Do you think that there is a chance that international cooperation endeavours can go one step further, towards joint enforcement?

I was very much part of the debate in the 1990s when experts were taking seriously the observation that transactions are global and law should be commensurate with their effects. I proposed a world framework in the WTO, which basically would adopt cosmopolitan (or community-regarding) principles, prohibit beggar-thy-neighbour restraints, and look at transactions from a community-wide view, much as Europe does for the European Union, but with national enforcement. Many Europeans were sympathetic (and they had their own proposal). Americans were not. And of course all such proposals are off the table now, and the WTO and internationalism in general are under intense stress.

International cooperation on a horizontal level is not a complete substitute, for it leaves lots of room for nationalism. But it should go further. Take, for example, the global mega-mergers such as *Holcim/Lafarge*, the biggest cement companies in the world in the most cartel-prone business in the world. It is astounding that the major enforcers all cleared the merger, with spinoffs that would (might) protect their countries' consumers, while leaving developing countries – the most vulnerable victims – to fend for themselves. That merger should not have been allowed. If affected jurisdictions collaborated in their merger reviews, they might have mutually gained the courage of convictions to prohibit the merger.

Recently you have published an important book, with Mor Bakhoum, on competition and markets in sub-Saharan Africa, and you have recently done a book tour in Africa. Can you tell us about the book, about the experience writing it, and why you decided to study the competition laws of the African nations?

Mor and I wrote the book, *Making Markets Work for Africa*. Mor (from Senegal) had just completed an assignment to review and write a report on all of the competition authorities in French West Africa. I had been doing work in South Africa and wanted to expand my scope; to learn about other African countries. For one thing, I was interested in the fit of Western law with developing country markets, and if not the Western standard, what standards? So, we undertook this project – to study jurisdictions in sub-Saharan Africa that already had competition laws, to find out what the authorities were doing, what were they doing well, what could they do better, what challenges they faced. We knew that their markets were different, they often hardly functioned, and in many areas the people were not sympathetic to markets. We had a hugely interesting time exploring the facts, discerning the narrative they told, and thus creating the book. We – or at least I – gained a new appreciation for the tasks of the competition authorities of sub-Saharan Africa. They have so many tasks to accomplish for progress in their work. They have a different balance of advocacy and enforcement, for they must be able to tear down some barriers before competition can function at all. For example, where governments are autocracies and leaders lavish the best market opportunities on their cronies, the space for competition is squeezed. The nations we studied ranged from those that still clung to colonial traditions of socialism with suspicion for markets, to those that had freed themselves from their colonial heritage and were working hard and wisely to open up the markets for their people. We also studied the regional free trade agreements and common markets in Africa and, while observing their drawbacks and dysfunctionalities, we still concluded that collaborations among the African nations is needed for effective cross-border enforcement and a voice of Africa.

You are a leading voice on the proposition that equality of opportunity is and should be a value of antitrust in the context of developing jurisdictions. Would you also recommend that developed jurisdictions take this path?

The growing literature on inclusiveness as a value in the competition laws of developing countries should have a positive spill-over effect in the developed world. The antitrust law of the United States, for example, needs to absorb these lessons in the law of exclusionary practices. Currently, US law weighs heavily on the side of dominant firms in having freedom to take strategies with exclusionary effects. It gives little regard to the exclusionary effects if the dominant firm tells a story about how it does not have the power to limit output and how its conduct is efficient and will enhance its incentives to invest and invent. This is the wrong emphasis for an antitrust law. The literature on inclusiveness – empirical, anecdotal and conceptual – shows how dominant firms erect and constantly reinforce barriers that protect them from competition and that keep at bay feisty and potentially efficient competitors with better ideas.

In light of your experience, how do you suggest framing the relationship between antitrust law and economics?

Antitrust and economics are and should be deeply linked. The problem is not that economics is deeply embedded in antitrust. The problem is with assumptions of some economists and assumptions of one very important school of economics (e.g. that markets almost always work if left alone, and economic power is hard to get and will be punished by the market if exercised). For antitrust *law*, the law part of the equation must be superior, for the law part sets the norms and generalises economics into rules and standards that are judicially administrable and easily enough understood for compliance. Economics should be in service of the norms.

I know you love being an academic. You were also a partner in private practice. Could you compare academia to practice and do you have advice for young women lawyers making the choice? What excites you most about your career?

I have been very fortunate in my career, and I love and have loved my career. It was of course beyond all of my expectations when I entered law school in 1958, because, as a woman, I had none. As a member of a law faculty, I am excited to interact with my colleagues and my students, to learn from them, and to help them. When they tell me I have made an impact on them, that is a great gift. My time for scholarship is a gift.

My practice was also very satisfying. I am always fascinated by the law, analysis of it and applications of it. As a practitioner, I loved the teamwork, and loved learning new markets (and people) with each new case. As an academic I have more space to contemplate what I think the law should be and thus to think about the values of law. Academia has also given me a platform for lecturing and giving technical assistance in all parts of the world and thus for developing an amazing network of friends and acquaintances, globally.

What (other) advice do you have for young people considering a career in antitrust law?

Antitrust is a great field. It is multifaceted, for it spans law, political economy, economics and even foreign relations. It offers opportunity for all of the practice skills as well as scholarship and teaching. It is a very interpersonal field, for it exposes you both to teamwork at home and new acquaintances abroad. Follow your star. Follow the path that suits you and excites you. And if you devote yourself to the task, you will be richly rewarded by the personal satisfactions that it brings.

Michal Halperin
Israel Competition Authority
Tal Eyal-Boger

Michal Halperin is director general of the Israel Competition Authority (ICA). For the past 28 years Ms Halperin has been practicing law, specialising in antitrust law. On March 2016, she was appointed director general of the ICA. In the beginning of her professional career, she worked at a leading Israeli commercial law firm and after five years, became a partner. In 2000 she moved to Boston and served as special adviser in one of the leading law firms in Boston. After returning to Israel in 2002, Ms Halperin served for four and a half years as chief legal counsel and deputy director general at the ICA. In 2007, Ms Halperin joined a leading Israel law firm as a partner where she established and led the firm's antitrust department.

Tal Eyal-Boger is a partner and head of the Competition and Antitrust group at FBC & Co. She is internationally recognised as one of Israel's leading competition and antitrust practitioners, focusing on various competition related matters – cartels and restrictive arrangements, abusive behaviour by monopolies, regulation of oligopolies and merger of companies. She regularly represents clients before civil, criminal and administrative courts, including before the Competition Tribunal. Her expertise is widely based on vast experience in complex litigation cases, including in class actions (defence side) and investigations by the Israeli Competition Authority, acting for global multinational clients as well as local companies from an array of industries. Ms Eyal-Boger earned her LLB degree (cum laude, 1994) from the Tel Aviv University and is finalising her obligations for the Kellogg-Recanati International Executive MBA programme.

In recent years there has been much discussion about rethinking competition policy. Ever since the 1970s, the Chicago school and its economically minded view of antitrust has dominated. The focus has been about protecting "consumer welfare", which mainly means keeping prices low. But today companies (especially in the technology sector) deliver services and products at an extremely low price, if not for free. Do you think new competition policy is also required in Israel?

There is no doubt that the digital economy, which includes what is often referred as – "zero" price services and products – challenges competition authorities worldwide. However, the classic competition assessment tends to analyse prices, not because it considers an increase of prices as the only possible harm caused to consumers, but rather because it is an effective proxy for examining competitive concern. Clearly, competitive harm can be reflected in various aspects, including, inter alia, the quality of a product, the level of service, the diversity offered, and in aspects relating to research, development and innovation. The point is that these aspects may be harder to assess. In this regard, in the context of the digital economy, many competition authorities worldwide, including the Israel Competition Authority (ICA), will have to overcome the challenge of examining various competitive issues, in markets where competition is not conducted over prices.

The ICA has stated that it examines the "digital economy" sector and its possible effect on competition. In September 2018 it invited interested members of the public to submit their comments regarding competition issues in the digital economy. Where does the ICA stand with regard to the matter? Does the ICA focus on potential competitive concerns arising from the "digital economy"? Is the general concern that regulatory involvement may harm competition and chill innovation more prevalent with regard to the tech industry? What are the insights that have been crystallised in this respect?

The ICA's role in the context of the digital arena is twofold. First, to allow the entrance of advanced and innovative technologies to the Israeli markets for the benefit of the Israeli consumer. Simply put, Israel is not where it should be in many industries, whereas advanced and new technologies should be much more prevalent in the local consumer's experience. This is the case, for instance in the fintech industry, in transportation, e-commerce and more. To this end, we invest efforts in removing barriers to allow the entrance of new technologies to the Israeli markets through various tools at our disposal, including advocacy. Second, and in parallel, ICA has an uncompromising responsibility to protect the Israeli consumer, including from the market power of the "Internet giants", to the extent that competitive harm is caused, or if competitors are prevented from entering or operating in the market. To this end, we have a duty to continue and acquire expertise and knowledge in this field. If there is a place where we believe the Internet giants, or any other company for that matter, harm Israeli consumers or prevent competitors from entering or operating in the market – we will certainly intervene.

It was recently announced that an interdisciplinary team of competition, privacy and consumer protection regulators was established to promote regulation, development and cooperation in major issues in digital economy. How is this going to work? What is the underlying vision with regard to the interdisciplinary team's work? Are we to expect a policy report?

On 18 September 2019, the establishment of an interdisciplinary team, including the Privacy Protection Authority, the Consumer Protection Authority and the Competition Authority, was announced. The team conducts joint meetings from time to time. It discusses issues, common to privacy, consumer protection and competition, notably issues which may draw mutual or opposing positions of the authorities. The underlying intention is to furnish joint position papers of various kinds on issues which the three authorities are entrusted with, and which interconnect with the digital economy. This may include legislative bills, best practices, guidelines and more.

In recent years we have experienced in Israel a trend of "follow-on" civil enforcement (class actions) following judgments of foreign courts and decisions of foreign competition authorities. What is the ICA's view on this trend?

The ICA supports this trend. Of course, each case should be grounded and justified in and of itself, and the burden lies with plaintiffs to prove their case. I believe that private enforcement complements public enforcement. Hence, class actions and other private civil enforcement, when justifiable, should be encouraged.

Will we see enforcement actions by the ICA following enforcement actions of foreign competition authorities (e.g. the European Commission, Federal Trade Commission or US Department of Justice)? In this regard, does the ICA have a specific approach with respect to the digital sphere and the big tech companies?

The ICA does not have a specific policy with respect to the digital sphere and the big tech companies. Each case is examined according to its own circumstances and merits.

On 28 July 2019, the ICA published new draft merger regulations for comments from the public. At first glance, the proposed amendments in the draft for increasing the sales turnover threshold may result in reduction of the regulatory burden. However, the other proposed changes raise the concern that the proposed amendments may significantly increase the regulatory burden both with regard to the increased scope of transactions that would require the director general's approval, and with regard to the increased scope of the disclosure obligation. This is especially burdensome taking into account foreign-to-foreign mergers. Can you share the thought process and considerations behind the suggested draft?

To be clear, there is no intention, on the ICA's part, to increase the scope of transactions which require the director general's approval. This cannot be done through an amendment to the merger regulations.

With regard to increasing the scope of the disclosure obligation in cases where filing is required, I will note the following: as a general rule, indeed, the disclosure obligation in the context of the merger review regime in Israel is much narrower than that which applies in leading developed countries. Peer competition authorities in leading developed countries require the submission of a significantly broader scope of information than does the ICA. One of our main goals in the proposed amendment to the merger regulations is to align the requirements set forth by the ICA, to those set forth abroad. In addition, we believe that for mergers that clearly do not harm competition – particularly "ultra-green" mergers, assessed through the ICA's fast track for the approval of mergers – this would mean a reduction in the time frame for the ICA's assessment and an easier decision-making process. This is the case, as the ICA's assessment in such mergers is based on the information provided by the parties. Thus, while it is true that the amendment may burden the parties in this respect, it will nonetheless allow them to receive approvals quicker. This is why we believe that, on balance, the business community will benefit from this proposed amendment.

With regard to foreign-to-foreign mergers, the claim according to which the obligations imposed on foreign parties are especially burdensome, compared with local parties, is not clear. As a matter of principle, we strongly reject the concept that foreign entities should be treated differently from local entities. Foreign entities which conduct business in Israel should comply with and are subject to same legal framework as local entities. We see no good reason to adopt a more lenient approach towards foreign entities in this regard or in any other aspect.

On 21 July 2019, the ICA published the final version of its guidelines on the matter of how to evaluate significant market power, following the broadening of the definition of a monopolist in the revised Israeli Competition Law (the revision establishes that a monopoly is not only an entity with a market share above 50%, but also any entity which has "significant market power").

Does this change arise from the ICA's difficulty to determine market shares in certain cases (for example in digital markets)? Will the future trend be to focus on "significant market power" rather than market share?

The amendment to the Economic Competition Law did not arise from any such difficulty to determine market shares. Rather, it arose from a deep understanding that there is no necessary connection between market share and market power. The phenomenon that is of real interest to the ICA is market power. Accordingly, the amendment to the law was enacted to allow treatment of this phenomenon. Indeed, looking forward, the ICA intends to focus more on significant market power, rather than on market shares.

In 2018 an amendment to the Israel Competition Law conferred on the director general of the ICA a new authority to instruct a direct importer of the concrete steps it must take, in instances where the director general considers that there is a risk of harm to parallel imports or personal imports, which will have a detrimental effect on competition in the relevant sector. Considering that direct import of international brands has many procompetitive advantages, when instructing a direct importer, how does the ICA ensure that it does not harm the benefits that direct importing brings to the Israeli public and economy?

As a matter of principle, we believe that blocking parallel import is not a legitimate action to protect the interest of an importer. That said, there can be specific circumstances where a parallel importer may act in a manner which may justify, to some extent, actions on behalf of a direct importer. As to your question, before we impose instructions, we conduct a hearing. To the extent that a direct importer has strong reasons explaining why it was justified in trying to block parallel imports, we will certainly take these under consideration. However, this does not change the main principle: blocking parallel imports is not a legitimate action to protect the interest of a direct importer.

In several recent decisions, the competition tribunal did not follow the ICA's approach, and overruled or limited the director general's decision. This was the case with respect to the *Price Squeeze* case (following the tribunal's remarks the ICA withdrew its decision against Bezeq, the largest telecom company); the *Colgate* case (in an interim decision the tribunal limited the scope of instructions the director general imposed on the direct importer of Colgate regarding its communication with Colgate); and the most recent decision in the banks sector (the tribunal overruled the director general's decision to block the merger between Bank Mizrahi-Tefahot and Bank Igud). What are the ICA's takeaways from these tribunal decisions?

Our most important takeaway is that we are very lucky and honoured to have an independent, expert competition tribunal, which does not always follow the ICA's position. This is how things should work. We are strong believers in the importance of judicial review. Even more so when it is conducted by a specialised tribunal, well equipped to engage in substantive deliberation on competition law and policy, such as the Israeli Competition Tribunal. The tribunal is a significant part of the competition regime in Israel. Over the years, it has acquired broad -knowledge and expertise in antitrust and competition law. Accordingly, it takes a major role in the creation of case law and the development thereof. Such a competition tribunal, which is able to oversee an agency's conduct, from a professional and knowledgeable standpoint – beyond the generally accepted administrative review standards such as due process, and correct administration – ensures that decisions made by a competition agency maintain their reasoned, well-founded and measured nature. Sometimes the ICA's positions are accepted, sometimes they are partially accepted, other times they are not. This is an inherent and important part of our well-balanced system.

How would you describe the cooperation between the ICA and specific industry regulators (e.g. communication, transportation, energy, banking etc.)? In areas subject to specific regulation, what is the weight of the insight provided by the relevant regulators in the ICA's work and in the director general's decisions?

The ICA invests considerable resources and efforts in advancing joint initiatives with many industry regulators in different fields. This includes, for instance the Capital Market, Insurance and Savings Authority, the Israel Securities Authority, the Israel Ministry of Environment Protection, and many more, all as part of ICA's attempt to create joint projects for the purpose of advancing competition and creating a procompetitive regulatory environment. Certainly, with reference to ICA decisions in areas subject to specific regulation, we conduct close dialogues with the relevant regulators, and significant weight is granted to their insight.

The ICA recently indicated that it is in the process of re-mapping regulatory failures in the Israeli economy, and requested public input to find solutions that will, on the one hand, protect the relevant regulators' interests and, on the other, reduce harm to competition. If possible, please share the background for this process, and did the ICA identify any "regulatory failures" which harm competition and require amendment?

The "Call for Contributions regarding Competitive Failures Originating in Regulation" was one of the very first initiatives of the ICA's newly established Markets Department. The Markets Department was established as part of the ICA's reorganisation process during 2018. This department – which is made up of sector-specific teams of economists and attorneys – was entrusted inter alia with the mission of overseeing the ICA's approval of transactions as well as with its advocacy mission, i.e., with advising the government and ministerial committees on regulatory and legislative proceedings, as well as providing specific competition consultation to various government offices. This was the background for publishing the Call for Contributions.

Notably, we were very much surprised by the volume of responses and inputs received. Over 90 responses were contributed from over 50 different entities in a broad array of markets, including finance, food, transportation, communications, health, retail, energy and more. The ICA followed up with a process of mapping these contributions and examining them. To date, the treatment of 7 responses was terminated after an initial examination; 17 contributions were added to an already existing inquiry conducted at the ICA; the issues raised in 2 contributions are being advanced by the ICA; and an additional 26 contributions are classified as issues for future inquiry by the ICA.

What are the future priorities for the ICA's work in terms of enforcement measures and relevant markets?

Enforcement against cartels and bid-rigging will always remain top priority, and will continue to be enforced with criminal measures. In parallel, the ICA increased its enforcement efforts against monopolies, an effort which will continue to remain at the heart of ICA activity.

Following the comprehensive reform to the Israeli Competition Law from earlier this year – are there any additional amendments to the Israeli Competition Law that we might expect in the coming years?

Currently, we are not working on an additional amendment to the Israeli Competition Law.

Laurence Idot
University Paris II Panthéon-Assas

Anne-Sophie Choné-Grimaldi

Laurence Idot became full professor (*Agrégée des facultés de droit*) in 1982 following a PhD on "The Control of Restrictive Business Practices in International Trade" (Paris II, 1981). She has taught EU and competition law, mainly for postgraduate students, at University Paris I Panthéon-Sorbonne (1993–2007) then at University Paris II Panthéon-Assas (2007–2018), before becoming emeritus professor in September 2018. She is also co-director of the monthly review *Europe* (1991) and director of the scientific committee of the review *Concurrences* since its creation. She had an active role in many academic associations, mainly as the president of the French Association on Competition Law (AFEC) before joining the French Competition Authority. She was a member of the college of the *Autorité de la concurrence* for two terms, from 2009 to 2019. Professer Idot has extensively published on EU competition law, and also in her other fields of interest which include arbitration law and private international law, and their interaction with competition law.

Anne-Sophie Choné-Grimaldi is full professor at Paris Nanterre University, where she heads the law – economics undergraduate programme. She is the director of the research centre CEDCACE (*Centre de droit civil des affaires et du contentieux économique*). She specialises in competition law, contract law, retail law, capital market law and freedom of movement. She co-authored, with Jean-Bernard Blaise, *European Business Law*, published in September 2017 (Presses Universitaires de France). She is a regular contributor to the review *Concurrences*.

Since the beginning of your career, you have seen the place of women evolve within the university. Has this changed anything in academic thinking and research?

It is true that more women are full professors nowadays, but the main change occurred in the 1970s. I am unable to answer the question probably because the parity has never been a concern for me. At Nanterre University (Paris Ouest), where I began my studies in 1969, there were already several women who were full professors, and still more associate professors. It was less true in Paris I and Paris II, for historical reasons. In France, academic thinking and research is less dominated by the gender, which for me is completely irrelevant, than by the distinction between private and public law. Everything in the law faculties of our universities – courses, diplomas, recruitment – is based upon this distinction and the problem is the parity between both which makes no sense nowadays. For years, there were more women in private law than in public law, but it has become less and less true (see the results of the last *agrégation de droit public* in 2020).

I would prefer to make some remarks on the change in the teaching of competition law in French universities. Here I have seen a major evolution. In the 1970s, competition law was only taught with European Community law, as a part of "European business law" and only in very few universities (mainly Paris I, thanks to the creation in 1964 of the *Centre Universitaire d'Etudes des Communautés Européennes* by Pierre-Henri Teitgen, who joined Paris I after the split of the old faculty of law of Paris in 1969). I had to leave Nanterre to follow the first postgraduate diploma (equivalent of a LLM) specialising in European law at Paris I. In the 1980s, courses in European law began to be organised in most universities, but the number of hours devoted to competition law remained limited. This automatic link between competition law and European law disappeared only in the 1990s, when French competition law began to be taught by some professors (not all) as a part of the general compulsory course in commercial law. Nowadays, all French students are taught know the fundamentals of French and European competition law. Many competition law courses are organised in various postgraduate diplomas (in private law, public law, of course in EU law, but also in the dual degrees of law/economics). Furthermore, specialised postgraduate diplomas have been created.

This huge change in the teaching is, unhappily, less visible in the research. The number of theses in this field is rather limited because of our academic structures. In France, you write a thesis to join an academic career, since it is a huge undertaking, if you compare this type of thesis with most Anglo-Saxon PhDs, but many students who are interested by writing a thesis in competition are reluctant because they fear the consequences for their academic career. Competition law belongs both to private law and to public law and this distinction may be an issue for our recruitment, as it is emphasised too much in France. Moreover, so far, good students have not had any problem in finding interesting jobs in the specialised departments of law firms.

In the organisation chart of the competition authorities, the concern for parity between men and women has become prominent. You have been a member of the board of the French Competition Authority. What has the greater presence of women in competition authorities brought?

Once again, I am unable to answer this question. There were already many women working for the French Competition Authority (college, investigation services, administrative services etc.), before parity became compulsory for the college in August 2014. The third president of the former *Conseil de la concurrence* (1998–2004) was a woman – Marie-Dominique Hagelsteen, as is the present president, Isabelle de Silva. The law has imposed parity in places where it was not necessary (public sector). Thanks to the way of recruiting our high officials and judges through specific examinations to join the specific schools (ENA, ENM), there are many women lawyers who now occupy the highest positions. It was less true in economics, but it began to change 10 years ago. The problem is probably different in firms, particularly in law firms, where fewer women become partners.

Requiring gender parity generally amounts to a form of positive discrimination in favour of women. Does this contradict the idea of competition based on merit, which is well known to experts in the field?

I am not at all in favour of positive discrimination and I agree with your analysis: it contradicts the idea of competition. That's not a good solution. The problem is elsewhere: it is necessary to give equal opportunities to all children as soon as possible, mainly at the first years of school. In France, we did better on this a century ago than we do now. That is a huge issue and I will make no additional comment.

Should competition law practice a kind of positive discrimination in favour of small and medium-sized enterprises, for example, by allowing them to consult each other under defined conditions?

Why? That's not an issue of size of the firm, but of position on the market. In EU law, we already have the tools to cover this situation and I don't see the need to go further. In French law, there is already a specific regime for so-called practices with a local dimension, which are dealt with by the Ministry of the Economy. I was against this solution, which was introduced by the 2008 reform. A decade later, I recognise that it alleviates the Authority's workload, but the applicable rules should be the same, and it is not true for the sanctions.

What has French academia contributed to European competition law over the last decade?

First, the contribution of French economists is well known. There is no need to mention Jean Tirole, the Toulouse School of Economics and many other names. Second, if I focus only on law, many recognised professors in French competition law are women. There are more women than men in this field. Third, we are less specialised that many of our European colleagues since we have to teach many different courses, mainly at the beginning of our career. It gives a broader view. French law academia is less technical but more conscious of interaction of competition law with other parts of the law. Your question is only on the last decade. I will make the comparison with the discussions following the White Paper of 1999. We were very few to join the debate, which in France was mainly dominated by officials (Ministry of the Economy, Competition Authority, some specialised judges at the Paris court of appeals and the commercial chamber of the *Cour de cassation*). A change occurred with the ensuing discussion on private enforcement. Competition law suddenly interested many colleagues, as well as judges, probably because it was necessary to deal with issues in civil law and to adapt our ordinary procedural rules. It looked like "true law", not a mix of law and economics.

Unhappily, French academia lacks visibility since in law we still mainly publish in French. As soon as you write a tiny note in English, you are read. If you write something clever and deeper in French, the impact will be limited and broadly ignored. German academia publishes more in English and your generation should follow the example. However there are two limits. First there is the compulsory use of the French language, which is still the law in France. Second, it's a pity not to use our continental languages in law. English terminology is rather poor, poorer than French and let alone German. I will only give two examples. The first one in competition law, there is no word in English to translate "*entente*": it is necessary to say "agreement and concerted practices with an anticompetitive effect". The word "cartel" is sometimes used, but it's a mistake since cartels are only a specific kind of *entente*. The second one is more general. In French law, we have different kinds of reviews of decisions or judgments (another example; a decision is not a judgment;

you cannot use the same word): *l'appel, le recours en annulation ou en réformation, le pourvoi...* All these different words, which have different regimes, are translated in a single word: "appeal". We shall resist the impoverishment of the legal language because of the general use of English language.

What can French academia contribute to European competition law in the coming years?

The recent evolution and the present consultations are interesting since they open the door to other issues like fairness, unfair commercial practices, the link between competition and international trade, the control of non-EU investments... We are rather familiar with these kinds of problems, mainly the first, and I hope that we will invest in these new fields of research, as we did two decades ago with the regulation issues in network industries, for example. French academia has already extensively written on some present issues, such as the concept of undertaking and the borders of the market, services of general interest or the interaction between competition law and environmental law. Unhappily, these works are often ignored outside France. We should use these previous works to contribute to the debate in a more active way. I recognise that it is difficult since the workload of French academics is very high with few means: no research assistant, no secretary... It is easier for a law firm to reply to the consultations of the Commission. It is a pity that the consultation took place in July and August... just after the COVID-19 containment! Happily, that is only the first step of the discussion.

You have seen the growing role of economists in the application of competition law. In your opinion, how should the roles of lawyers and economists be defined?

There is a lot to say. First I will distinguish between the respective roles in the adoption of new texts and the application of law in individual cases. In the first situation, the role of economists is fundamental. They should explain what is good and bad for competition: for example, what about resale price maintenance (RPM)? From an economic point of view, is it justified to qualify RPM as an hard-core restriction? Then, following the political choice, lawyers should translate the best solution based upon this economic analysis in the texts. However two conditions should be met. First, economists must understand that we cannot have an individual analysis in each situation. The rule of law must be general by nature and it is necessary to have a minimum standard to maintain legal safety. Second, to be more convincing, economists should make more studies on the actual consequences of previous policies. There is presently a lack of *ex post* analysis, for instance, few economic studies on the consequences of merger decisions, on the consequences of BER.

As far as the application of competition rules in individual cases is concerned, I will make a second distinction between merger control and antitrust. In merger control, either there is no issue (more than 50% of cases are dealt with by simplified proceedings, which raises the issue of the adequacy of the thresholds... and we go back to the previous comment) and we don't need economists, or there is an issue. Here that is clear. The competition analysis is more and more sophisticated and economists have a major role to play, but in the legal framework controlled by lawyers (of the Authority and private practice). The role is clearly complementary. In antitrust, I am more reserved, making another distinction between public and private enforcement. In public enforcement, one shall not forget that most cases opened by competition authorities are clear-cut infringements. In cartel cases, proof issues do not concern the qualification of the conduct and have been partly solved by procedural devices like leniency programmes and settlements. When I was member of the college, economists attended to discuss the amount of the fine and the quantification of the injury to the economy. I will be very frank: it is a huge waste of time and money, except for the economists who work for defendant firms, since it is a very lucrative market. I hope that the next reform of French law will suppress the reference to this element of the pecuniary sanction. In antitrust cases, we need economists, not to calculate the amount of the fine in individual cases (once again, they have to intervene upstream to define the elements that lawyers take in consideration), but to help to qualify the conduct, when necessary. It is very rare for article 101 TFEU to be applied, mainly concerning abuse of dominant position. Here, once again, economists have a role to play. We need them for instance to calculate a margin squeeze… In private enforcement, there is the traditional issue of quantification of damages: it is not new, but private enforcement is a new market both for economists and lawyers. There is room for all, but at the end the rule of law will prevail.

Would you say that by allowing American digital giants to grow, European competition law has missed the digital shift?

Certainly not. European competition law is not liable for the present situation. Maybe it is the fault of the EU, which did not protect its market enough, opened its borders too broadly without requesting reciprocity, did not encourage enough innovation in Europe… That is a huge debate and in any case, it will be more the fault of the Member States, who didn't give the EU the means to act. As an enforcer of competition rules, the European Commission have done the job and applied the EU merger regulation as it has been written. That is law. It is now rather clear that we have to change and complete the rules, but it takes time. It is not new: the economic world, innovation, always precede law.

What is your opinion on the "digital package" on which the European Commission has launched a broad consultation?

First, you need to know rather well the way any economic sector functions, before adopting categorical judgments. Some younger colleagues are much more familiar with this new world than I, a single user without any particular technical knowledge of the field. Therefore, I will be very cautious. I have read the documents, which are rather light at this stage of the discussion, and some comments.

Second, on the Digital Services Act package, the principle of an *ex ante* regulation does not shock me in itself. It is necessary. I have no problem with the different proposed options: enlargement of the n° 2019/1150 regulation (Platform to Business), empowering regulators to collect information, adoption of a new regulatory framework with blacklisted practices and specific remedies. I fully agree with reference of the Commission to the previous example of telecommunications services. Of course, it will necessary to precisely define the scope of the new tool and the powers of the regulator. As we say in French, "the devil is in the detail". However, the articulation between regulation and competition law is a well-known issue and we have more than 20 years of practice.

Third, at this stage it is very difficult to have an idea on the new competition tool (NCT). In the four proposed options, the Commission could address competition concerns arising either from unilateral conduct by dominant companies (options 1 and 2), or as soon as there is a risk for the market structure (options 3 and 4). Two main characteristics are similar in all scenarios: first, the Commission could intervene without any prior finding of an infringement pursuant to article 102 TFEU and, second, could impose remedies, including structural remedies. The first French academics' comments were rather hostile and focused on the possible structural remedies. I will be less critical at this early stage. Of course, the new tool must respect the general principles of law, but before any negative judgment, we need to study the efficiency of similar existing tools, like, for instance, the UK market studies and investigations. It is clear that we could not only rely any more on the prohibition of an abuse of dominant position. We need another tool, probably based more on the risk for the market structure.

Finally, what advice would you give to young French women starting a university career?

If it is in competition law, first, to become fully fluent in English and to publish at least half of her research in English, second, to follow some classes with economists in competition law and regularly exchange with them, to become familiar with their way of thinking and working, third, to try to spend as much time as possible teaching or researching abroad, in a Member State, outside Europe – anywhere, to enlarge her horizon. Fourth, to join networks, either academic, or professional associations, to work on files and to meet and exchange with practitioners.

The choice of the topic of the research is also of course important. It should not be limited only to competition law. It's important to try to keep as broad as possible a view on our legal system and to think competition law like a small part of a huge ensemble. Some topics are extensively covered since they are fashionable, but it is more interesting to work on unexplored issues, to work on raw materials (decisions…).

To conclude, I would like to say a few words on the spectacular change I have seen during my career in the evolution of EU competition law itself. When I wrote my thesis at the end of the 1970s, I quoted less than five judgments of the Court of Justice, always the same on non-EU firms. A first major change occurred in the mid-1980s both at EU level with adoption of the merger regulation, the creation of the Court of First Instance and the opening to competition of former state-owned enterprises in network industries; and at the French level following the 1986 reform. Then the new century began with the revolution that led to Regulation no 1/2003 and the European Competition Network. It was a fascinating period with many interesting exchanges with all stakeholders. Very quickly, a new debate began with the role of private enforcement. We have now these new projects linked to digital (Digital Services Act package), but also to fairness in international trade. We are very lucky to work in this field. It is not possible to get bored.

Birgit Krueger
German Competition Authority

Sarah Blazek

Birgit Krueger has been chairwoman of the 9th Decision Division at the German Bundeskartellamt since May 2019, in charge of the tourism, hotel, restaurant and catering sector, transport, postal service, financial services, insurance and App Stores. Prior to that, from 2015 to 2019, she was head of the General Policy Division; and from 2007 to 2015, she was chairwoman of the 2nd Decision Division in charge of wholesale and retail, the consumer goods industry and agriculture. After studying economics at the University of Cologne, she joined the Bundeskartellamt in 1991. She was a rapporteur on various sectors (automotive, waste management, engineering, electricity, medical devices) and served as head of the merger control unit.

Sarah Blazek is an associate partner in the competition law team of law firm Noerr LLP in Munich, Germany. Previously, she worked for a number of years as a competition lawyer for the Brussels office of Freshfields Bruckhaus Deringer. Sarah advises clients on all aspects of European and German antitrust and competition law and also focuses on state aid matters. She has been recognised by *The Legal 500* (2020) as an "up-and-coming lawyer with profound expertise in German and European antitrust law" and has in particular been a keen participant in the second W@CompetitionDE talk in Germany.

From Food Retail to Digital Economy

Before heading the Bundeskartellamt's General Policy Division, you helped shape its approach to antitrust in the food retail sector during your time as head of the 2nd Decision Division. You led spectacular proceedings, such as the one leading to the Bundeskartellamt's prohibition of the *Edeka / Tengelmann* merger, and provided guidance on the prohibition of vertical price fixing in the bricks-and-mortar food retail sector. Can you give us a short retrospective of this time?

I chaired the 2nd Decision Division for eight years until the end of 2015. It was a very exciting position that comprised a multitude of interesting competencies throughout the value chain in food manufacturing and distribution, from the agriculture sector and the entire food industry through to the highly concentrated food retail sector. The way in which case-handling and independent decision-making are organised in the Decision Divisions already ensures that the heads of divisions are always highly involved in practical case work and have to know the facts of the cases in detail.

Certainly the prohibition of the *Edeka/Tengelmann* merger and the subsequent ministerial authorisation received a high level of public attention. The fine proceedings for vertical price-fixing in the food retail sector were important pilot proceedings to punish companies for their clearly prohibited pricing practices, which harmed consumers in important product areas. However, these fine proceedings were not conducted by my former Decision Division, but by our 10th Decision Division, which specialises *in fine* proceedings. Such major proceedings of course call for guidelines and guidance for the economic sectors involved. You have mentioned the example of our guidance note on the prohibition of vertical price-fixing that made the most important information on the scope of the prohibition of vertical price-fixing in the food retail sector accessible to the public. With the guidance note, the Bundeskartellamt intended to provide the sector and anyone interested with practical examples of the possibilities and limits of coordination between retailers and manufacturers.

Which general antitrust concerns regarding vertical restraints have manifested themselves or arisen since then due to the growing world of online trade and the ensuing restrictions on online distribution?

The "digital" part of my work for the 2nd Decision Division originated in the increasing digital transformation of distribution channels in the general consumer goods industry rather than in the food retail sector. To this day I consider the antitrust law debate of vertical restrictions imposed by powerful manufacturers on online sales one of the most important aspects of my career.

Over the last two decades e-commerce has become a supplementary distribution channel of great importance, which allows even smaller retailers to extend their reach on the market. It has also enhanced (price) transparency across different products and different retailers. This has often increased the competitive pressure on both manufacturers and retailers; several of them have responded with new forms of restrictive practices in order to secure their margins. Here the competition authorities in Europe have an important role to play. While restrictions addressing legitimate concerns by manufacturers about the quality of distribution usually do not raise competition concerns, we closely examine restrictions which have the sole purpose of reducing price pressure from online competition on the merits. The latter applies in particular to per se bans on online-specific distribution or search formats that can be considered essential for a dealer's reach, and transparency on the range offered to the end customer. We have therefore worked on several cases primarily involving selective distribution agreements and unlawful restrictions of online sales. One example was the *ASICS* case.

Despite court decisions at European and national levels, the discussion on how to deal with such online restrictions is still ongoing. It will be one of the key issues in the upcoming amendment to the Vertical Block Exemption Regulation and its accompanying guidelines and we (inter alia) suggest amending the Vertical Guidelines with a more nuanced position on online restrictions and, in particular, platform bans.

You currently head the Bundeskartellamt's 9th Decision Division. Can you share a brief overview with us of how digitalisation and the typical features of our new digital economy have impacted your work there? Can you illustrate this with a concrete example or a specific case?

In my current position as head of the 9th Decision Division, whose competencies include transport and Mobility as a Service (MaaS), the rise of the platform economy with intermediaries increasingly replacing the traditional purchase – resale distribution models is a hot topic. One ongoing set of proceedings concerns the sale of tickets of Deutsche Bahn via so-called mobility platforms. On mobility platforms, travellers can search for travel information either online or via apps: they can compare routes and book tickets. Some mobility platforms even offer to organise a complete journey with different means of transport. Digital platforms through which travellers can book all means of transport to their destination from a single source will be an important market in the future. In Germany, these providers rely on Deutsche Bahn for tickets and information. As things stand at present, mobility platforms do not, for example, receive real-time information about departures and delays. What is more, Deutsche Bahn's requirements for online marketing and granting rebates are extensive. We are following up these allegations and will examine whether Deutsche Bahn is unlawfully restricting the visibility and attractiveness of mobility platforms for consumers.

You headed the Bundeskartellamt's General Policy Division from 2015 until 2019. This period was characterised by intense discussions about whether adjustments of the regulatory framework were required in view of the internet economy. Against this background, in 2015 the Bundeskartellamt established an in-house project group, the Internet Platforms Think Tank, to develop competition law strategies to deal with the digital economy and platform markets. It led to the publication of a corresponding working paper. Can you explain how the Bundeskartellamt has built on this early conceptual work and how it has organised its approach to digital matters?

While I was head of the General Policy Division, I of course dealt intensively with antitrust phenomena in the context of a significant digital transformation and a platform economy that is gaining strength. It has to be emphasised that general policy work is always closely linked to the Decision Divisions' case work. The Internet Platforms Think Tank you mentioned was created based on the case practice of and questions raised by the 6th Decision Division, which is responsible for a number of platform-related issues. Since 2015, the working groups have prepared practice-orientated working papers, some of them in close cooperation with the French *Autorité de la Concurrence*: "Market Power of Platforms and Networks" and "Competition Law and Data" in 2016, and "Algorithms and Competition" in 2019. The latter two are about data and algorithms as technological drivers of digitalisation and understanding technical aspects of current business models, in particular topics like data analysis and software tools used by companies. Basically, we always follow the same approach when preparing working papers. Our aim is to (a) expand antitrust expertise regarding the digital economy and provide an analysis of current literature and other materials, (b) develop examination concepts for the quick and efficient processing of digital economy cases and (c) trigger the legislative measures we consider necessary.

The digital economy of course also influences the way in which we organise our work.

Almost every industry division in my authority now deals with digital matters, from the platform economy and numerous multi-channel sales systems to all digitalisation initiatives in the context of "Industry 4.0". This obviously requires more internal coordination but also leads to many fruitful discussions about the "correct" antitrust approach to these cases, which sometimes involves new theories of harm. I enjoy this close cooperation within the authority on the digital economy.

We have also created a new Digital Economy Unit (G6) under the umbrella of the General Policy Division. The unit is composed of an interdisciplinary team of lawyers, economists and mathematical/technical experts. Not only did this unit co-author and coordinate the paper on algorithms, but it also represents the Bundeskartellamt in European Competition Network working groups and advises the Decision Divisions in cases involving multisided markets or platforms, algorithms used by companies and in matters of access to competitively relevant data. Many authorities are currently gaining knowledge and experience on how to promote an interdisciplinary exchange within established organisational structures and make cooperation even more effective. We are of course also discussing these matters with other authorities.

The digital economy is characterised by incredibly fast technological developments. Digital power, including in terms of data collection, and economic power increasingly go hand in hand. This trend and the best way to "tame" digital giants have been debated by the global antitrust community intensely and quite controversially. Against the background of the newer legislative developments, as well as developments in enforcement and your conceptual work and insights on these matters, do you believe that antitrust law in Germany (and the EU) is now on the right path to finding appropriate answers? What efficient and adequate tools are still missing to avoid a potential "digital underenforcement"?

Things are on the move, both in Germany and in Europe. I would even go so far as to say that so many initiatives have been started, both in competition law and in the area of potential regulation, that we should wait and see how effective the underlying concepts actually are before considering further initiatives.

The (upcoming) 10th amendment to the German Competition Act (GWB) will see a considerable change to the abuse provisions in sections 19 and 20. To give you an idea of the scope involved, I will simply list the relevant aspects at this point.

The new law would go far beyond our traditional rules on abuse of dominance. Our tools will likely be sharpened to put us in a more comfortable position to tackle our challenges. The following examples illustrate the range:

- The Bundeskartellamt can declare a company to be "of paramount significance for competition across markets". Once such a paramount significance is determined, we can prohibit practices like self-preferencing, market envelopment, establishing entry barriers related to data, hindering interoperability or data portability, even on markets where the company in question is not yet dominant.

- The new law facilitates interventions below the dominance threshold by proving dependency on stronger platforms and their competitive advantage in controlling big data.

- It broadens our national essential facilities doctrine by explicitly referencing access to data.

– It clarifies that intermediation power (gatekeeping) is a special factor contributing to market power.

Even if our toolkit allows us to capture data-related concerns, finding good remedies is still not an easy task. But we do have some experience in this. In our *Facebook* case we placed restrictions on the use of data and prohibited Facebook from combining user data from different sources without the user's consent. Although the Federal Court of Justice rejected Facebook's request to order the suspensive effect of its appeal, the main proceedings are still pending before the courts.

DG COMP is also considering new tools to facilitate intervention, in particular in "structural antitrust issues" like monopolisation strategies or the transfer of market power below the threshold for market dominance. DG CONNECT is simultaneously discussing the introduction of a tool for platform-specific *ex ante* regulation.

In the past, there have been demands for exemptions from antitrust law for "traditional" industry players in Germany, sometimes disguised in a "national champions" argument, to protect them from online competition. You talked about this "spectre of digitalisation" which would continue to haunt us further in the form of extensive exemptions claims. What is your position on these discussions today?

Indeed. The spectre of digitalisation is often used as an argument by traditional industries when demanding far-reaching exemptions from competition law. Established economic actors do not always find it easy to keep up with the digital big techs, even when it comes to specific projects they discuss with us. They do not necessarily fail to implement the technological aspects involved; however sometimes the interests behind and strategies in favour of a joint initiative just differ considerably. As an example, I would like to mention digital payment systems, which fall within my Decision Division's area of competence.

Antitrust law in principle provides for cooperation opportunities to counterbalance dominant platforms, both on a European and a national level. A critical mass is often required to achieve the necessary network effects without losing the essential entrepreneurial variety. However, antitrust guidelines are just as essential. Cooperation between major suppliers may not hinder new competitors from entering the market and may be non-discriminatory. We also have to ensure that there is no limitless flow of competitively significant data. Over the last few years, the Bundeskartellamt has developed practice-orientated approaches towards quick examination involving guidance and informal procedures. However, success or failure often does not depend on the possibilities provided for by competition law.

The German banking industry, for instance, is under considerable competitive pressure from powerful payment systems, most of which are operated by US companies, e.g. Apple Pay or PayPal. Some payment models launched in Germany are very successful at the point of sale, e.g. Girocard, whereas others like Paydirekt or Giropay are less successful. In any case, these models are not a real counterweight.

#DK is one new business case of the German Banking Industry Committee. However, it is not easy to pool the various interests and strategies of the participating associations and individual banks. In my opinion, an innovative and quick leap forward is essential. Such a leap would involve the development of a payment system that can be used on an international scale and on all types of devices, both digital and mobile, i.e. an "omnichannel" system that should also provide for an instant payment function. The structure must be quick and effective, focus on payment and work in an open and non-discriminatory way. Efficiencies for commerce and consumers must be the priority, and they are also important for examination under competition law. We are ready to accompany the process from an antitrust perspective.

Reflections and Advice to Antitrust Practitioners

Your 30th anniversary with the Bundeskartellamt is approaching. During this time, you have been at the forefront of national and international antitrust law debates, shaping antitrust law policy and enforcement in Germany and beyond. If it is at all possible for you to single out any particular highlights or achievements from all this time, what would these be? Are there any specific cases, discussions or developments that have particularly influenced your approach to antitrust matters?

Merger control certainly is solid ground for me. I have been involved in many difficult merger control proceedings in very different functions right from the start of my work with the Bundeskartellamt. I started as a young case handler, later became a rapporteur before heading a Decision Division and advised colleagues as a member, later as head, of the General Policy Division. I enjoy case work a lot, particularly when it comes to often very facts-based discussions with the companies concerned. I support a stringent and effective approach to merger control, because it allows us to detect threats to competition and imminent concentrations at an early stage and take corresponding action before it is too late. In my view the introduction of the European SIEC test to German merger control has expanded our definition of market dominance in a reasonable way. I believe that the basic concept gives us more leeway when addressing imminent market concentrations, which may in some borderline cases also involve a powerful group of companies, because we do not have to prove the existence of a dominant oligopoly.

Teamwork is essential when deadlines are tight in the decisive phase of a potential prohibition case. Pressure was enormous in the *Edeka/ Tengelmann* case, both during the proceedings themself and from the political side. From the back office to case handlers and colleagues in the General Policy Division, the case team always worked constructively together, even in the most difficult situations, and always focused on making the right decision, taking all investigation results into account. For me this was a great experience I would not have wanted to miss.

Can you share a little bit about what professional experiences – positive and negative – have made a special impact on you and helped you progress in your professional development? What advice can you pass on to female antitrust practitioners? And last but not least: After, as it seems, having "seen it all", what still excites you, motivates you or even surprises you about antitrust issues in your daily work? What would you tell women who are thinking about taking up a career as an antitrust practitioner about why this is a fascinating and fulfilling area of law or, for more experienced practitioners, why this is an area of law worth continuing to be involved and invested in?

Joining the Bundeskartellamt in 1991 was the right decision for me. Competition law is fascinating. Even after almost 30 years, new legal issues keep coming up and special market conditions and cases pose new challenges. An economist myself, I have always enjoyed interdisciplinary work at the interface between application of the law and our economic approach to market investigations and analyses. Competition law brings you very close to economic decision-making and markets and what you do can have immense effects on economic processes, consumers and entrepreneurial decisions. This is a privilege but it also comes with great responsibility and can involve difficult, conflicting disputes either during the procedure or in court. Besides sound facts as a basis, a knack for persuasion and negotiations can be an advantage in some situations.

Of course not every step of a long-standing career in a public authority may seem particularly exciting and challenging at first glance, and maybe sometimes also not at second glance. The ability to tolerate such phases is important, because, at least in Germany, you either sign up for only a few years or an entire career in the competition authority. This is the price you pay. In Germany, unlike other European countries, there are very limited opportunities for gathering experience in a company after joining the competition authority and then coming back to the authority. However, I have never regretted my decision to spend my career in *one* single authority and I very much enjoy going to work (almost) every day.

Gail Levine
Federal Trade Commission

Amanda Reeves & Elizabeth Prewitt

Gail Levine is a Deputy Director for the Bureau of Competition at the Federal Trade Commission (FTC). She oversees a variety of mergers, conduct investigations and litigation, particularly in health care and tech. Gail joined Uber in 2016 as the head of US regulatory affairs, and later served as director of US competition law. Before that, Gail was vice-president and associate general counsel at Verizon, where she handled patent and antitrust matters. Gail has also served as attorney advisor to the FTC chairman, and as FTC deputy assistant general counsel. She began her career as a litigator in the US Department of Justice's Civil Division.

Amanda Reeves is the Global Chair of the Latham & Watkins Antitrust & Competition Practice. Mandy Reeves is a globally recognised litigator particularly focused on the application of the antitrust laws to the healthcare, life sciences and high technology industries. Her practice runs the gamut – from representing clients in FTC and DOJ investigations into mergers and alleged anticompetitive conduct, to defending clients in antitrust litigations, raising novel issues. She has experience at all phases of government antitrust investigations and is an experienced litigator. Mandy re-joined Latham in 2011 after two years serving as attorney adviser to commissioner J Thomas Rosch at the FTC.

Elizabeth Prewitt is a Partner in the Latham & Watkins Antitrust & Competition Practice and leads the defense of major global and domestic corporations and executives facing complex and often cross-border antitrust investigations initiated by US federal (DOJ), state, and foreign competition enforcement agencies. Prior to transitioning to private practice, Liz spent 16 years as a trial lawyer in the Antitrust Division of the DOJ. She served as Assistant Chief of the Antitrust Division in the New York office from 2012 to 2014 and as a Visiting International Enforcer to the European Commission's Directorate-General for Competition in Brussels. Liz is a first-chair trial counsel and two-time recipient of the Attorney General's Distinguished Service Award (the DOJ's second highest award) and the Assistant Attorney General's Award.

There have been recent episodes where the overlap and tension between the Federal Trade Commission's (FTC's) antitrust arm and the Department of Justice's Antitrust Division has been exposed, most notably in the context of the *Qualcomm* litigation. What is your view on whether that will be a feature of the enforcement landscape moving forward and how the agencies should navigate points of possible friction or divergence?

There is plenty of antitrust work to keep both of our agencies busy. We spend our taxpayer money best when we are each investigating challenging areas vigorously. But it's not uncommon for federal agencies to disagree with each other. They do that all the time. In fact, when those differences in policies and principles are aired well internally, it helps the government ensure it is reaching the right decision.

Focusing on the level of interaction between the FTC and the EU's DG COMP, in what matters do you foresee there would be more active engagement between the FTC and DG COMP and why?

We communicate closely with DG COMP on a wide range of matters today, from cross-border mergers to conduct cases. We are building on that tradition of communication and cooperation now that we have established our Technology Enforcement Division. The TED, as it's known, communicates frequently with other enforcers, including DG COMP. Having said that, we always keep in mind that the facts in the EU and the US may be different, and the competition legal frameworks certainly are. We can inform one another's work, but neither of us can make anyone else's analysis a substitute for our own, independent review.

State enforcers have become increasingly active in enforcement, and have at times joined forces with private plaintiff in civil litigation. Do you have any concerns about this trend?

To the contrary, we're really proud to be building on a long tradition of successful federal/state collaboration. We're at our strongest when we work together, particularly since state enforcers know the local markets and add critical resources to prosecute key cases. When we team up with the states to litigate national issues at the local level, we have met with considerable success. For example, in June 2019, the 8th Circuit agreed with our arguments in *FTC v Sanford Health*, affirming an injunction blocking an anticompetitive physician group and hospital merger in North Dakota. It meant a lot that North Dakota's state attorney general joined our challenge there. Likewise, 11 state attorneys general – from Arizona to Washington – participated in our investigation of *Fidelity/Stewart*, a US$1.2 billion title insurance merger that would have reduced an industry dominated by "the Big 4" players to "the Big 3", we alleged. (The parties later abandoned the transaction.) This trend extends beyond our merger work, as well. Seven states have joined our challenge to an alleged illegal course of conduct to maintain high prices for an off-patent drug. That case, *FTC v. Vyera*, is pending in federal court now.

The FTC's Technology Task Force has been in place since February 2019, what do you see as its biggest challenge and how do you plan to overcome that challenge?

Possibly our biggest challenge is the fact that we have limited resources. As you may know, we shifted resources within the Bureau of Competition in 2019 to create the TED. (It started life in early 2019 as the Technology Task Force. It's now the TED, a name change that reflects that it is now a permanent division of the FTC's Bureau of Competition.) The group is dedicated to monitoring competition in US technology markets and recommending enforcement action when warranted. It's staffed by seasoned career attorneys who know how to analyse complex markets, including in the tech space.

What is your view regarding how the FTC should engage with complainants, given that their interests may not always align with the FTC's enforcement mission?

Our door is always open to those who have competition complaints. Complainants can be one of the best sources of the kinds of facts on the ground that are critical to our investigations and enforcement actions. Those facts are rarely self-evident. We have to go out and find them, through document review, interviews – and, when we're lucky, well-informed complainants.

Not every complainant brings us the kind of competition problems that the FTC Act allows us to challenge. But that's fine. Where the complaints don't state an antitrust complaint but still sound in competition policy – say, unnecessarily burdensome state licensing requirements designed to impede competition – we can refer the complainants to our colleagues in the FTC's Office of Policy Planning, which specialises in powerful advocacy against practices like that.

You have had a varied career, moving between the public and private sector, but are there any guiding principles that informed your career choices and the path you have charted?

I have always sought jobs that would let me work with good people to tackle hard problems. As a litigator at the Department of Justice, I fought constitutional challenges to new federal data privacy laws. At Verizon, I advocated to reform patent laws that were getting in the way of innovation. At Uber, I led the US regulatory team at one of the company's most contentious times. I'm privileged now to oversee the FTC's new Technology Enforcement Division as it takes on some of the highest-profile investigations in the nation, the FTC's Health Care team as it fights anticompetitive drug-pricing practices, and some of the top merger-review teams in the country. All along, I've gotten to work with amazing people at each institution, and that's what made each job a pleasure.

Among the key learnings from your private sector experience that you bring to your role as an enforcer, are there some that you draw upon more regularly?

Yes. From my time in the private sector, I know how much facts, and speed, matter. Theory and principles are important, but facts tend to be critical to top decision-makers, from CEOs and board members to judges and juries. I learned early on as a trial lawyer that you need to know the facts better than your witness does – and you need to be able to make them simple and easy to understand. Moreover, you need to be able to gather the right facts and marshal the right people to make decisions quickly. If you or your CEO or board or judge can't decide quickly enough, the market may move without you – rendering your careful deliberations moot. In other words, it all comes down to speed and facts.

You have witnessed a range of advocacy styles, and more recently one of your colleagues has spoken about the benefits of allowing less senior attorneys take on more prominent advocacy roles: are there any particular ways of engaging with enforcers that you find more effective? Can you share some examples of advocacy that you found to be particularly effective or ineffective?

True to my answer above, I find that the most impressive presentations are the ones that reflect a deep knowledge of the facts. Outside advocates do their clients the greatest service when they can help us understand the facts. Within a lot of organisations, it's often one of the most junior people on the team who knows the facts best. When that's true, that's the person I want to hear from directly.

What were your first observations about re-joining the FTC in 2018?

When you visit the Bureau of Competition's main conference room at the FTC, you'll see on the walls the Gilded Age political cartoons from the early days of antitrust. One shows fat cat oligarchs controlling the Senate from the back row. Another shows the personification of Liberty threatened by an anticompetitive gorilla, like some kind of antitrust King Kong. Antitrust was a political-campaign issue back in those days, and it's a headline-grabbing issue again today. The fervour of public attention paid to antitrust today is perhaps matched only by the days of President Theodore Roosevelt. We at the FTC take that mission as seriously as the original trustbusters, and we're proudly building on that tradition.

Gabriella Muscolo
Italian Competition Authority

Lindsay Lutz

Gabriella Muscolo is a commissioner of the Italian Competition Authority. As a judge, she sat at the specialist section for IP and competition law at the Court for Undertakings in Rome. She was member of the enlarged Board of Appeal of the European Patent Office. She is currently a fellow of the Centre of European Law of King's College London, a member of the Board of Trustees of ERA and of the advisory boards of the ERA Forum and of *Concurrences e-Competitions Bulletin* boards. She is a lecturer of competition and IP Law at Italian and foreign universities and publishes in Italian and English in the fields of competition and IP law.

Lindsay Lutz is an associate director at Intel Corporation, advising sales teams on antitrust and commercial matters. Before Intel, Lindsay was global competition counsel at eBay, where her portfolio included antitrust counselling, regulatory, litigation, M&A and compliance; she also previously worked as counsel at Pillsbury Winthrop Shaw Pittman and clerked for US federal Judge David O Carter. Lindsay is a graduate of Harvard Law School and the University of Notre Dame.

The Italian Competition Authority (ICA) recently published a set of Guidelines and Policy Recommendations relating to the Digital Sector, which was the culmination of a multi-year, multi-agency effort. Why has the agency put such a priority on digital issues?

The emergence of the digital economy poses new challenges for the enforcement of competition law and has indeed become one of the main priorities of the ICA. Digital transformation blurs the boundaries between the material and virtual dimensions of the economy. Indeed, in order to engage in the material dimension of business, it is increasingly necessary to use online platforms.

As far as big data is concerned, it represents an important component of knowledge capital, a relevant asset for digital enterprises, and they affect the whole economy. They have been defined by the Organisation for Economic Co-operation and Development (OECD) as "the information characterised by such assets in high volume, velocity and variety to require specific technology and analytical methods for its transformation into value". Hence, big data is not just a mere collection of data in large datasets. It involves highly sophisticated technologies, such as cloud computing, which allow a large and varied amount of data to be processed at high speed in real time.

Online platforms provide targeted services, which are an important source of consumer welfare. At the same time, their business models are characterised by (i) services which are apparently offered free to consumers in exchange for data and attention, and (ii) advertisers subsidising the service free of charge in exchange for the possibility to target consumers with advertising.

In this context, non-price parameters, such as quality and data protection, may become relevant for the competitive process. Therefore, big data is among the factors which paved the way for the emergence of online giants, such as online platforms, and may raise competitive concerns. This has led to the development of new theories of harm and new challenges for competition authorities. Indeed, as far as the competition sector is concerned, it is debated whether a breach of data protection by a company in a dominant position may be considered an exploitative abuse.[1]

Building such theories of harm has raised some challenges, especially with regard to the definition of the relevant market and the assessment of market power.

Particularly, in identifying the relevant market, a service offered free of charge makes the application of the traditional SSNIP test difficult. Therefore, it has been suggested that a quantitative assessment of quality be introduced, for instance by using the Small but Significant Non-transitory Decrease in Quality (SSNDQ) test.[2]

Regarding the assessment of market power, a service offered at no charge makes it difficult to assess dominance; the exertion of market power may take place in other parts of the market or through non-price dimensions of competition. Therefore, it has been stressed that focusing on promoting market contestability is crucial (for example, favouring the incentive and the ability of consumers to multi-home) since these markets tend to favour a winner-takes-all outcome.

---

1   See Orla Lynskey and Francisco Alves Da Costa Cabral, *Family Ties: The Intersection Between Data Protection and Competition in EU Law* (Wolters Kluwer, 2018). See also Giulia Schneider, "Testing Art. 102 TFEU in the Digital Marketplace: Insights from the Bundeskartellamt's investigation against Facebook" (2018) 9(4) JECL & Pract. 213. In particular, p 221, whereby can be found a list of cases of infringement of other branches of law for competition law assessments, i.e. Case 127/73 *Belgische Radio en Televisie v SABAM* ECLI:C:1974:25; *Banghalter & Homem Christo/SACEM* (Case COMP/C2/37.219) Commission Decision SG(2002)231176, <http://ec.europa.eu/competition/elojade/isef/case_details.cfm?proc_code=1_37219>; Comisiòn Nacional de la Competencia, Resolución Expediente, S/0466/13 SGAE Autores. Regulation (EU) 2016/679 of the European Parliament and of the Council on the protection of natural persons with regard to the processing of personal data and on the free movement of such data, and repealing Directive 95/46/EC (General Data Protection Regulation) [2018] OJ L119/1, recitals 7, 58 and 60.

2   Suggested also by Michal Gal and Daniel Rubinfeld, "The Hidden Costs of Free Goods: Implications for Antitrust Enforcement" (2016) 80(521) Antitrust LJ. For an alternative, similar, approach, see the attentional version of the SSNIP test, which "tries to determine how consumers might react to a small but significant and non-transitory increase in undesired messages or advertising load for a given product" proposed by Wu. This test would be used to assess the "attention market", defined on the "time spent" by consumers, Tim Wu, "Blind Spot: The Attention Economy and the Law" (26 March 2017), Antitrust LJ (forthcoming), <https://ssrn.com/abstract=2941094>.

Moreover, with regard to the notion of market power, some scholars[3] have pointed out that relevant markets might no longer be the starting point of competition analyses. Thus, the assessment of market power should go beyond traditional parameters, such as market shares, and be more focused on the strategies adopted by players in order to capture value within a certain framework. Hence, competition law tools should also be able to capture interactions among players which take place outside the relevant market.[4]

Algorithms may raise competition concerns especially when assessing collusive practices. The proliferation of data has boosted the adoption of data analytics techniques and algorithms. Thus, artificial intelligence has developed remarkably in recent years.

Very often, the term "algorithm" is used improperly. When we imagine the cartels of the future, we are not talking, in fact, about a simple "algorithm", which in itself is a neutral instrument. Rather, we refer to much more specific techniques for implementing artificial intelligence: we are talking about machine-learning algorithms or, better still, deep learning. The OECD has tried to define algorithmic collusion thus: "algorithmic collusion consists in any form of anticompetitive agreement or coordination among competing firms that is facilitated or implemented through means of automated systems".

Algorithms change certain structural characteristics of the market, such as transparency and frequency of interaction. As a result, they increase the likelihood of collusion. Indeed, if markets are transparent and companies react instantaneously to any deviation, the pay-off from deviation is zero. Therefore, collusion can always be sustained as a balancing strategy.

---

3   See among others, Ioannis Lianos, "Blockchain Competition Gaining Competitive Advantage in the Digital Economy: Competition Law Implications" (BRICS Competition Law centre, research paper series: 1/2018); Rupprecht Podszun, "Innovation, Variety & Fair Choice – New Rules for the Digital Economy: Expert Opinion for Finanzplatz München Initiative (FPMI)" (1 December 2017) <https://ssrn.com/abstract=3243403>.

4   G Muscolo and G Pitruzzella, "From Web 2.0 To Web 3.0 And Crypto: Is There Room For The Distributed Ledger Technology In The Telecommunication And Media Sector?", in *Media Markets 3*.

At the international level, especially in the OECD, we are debating whether these types of risks could have similarities with the classic oligopoly problem, that is, tacit collusion between companies, underlining how this problem could be extended to non-oligopolistic market structures. However, the difficulty of identifying the exchange of wills as a decisive ingredient for a violation of art 101 TFEU (Treaty on the Functioning of the EU) in the presence of sophisticated algorithms is, at this stage, complicated.

Therefore, within this challenging environment, the Authority has decided to launch a sector inquiry on big data. In particular, it decided to do it with the Authority for Privacy Guarantees and of the Authority for Communications Guarantees since big data and, in general, the digital and data-driven economy, pose multidisciplinary issues.

The ICA Guidelines suggest strengthening the ICA's powers in acquiring information beyond formal proceedings, such as sector inquiries or preliminary proceedings. What is the rationale behind this policy recommendation?

During the sector inquiry on big data, the three Italian authorities struggled to find information on the markets of the digital and data-driven economy. Indeed, digital operators tend not to publicly disclose the information necessary to obtain a complete idea of the quantitative dimension of the big data phenomenon and the digital economy markets in general. Moreover, digital operators are reluctant to provide sensitive information during sector inquiries if they are not obliged to do so.

Therefore, the three agencies have proposed that their powers be strengthened – notably those of the ICA and the Communications Authority – in the acquisition of information beyond formal proceedings. This should also include the possibility of imposing administrative sanctions in the event of refusal or delay in supplying the requested information, or in the presence of misleading or incomplete information.

Increasingly, the ICA has been collaborating with other agencies, such as the Italian Communications Industries Authority and the Italian Data Protection Authority, on issues relating to the digital sector. What opportunities do you see to work with other agencies to jointly advocate for regulatory changes?

What we should understand is that antitrust policy plays a crucial role in a broader context in which other regulations also play an important role, such as privacy and telecommunications rules. Therefore, what should concern policymakers is finding a common *fil rouge* to pursue through a virtuous coordination of all these regulations.

The inquiry into big data carried out by the ICA, the Authority for Communications Guarantees and the Authority for the Protection of Personal Data is a valuable example to follow and, in particular, is a baseline from which to start.

Indeed, through this sector inquiry, the three authorities tackled big data issues from three different points of view and managed to find a shared perspective on what the main actions to adopt in the near future should be. These actions are summarised in the Guidelines and Policy Recommendations which were published at the beginning of July 2019.[5]

In particular, the Guidelines underline that each authority, within the sphere of its respective competence, "can better guarantee its institutional objectives, as far as it is able to take full advantage of a fruitful cooperation with the other two authorities. To this end, the ICA, the Authority for Communications Guarantees and the Authority for the Protection of Personal Data, in the exercise of the complementary competences assigned to them and which contribute to tackling the critical issues of the digital economy, commit themselves to a closer collaboration on digital markets, also through means of a memorandum of understanding".[6]

---

5   Guidelines and Policy Recommendations for Big Data (July 2019), <https://www.agcm.it/dotcmsdoc/allegati-news/Big_Data_Lineeguida_Raccomandazioni_di_policy.pdf>.

6   *ibid.*

As for possible regulatory changes, the Guidelines observe that an effective public policy for big data and the digital economy requires not only enforcement, but also adequate advocacy aimed at: (i) countering the rules and regulations which protect traditional/mature markets against the costs of innovations brought about by digitalisation, which enhance competition and increase consumer welfare; (ii) defining a regulatory level playing field – tax regulation and other industrial advantages which may benefit the main digital operators; (iii) stimulating and raising public awareness of both the benefits and the risks of digitising the economy.

Several Member State competition authorities are considering or have already implemented changes to merger review thresholds to enable the review of acquisitions of smaller start-up-type entities by large players in the digital sector. Part of this change has been driven by a conversation about whether, especially in digital sector two-sided markets, current turnover thresholds are an accurate indicator of the potential strategic importance of transactions within an industry. The ICA recently endorsed a change itself, suggesting modifications to the Italian merger control regime. What are the key factors prompting this recommendation?

Online giants have been involved in numerous merger and acquisition (M&A) operations over the past decade. From 2008 to 2018, Amazon, Facebook and Google concluded 299 operations which have been grouped in the following clusters: physical goods and services; communications apps and tools; artificial intelligence, data science and analytics; tools for developers; home wellbeing and other personal needs; digital content; advertising tools and platforms; and remote storage and file transfer.

The pace of these operations was, on average, 5, 6 and 15 M&As/year respectively for Amazon, Facebook and Google. Most of these transactions are not horizontal and are targeted at very young businesses, typically no older than four years (60% of cases).[7] Thus, online giants are expanding their activities in several markets. They are building real ecosystems where users are provided with a wide range of online and non-online products and services.[8] Not surprisingly, some scholars have observed that the starting point of competition analysis will no longer be based solely on defining relevant markets, but rather on strategies adopted by the players in order to capture value within a certain framework.[9]

These acquisitions may hamper competition. This is particularly true in market settings with strong network effects and data-driven feedback loops that act as barriers to entry, leading to high concentration.[10] The dominant firm could hamper competition by both: (i) acquiring small innovative start-ups in adjacent or overlapping markets, "killing off" a potential future threat; (ii) exploiting the acquired firm to harm rivals in the downstream market (or in other markets adjacent to the ecosystem of dominant firms).[11]

Therefore, the ICA suggested, in the Guidelines and Policy Recommendations for Big Data, "a reform at national and international level that allows the competition authorities to fully evaluate those mergers that have the potential to lead to a substantial decrease in competition even if their turnovers fall below the current thresholds".[12]

Some possible strategies for the competition authorities may be: (i) directly tackling the issue, by introducing transaction value – based thresholds

---

7   For further analysis see Elena Argentesi and others, "Ex-post Assessment of Merger Control Decisions in Digital Markets: Final report" (prepared by Lear for the Competition and Markets Authority, 9 May 2019).

8   Gabriella Muscolo and Alessandro Massolo, "Data Driven Economy. Trade-off Between Competition and Cybersecurity" (2019) 1 Analisi Giuridica dell'Economia, 189.

9   See Lianos, note 3.

10   See Jacques Crémer, Yves-Alexandre de Montjoye and Heike Schweitzer, *Competition Policy For The Digital Era* (European Commission 2019).

11   See Jason Furman and others, *Unlocking digital competition: Report of the Digital Competition Expert Panel*, (HM Treasury 2019).

12   Guidelines and Policy Recommendations for Big Data, note 5, IC53 – policy 8.

(as Austria and Germany have recently done); (ii) introducing a "market share" test similar to the Spanish one which has enabled the Spanish authority to deal with the *Facebook/WhatsApp*[13] and *Apple/Shazam*[14] cases; (iii) introducing a "share of supply" test similar to the UK one which allowed the *Facebook/Instagram*[15] and *Google/Waze*16 cases to be dealt with; (iv) introducing an *ex post* evaluation, as the French authority is considering, among other possible solutions;[17] (v) revisiting the theories of harm18 and asking digital dominant firms to provide evidence of merger-specific efficiencies that offset potential harms to competition, as proposed in *Competition Policy For The Digital Era.*[19]

That report also pointed out that designing a suitable transaction threshold is controversial, especially when striking a balance between the level of the threshold and the risk of "false negatives". Moreover, this kind of threshold may pose legal certainty issues.[20]

In the UK, the Digital Competition Expert Panel highlighted that the voluntary notification system should enable the Competition and Markets Authority (CMA) to assess more mergers. This, as acknowledged by the CMA, should be feasible thanks to the flexibility given by the share of supply test. Should this test not work, the Panel suggested that the government consider introducing a threshold based on the value of

---

13   *Facebook/WhatsApp* (Case M.7217) Commission Decision C(2014) 7239 final, <https://ec.europa.eu/competition/mergers/cases/decisions/m7217_20141003_20310_3962132_EN.pdf>.

14   *Apple/Shazam* (Case M.8788) Commission Decision C(2018) 5748 final, <https://ec.europa.eu/competition/mergers/cases/decisions/m8788_1279_3.pdf>.

15   *Anticipated acquisition by Facebook Inc of Instagram Inc*, OFT ME/5525/12, 14 August 2012, <http://webarchive.nationalarchives.gov.uk/20160815232112/https://assets.publishing.service.gov.uk/media/555de2e5ed915d7ae200003b/facebook.pdf>.

16   *Completed acquisition by Motorola Mobility Holding (Google, Inc.) of Waze Mobile Limited*, OFT ME/6167/13, 11 November 2013, <https://assets.publishing.service.gov.uk/media/555de2cfed915d7ae2000027/motorola.pdf>.

17   For further analysis, see *Ex-Post Review Of Merger Control Decisions: Pros And Cons* (Law & Economics workshop, Concurrences in partnership with Cleary Gottlieb and Compass Lexecon, Paris, 2019).

18   Before introducing new thresholds.

19   Crémer, de Montjoye and Schweitzer, note 10.

20   *ibid.*

the transaction. Furthermore, it proposed the creation of a Digital Market Unit with the task, among others, of identifying digital firms with strategic market status. These firms should then notify their acquisitions.[21]

The Stigler Center seemed to be in favour of the introduction of a transaction-based threshold "or some other criteria". However, as underlined by the European Commission Report, the Stigler Center suggested that the burden of proof should fall on dominant platforms.[22]

Relatedly, what tools at the competition authority's disposal do you think are most valuable in assessing potential harm to competition in digital market merger reviews where the acquisition target is not yet generating substantial revenue? When services are being provided for free to consumers, does potential harm to innovation receive more weight in the analysis? What theoretical concepts do you find useful when analysing the effect of a transaction upon innovation?

The assessment of digital market mergers poses new challenges beyond the fact that the acquisition target is not yet generating revenue. Indeed, competition authorities have to take into account new parameters, such as likely non-price effects, including quality or guaranteed privacy. Most importantly, the target could allow the acquirer to collect and/or compute new valuable data which could represent an important competitive variable.

Due to strict time constraints, both EU and Italian merger assessments heavily rely on companies' own documents. Therefore, considering the complexity of fast-moving digital markets, early cooperation with companies has become even more crucial in order to better target internal document requests and, in turn, to carry out effective analyses.

---

21   Furman and others, note 11.

22   Stigler Committee on Digital Platforms, *Final Report* (Stigler Center for the Study of the Economy and the State 2019).

This is because accurate information makes it possible to assess, for instance, whether the parties are close competitors, whether there are overlapping innovation efforts and, especially, whether the parties are planning to undermine these efforts (i.e. by reducing R&D investments). For example, the EC has recently carried out such in-depth analyses in the *DuPont/DOW* and *Bayer/Monsanto* merger cases.

Some academics suggest that the set of information available should be improved by not relying too much on the information provided by the parties because it may be biased. Hence, they advocate the use of dawn raids or new sources of information, such as calculating the value of the target acquisition. In other words, the present value of the target's future profits. Thus, the higher this value, the more likely it is that the merger is liable to raise competition concerns.[23]

Furthermore, in the context of digital mergers, the trade-off between competition and innovation is exacerbated.

The extensive economic literature shows how this trade-off should consider a variety of complex aspects. In particular, the need to make prospective assessments in such dynamic markets. In digital industries, as stated in *Competition Policy For The Digital Era*, innovation differs in many dimensions from other industries. Indeed, a platform is a unique blend of constantly evolving features, which are often implemented and tested simultaneously with their development.[24]

---

23   See note 7. Moreover, analyses such the one carried out by the European Commission in *Apple/Shazam* are beneficial. Indeed, in this case, the Commission considered that the operation would have raised alleged anticompetitive effects relating to the automatic music content recognition system (ACR). More specifically, Apple could have hindered competitors in the markets for the supply of ACR and digital music streaming apps. The Commission also carried out an in-depth analysis of the data. In other words, the Commission assessed whether the data that Apple would have purchased from Shazam could be considered an essential input for digital music distribution and that Apple therefore exploited this competitive advantage without giving access to Shazam's data to its competitors. However, the Commission found that this data was not unique and that Apple's competitors also had significant data on their users. The Commission then authorised the concentration.

24   Crémer, de Montjoye and Schweitzer, note 10.

On the one hand, as pointed out by several scholars,[25] effective rivalry spurs firms to innovate. In this fundamental way, competition promotes innovation. Specifically, contestable markets (firms competing for profitable future sales) foster innovation. Following this view, a merger between rivals triggers two effects:[26] i) it internalises business-stealing effects and thus tends to depress innovation incentives; ii) it strengthens synergies specific to the merger, such as the internalisation of unintended spillovers or productivity gains, which can offset the negative effect of a merger on innovation.

As a result, there could be a misleading narrative that *"too much competition might be bad for innovation"*.[27] Instead, empirical evidence shows that greater competition, meaning that future sales are contestable, spurs innovation. These studies criticise the models used in the literature to analyse the effects of mergers, underlying that they typically do not take into account the impact of coordination in R&D activities (which a merger would bring about). This approach can provide, at best, a partial view of the impact of a merger on R&D incentives.

On the other hand, it is possible that a merger could lead to an increase in the ability to innovate, for example through the growth of the company and the combination of complementary activities, even in the light of a possible reduction in competitive pressure. However, the difficulty in quantifying these positive effects, in particular spillover effects, makes it even harder to evaluate the balance between dynamic efficiencies and the static effect of a merger. Thus, authorities have to develop an in-depth, qualitative, case-by-case assessment in order to solve this issue.[28]

---

25   Giulio Federico, Fiona Scott Morton and Carl Shapiro, "*Antitrust and Innovation: Welcoming and Protecting Disruption*", in Josh Lerner and Scott Stern (eds), *Innovation Policy and the Economy 20* (University of Chicago Press 2019).

26   *ibid.*

27   *ibid.*

28   See OECD, *Policy Roundtables: Dynamic Efficiencies in Merger Analysis*, (DAF/COMP(2007)41, 2007) <http://www.oecd.org/competition/mergers/40623561.pdf>.

How is economics important to your analysis within an effects-based antitrust framework? What advice do you have for other agencies on how best to apply economic analysis in their work?

Economics is important in antitrust analyses, especially when it comes to assessing exclusionary conducts. The ICA has particularly used economics when assessing price conducts and in vertical agreements.

Concerning the former conduct, I can cite case A428.[29] In this case, Telecom Italia abused its dominant position as a vertically integrated operator in the provision of wholesale access services to the local network and broadband, with two distinct behaviours. Telecom Italia – while giving an unjustified number of refusals of access to its wholesale network to competitors – applied a discount policy for large business customers for retail access service to the fixed telephone network. In this way, Telecom Italia inhibited an equally efficient competitor from operating profitably in the same market. In applying the as-efficient-competitor test, the ICA calculated the LRIC (long run incremental cost) for the incumbent and took as wholesale price "the retail price minus", set by the regulators for the infringement period, verifying the margin squeeze conduct.

By the same token, in another case of abuse, the ICA ascertained the exclusionary strategy adopted by Poste Italiane which had been implemented since 2014.[30] Poste Italiane limited the offer in the upstream market to their *Posta Massiva* service – rejecting the better *Posta Time* service – to its competitors who were forced to use Poste Italiane's services in rural or less populated areas. Moreover, in these same areas, Poste Italiane offered the *Posta Time* service to final consumers at lower prices than *Posta Massiva*, sometimes even with *ad hoc* rebates.

---

29   Case A428, decision of the Italian Antitrust Authority No 24339, 9 May 2013 <https://www.agcm.it/media/comunicati-stampa/2013/5/alias-6433> (in Italian).

30   Case A493, decision of the Italian Antitrust Authority No 26900, 13 December 2017 <https://www.agcm.it/media/comunicati-stampa/2018/1/alias-9113> (in Italian).

The ICA applied the as-efficient-competitor test and verified that competitors of Poste Italiane were not able to profitably replicate its offers, thus ascertaining the margin squeeze conduct.

Regarding vertical agreements, the ICA found that the vertical agreement adopted by companies operating radio-taxi services in Rome and Milan (cases 1801 A–1801 B)[31] infringed article 101 TFEU (Italian Law 287/90, article 2). The firms prohibited their own member drivers from using other applications in order to maintain their market position and prevent potential competitors with the "open platform" model (such as the Mytaxi app) from entering the market. The ICA assessed with the *Delimitis* test the foreclosure effect of these agreements, and then also rejected the efficiency defences put forward by the radio-taxi companies. For similar agreements, the ICA recently opened a proceeding against four radio-taxi companies in Naples (1832).[32]

Moreover, as I will explain more in detail in the next question, the ICA struck a balance between efficiency and exclusionary effects in the *Booking* case.

All in all, when using economic analysis as a tool to improve decision-making in competition cases, we should see economics as a method of thinking, specifically, as a theoretical framework to understand why given situations give rise to anticompetitive effects. In other words, economics should be a way of accessing appropriate evidence with which to examine whether such effects occur or may be expected to occur.

Hence, in order to develop a sound and strong economic theory, it is important to clearly identify the theory of harm and the type of evidence needed to confirm or dismiss it. For this purpose, *ex ante* and *ex post*

---

31   Cases I801A – I801B, decisions of the Italian Antitrust Authority No 26340 and 26345, 27 June 2018, <https://www.agcm.it/media/comunicati-stampa/2018/7/alias-9387> (in Italian).

32   Case 1832, provision of the Italian Antitrust Authority No 27553, 13 February 2019, <https://www.agcm.it/dettaglio?db=41256297003874BD&uid=E7B2BD080673DA7CC12583AC0059209B&view=&title=I832> (in Italian).

validations are important. The former prove that the theory should be consistent with the facts and the market environment. The latter confirm that the observed market outcomes should be consistent with the predictions of the theory.

When it comes to applied economics, it is key to understand all the relevant aspects of the markets. In particular, for supply and demand, elements such as demand substitutability, costs, barriers to entry and to exit, and the firm's strategies should be examined. In this way, it is possible to understand the extent of the impact of an agreement or unilateral conduct on the specific market. Furthermore, quantitative analyses, such as quantitative tests or data, or econometric analyses, should be carried out carefully. For this purpose, the data gathered should be necessary to assess how the market works: defining market boundaries, understanding competitive constraints, and assessing the impact of a merger.

As a public enforcer and, especially, as a former judge, I can say that sometimes decision-makers may not be experts in evaluating complex economic analyses. As a matter of fact, they may give it too little weight. It is, indeed, often easier to criticise complex economic work than to produce a positive alternative. Decision-makers may be tempted to dismiss an imperfect analysis altogether and this could be an issue, particularly, when assessing certain types of abuses – most notably price abuses – which require quantitative analyses. In this regard, it is also tempting to rely on analysis that suggests the solution is based on a certain number or to put undue weight on evidence that lacks robustness or significant qualitative evidence.

In conclusion, I would say that a careful assessment of what "evidence" is provided by economic analyses could encourage "sophisticated" analyses. However, these should face procedural time constraints, overcome the risk of eroding the ability to prove why no economic analysis is "bullet proof" and ensure the right of defence.

Price parity clauses have been a hot topic amongst competition authorities for several years now and have been cited as an area of considerable divergence in approach among competition authorities worldwide. One of the most prominent European investigations into price parity clauses was the online hotel bookings case, with investigations commenced in a variety of countries including France, Germany, Italy, Sweden and UK. Other international competition agencies, notably the United States, chose to take no action.

The ICA closed proceedings against Booking.com in 2015 by accepting commitments the company offered to narrow the scope of price parity clauses. In 2017, the Italian parliament went a step further by prohibiting hotel price parity clauses altogether. The controversy continues in Europe – in June 2019, the Düsseldorf Higher Regional Court overturned a 2015 decision of the German competition authority to ban Booking.com from imposing narrow price parity clauses, and the Regional Court's decision is now under appeal. What is it about parity clauses that has led to such spirited disagreement about when they are likely to infringe competition law rather than serve as a necessary measure to prevent free-riding behaviour?

Speaking of price parity clauses, the main argument that arouses disagreement among scholars and competition authorities on whether to intervene, and how, and the weight given to the possible efficiencies in the analysis.

On the one hand, in fact, economic literature has provided evidence on the different ways in which MFN (most favoured nation) clauses can hamper competition: both in a collusive or exclusionary way, and at platform or seller level. They could therefore be considered as a breach of both articles 101 and 102 TFEU.

For instance, in the case analysed by the ICA, the clauses were investigated as a vertical agreement with possible anticompetitive effects both on the upstream and downstream markets, thus potentially infringing article 101 TFEU (Italian Law 287/90, art 2). In detail, the price parity clauses imposed by online travel agencies (OTAs) on hotels could have led to a restriction of (i) competition between platforms on fees; (ii) competition on final prices within the OTA; and (iii) a potential foreclosure of the OTA market.[33]

On the other hand, there are potential efficiencies concerning the protection of investments. In *Online Hotel Booking*, specifically, both Booking.com and Expedia argued that the inclusion of MFN clauses in the contracts with hotel partners was aimed at protecting the correct functioning of their business models, and particularly at avoiding "free-riding" issues, i.e. consumers checking offers on the OTA website, but later booking rooms elsewhere at lower prices. The OTAs also argued that the MFN clauses were indispensable to protect investments in their own platforms and to offer consumers innovative services (such as a user-friendly review system), while ensuring that they can book rooms at the lowest prices.

The ICA decided to accept the commitment made by Booking.com to significantly limit the scope of its MFN clauses (from wide MFNs to narrow MFN). Furthermore, the commitment ensured "that consumers can continue to use free of charge the comparison, search and reservation services provided by [the OTA]" *Online Hotel Booking* [65]). Although the ICA did not state its view, it seems to have taken into consideration the validity of the OTAs' concerns, while balancing them with the need to guarantee a more competitive marketplace.

The ICA conducted this investigation and undertook the commitment decision in collaboration with the national competition authorities of France and Sweden and the coordination of the European Commission. This case showed the importance of sharing common rules and procedures and enjoying a European cooperation network. If the potential harm to competition of these clauses is widely supported, the debate on possible solutions to address the problem will remain open.

---

33   See OECD, *Hearing on Across Platform Parity Agreement: Note by Italy* (DAF/COMP/WD(2015)58).

WOMEN & ANTITRUST, VOL. II

Among those who suggest a case-by-case approach include, for example, Crémer, de Montjoye, and Schweitzer. In fact, in their report for the European Commission, *Competition Policy For The Digital Era*, the authors stated that if competition among platforms is vigorous, then it might be sufficient to prohibit wide MFNs; while if competition is weak, prohibition to narrow MFNs might be appropriate because other sales channels are the only competitors.[34]

Similarly, Baker and Scott Morton pointed out in "Antitrust Enforcement Against Platform MFNs", that there are relevant points to consider when analysing free-riding defence in the context of OTAs. They highlighted that: firstly, the transaction cost of searching among websites could prevent consumers from going further in their search; secondly, hotels may differentiate the provision of certain rooms on OTAs and not on their own site; thirdly, hotels could have advantages in using services offered by the platforms. They concluded that "if the OTA is paid for the value of those services, consumers that search the OTA but purchase on the hotel site would not be free-riding".[35] Anticompetitive issues may therefore override the efficiencies brought by price parity clauses.

Another solution could be the prohibition *tout court* of these clauses, both narrow and wide, as several national legislators have done, including the Italian one, at least for the online hotel booking industry. There is empirical evidence, although still at an early stage, that seems to show limited effects of the ban of these clauses.

For instance, Hunold, Kesler, Laitenberger and Schlütter in "Evaluation of Best Price Clauses in Online Hotel Booking" found that "BPCs (best

---

34   Crémer, de Montjoye and Schweitzer, note 10.

35   Jonathan B Baker & Fiona Scott Morton, "Antitrust Enforcement Against Platform MFNs" (2018) 127 Yale LJ 13, <https://digitalcommons.law.yale.edu/ylj/vol127/iss7/13>.

price clauses) influence the pricing and availability of hotel rooms across online sales channels" and that "direct channel of chain hotels has the strictly lowest price more often absent BPCs".[36]

More recently, Mantovani, Piga and Reggiani from the University of Bologna in their paper "Much ado about nothing? Online platform price parity clauses and the EU Booking.com case" provided quasi-experimental evidence on the full removal of price parity clauses in France in 2015 and in Italy in 2017 for hotels listed on Booking.com. Their analysis, while showing limited effects on prices both in the short and medium run, finds that "hotels affiliated with chains significantly decreased their prices in the medium run", even though "the benefits were restricted to a subset of consumers using Booking.com".[37]

Maybe further empirical evidences will lead the debate towards a clearer direction.

The ICA adopted its Guidelines on Antitrust Compliance in 2018. The guidelines indicate that one of the hallmarks of an effective compliance programme is that it must become an integral part of a company's culture and policy. In your experience, how have the most successful corporate compliance programmes been able to ingrain antitrust compliance into their corporate culture?

In September 2018 the ICA adopted the Guidelines on Antitrust Compliance.[38] The goal is to promote a better diffusion of antitrust awareness among all employees of companies with a series of incentives that result in a reduction of the fine.

---

36   Matthias Hunold, Reinhold Kesler, Ulrich Laitenberger and Frank Schlütter, "Evaluation of Best Price Clauses in Online Hotel Booking" (2018) 61 Int. J of Industrial Organization, 542, <https://www.sciencedirect.com/science/article/abs/pii/S016771871830033X?via%3Dihub>.

37   Andrea Mantovani, Claudio Piga, and Carlo Reggiani, "Online Platform Price Parity Clauses: Evidence from the EU Booking.com case" (August 2020), <https://ssrn.com/abstract=3381299>.

38   AGCM, *Guidelines on Antitrust Compliance* (2018) <https://en.agcm.it/dotcmsdoc/guidelines-compliance/guidelines_compliance.pdf>.

The document highlights a decisive point for undertakings requiring the mitigation of the fine: designing a compliance programme is not enough. Indeed, an effective and efficient implementation of such a programme is necessary. Furthermore, the firm has the burden of proof that an adequate programme is in place in order to qualify for mitigation of the fine.

In order to ingrain antitrust compliance into their corporate culture, therefore, firms should make a serious continuing commitment, allocating resources and identifying an autonomous, independent and well-equipped "programme manager". The manager will have the task and responsibility of ensuring both the vertical knowledge transfer, from top to bottom management, and a sufficient diffusion of awareness among all exposed employees.

Another crucial point, in this regard, is the periodic monitoring and updating of the programme: a credible compliance programme cannot be limited to one-off activities. Employees should be trained on a consistent and regular basis in order to develop thorough knowledge on the matter and the risks to which they are exposed.

Furthermore, an adequate scheme with appropriate disciplinary measures and incentives should ensure that employees and the programme manager make sure that antitrust compliance guides their behaviours. Finally, they must be equipped with effective compliance tools, such as internal reporting or whistleblowing systems.

A good compliance programme should also comprise management processes suitable to reduce the risks of critical behaviours: these rules should become part of normal business activity in order to fully embody the matter in the corporate culture.

If continuous implementation is the core element for firms to make antitrust compliance a part of their business ethics, it is also true, of course, that the programme has to be carefully designed. In this regard, an in-depth analysis of the risks to which firms are exposed becomes fundamental. Each undertaking will therefore need to identify the most problematic areas and the most appropriate prevention actions.

A complete assessment of their particular market environment and the undertaking's own characteristics is therefore essential. A compliance programme, indeed, is only effective if it is tailored to the specific firm. It must therefore be based on its nature, dimension and market position, along with the concrete features of the market in which it operates (e.g. number and size of undertakings, transparency, relations with suppliers and consumers).

The authority will therefore assess all these elements when evaluating a request for mitigation. In particular, once the suitability and effective implementation of the programme has been verified, it could allow mitigation of the fine: up to 15% if the programme has been adopted before the opening of the proceedings, up to 5% if adopted *ex novo* after the opening.[39]

The ICA has been the first competition authority to have introduced, in antitrust compliance guidelines, the concept that the adoption of these kind of compliance programmes could mitigate the sanction awarded by the authority.

You have published extensively at the intersection of intellectual property (IP) law and competition law. What issues at this intersection do you think are most ripe for further examination and legal development?

In principle, competition law and IP law do not have conflicting goals: indeed, the two systems are synergic because both aim to foster economic growth and protect consumer welfare. In exceptional and specific circumstances, however, an abuse of IPRs may result in illicit anticompetitive behaviour. The main criteria for striking the balance between exceptionally conflicting interests should be to keep markets open and contestable without hindering innovation.

---

39   *ibid.*

One sector in which the conflict between IP and competition law has emerged in recent times is the pharmaceutical market: however, it is of the utmost importance to underline how the recent excessive prices cases in Italy and the UK concern medicines that have long since been off-patent, for which it has not been necessary to remunerate R&D expenditure and, consequently, the case presented no risk of distorting innovation.[40]

As was highlighted by the European Commission's inquiry into the pharmaceutical sector in 2009, effective competition from generic medicines and, more recently, biosimilars, typically represents a vital source of price competition in pharmaceutical markets and nowadays significantly drives down prices for generics by an average of 50%.

However, anticompetitive behaviour may also occur with generic drugs. For example, reference could be made to pay-for-delay agreements whereby the generic company agrees to limit, or delay, its independent entry into the market in exchange for the benefits transferred by the originator. Over the last decade, pay-for-delay agreements have been found to be ant-competitive in a number of proceedings, including those concluded by European antitrust authorities. As an example, which at first glance seems very similar to a recent US case, one could cite the *Servier* case in 2014.[41]

Moving to a different market, that of high technology, enforcement actions on digital markets should also ensure that the potential for innovation, and hence consumer welfare, is fully protected.

---

40 See Case A480, decision of the Italian Antitrust Authority No 26185 *Price increase of Aspen's drugs*, 29 September 2016, <https://en.agcm.it/dotcmsDOC/pressrelease/A480_eng.pdf>. Other similar cases followed the Italian Aspen case: see the decision of the UK CMA, where the CMA found that Pfizer and Flynn each abused their respective dominant position by imposing unfair prices for phenytoin sodium capsules manufactured by Pfizer (*Unfair pricing in respect of the supply of phenytoin sodium capsules in the UK*, CE/9742-1, 7 December 2020, <https://assets.publishing.service.gov.uk/media/594240cfe5274a5e4e00024e/phenytoin -full-non-confidential-decision.pdf>). However, on 7 June 2018, the UK Competition Appeals Tribunal (CAT) set aside part of this decision, *Flynn Pharma and others v CMA* [2018] CAT 11 <https://www.catribunal.org. uk/sites/default/files/2018-08/1275-1276_Flynn_Judgment_CAT_11_070618.pdf>.

41 *Perindopril (Servier)* (Case AT.39612) Commission Decision C(2014) 4955 final, <https://ec.europa.eu/ competition/antitrust/cases/dec_docs/39612/39612_12422_3.pdf>.

2019 marked your five-year anniversary at the ICA. What do you think the key challenges facing the ICA will be in the coming five years?

With the advent of the new digital and data-driven economy, which paved the way for the emergence of online giants,[42] the consumer welfare approach has been severely criticised.

Indeed, several scholars have observed that the consumer welfare principle is excessively based on economics. In fact, antitrust should also be guided by political theory and should consider other objectives such as product quality, variety, innovation, fairness, employment, protection of small businesses and limitation of the political power of large businesses.[43]

Most importantly, these scholars stated that "antitrust law and competition policy should promote not welfare but competitive markets. By refocusing attention back on process and structure".[44] Suffice it now to say that these assessments clearly distance themselves from efficiency theories developed by renowned schools such as the Chicago school.

In particular, this new approach, also renamed as "neo-Brandeisian"[45] or "hipster antitrust" for some of its corollaries, found that incumbents could abuse their dominant positions in several ways which are not directly related to the effects of prices and output. Therefore, the risk is that antitrust enforcement may intervene when competition is already unduly harmed. This approach introduces new ways of assessing exclusionary strategies, such as predatory pricing or suspicious vertical integrations.

---

42   Whose business models, based on free or "freemium" services – i.e. provision of services in exchange for user profiling or with the additional monetary payment for premium services – and characterised by network effects, economies of scale and lock-in effects, are causing the so-called "winner takes all effects".

43   E.g., Zephyr Teachout & Lina Khan, Market Structure and Political Law: A Taxonomy of Power, 9 DUKE J. CONST. L. & PUB. POL'Y 37 (2014).

44   Lina M Khan, "Amazon's Antitrust Paradox" (2016) 126(3) Yale LJ 3.

45   See Herbert J Hovenkamp, "Is Antitrust's Consumer Welfare Principle Imperiled?" (2019) U Penn, ILE Research paper No 18-15. See also, Herbert Hovenkamp, "Whatever *did* happen to the antitrust movement?" (2018) 93 Notre Dame L Rev 583.

However, the neo-Brandeisian position has already found some fierce criticism in the name of the consumer welfare principle. In particular, it has been argued that the wide range of antitrust goals should be weighted and balanced.[46] And this is extremely complicated to do when assessing alleged anticompetitive practices.

In the *Guidelines and Policy Recommendations for Big Data*, the three authorities stated that in order to pursue the goal of consumer welfare, the analysis of anticompetitive practices in the digital economy may imply the inclusion of factors other than price and quantity, such as quality, innovation and fairness.[47]

Indeed, in the next five years, competition authorities should seek to provide concrete answers to issues raised by hipster antitrust. For example, when assessing mergers, in particular conglomerates or vertical integrations, competition authorities should assess competitive constraints considering medium-to-long-term periods.

For this purpose, it is of the utmost importance that the parties provide detailed information, especially concerning the analyses of big data which can facilitate the assessment of market power. Moreover, as recommended in the *Guidelines on Big Data*, since digital markets are not only multisectoral but also transnational, competition authorities should also cooperate internationally with their foreign counterparts or international organisations.

Indeed, the ICA has joined the European Competition Network (ECN), which brings together the European Commission and the national antitrust authorities of the European Union, applying the competition rules established by the TFEU.

Within the framework of the ECN, a working group called "ECN Digital Markets" was established to facilitate the sharing of ongoing work on

---

46   *Ibid.*

47   Guidelines and Policy Recommendations for Big Data, note 5, IC53 – policy 7.

the enforcement of competition rules concerning digital operators. The purpose of setting up this working group is, on the one hand, to promote cooperation among Member State authorities and, on the other, to encourage the correct allocation of investigative procedures concerning the digital economy.

In addition, thanks to the rapid development of digital markets, the EU Directive 2019/1 (also called ECN+) was enacted, which grants national antitrust authorities greater enforcement powers. Indeed, the ICA takes part in the Digital Clearing House, established on the initiative of the European Data Protection Supervisor. The initiative also assesses the implications of big data for consumer protection, competition and personal data protection.

In the non-European context, multilateral cooperation among antitrust authorities is implemented in three main contexts: the OECD, the International Competition Network (ICN) and the United Nations Conference on Trade and Development (UNCTAD).

Sofia Oliveira Pais
Catholic University of Portugal

Franziska Zibold

Sofia Oliveira Pais is professor of law at the Universidade Católica Portuguesa and the coordinator of the Católica Research Centre for the Future of Law. She holds a Jean Monnet Chair, awarded by the European Commission, and won the Antitrust Writing Award 2018 for the best academic article. She coordinated several projects in EU Competition Law co-financed by the European Commission. She is editor-in-chief of *Market and Competition Law Review*.

Franziska Zibold is an independent consultant for EU matters at Cruz Vilaça Advogados and others. She previously worked as an adviser in the cabinet of the president of the Portuguese Competition Authority, as a case handler at DG Competition in the fields of antitrust and state aid, as a briefing author for legislative matters at the European Parliament and in the private sector. She studied law at the University of Freiburg and holds an LLM from the College of Europe.

What was your main motivation to become a professor?

When I went to law school I planned to be a corporate lawyer. I had an uncle and several cousins already practising in that field and I wanted to follow in their footsteps. But, after graduation, I was invited to lecture at the university and when I was preparing my research and my classes in EU law and competition law, I started asking questions: why we need EU law and competition law, what goals they pursue, how we got here, where we are going to, what are the reasons underlying competition law. I started writing about these issues, and publishing, and I became passionate about them. I was also lucky enough to have the opportunity to involve my students in these problems, enjoying interesting and lively discussions in class, and preparing challenging research projects with them. Besides being intellectually stimulating, I could also engage students to be active and be part of the changing society. In classes they are learning not only how to apply the law but also to have a critical view; they are stimulated to think how the law should be applied to improve freedom, fairness and equality of opportunities. To sum up, being a law professor allows me to deepen my knowledge of EU and competition law with interesting discussions with my colleagues, my students or any other person interested in these topics, to enjoy flexibility and autonomy in setting my own research agenda and to travel and participate in interesting research projects.

Do you think that the current research landscape is favourable for young graduates who want to follow your path? If you wanted to change something, what would it be?

I think that the appeal today is even stronger. First, there are many new interesting areas in competition law and EU law to be engaged in, allowing young graduates to find their role in the world. Second, the increasing internationalisation of universities, noticeable in the curriculum of law faculties or in the partnerships developed with other institutions, as well in Erasmus programmes or similar, opened the universities to new worlds and enriched them with new ways of thinking, teaching and learning.

Finally, we live in a digital world and we can use new instruments to deepen and share our knowledge. With the coronavirus pandemic all universities needed to move closer to the digital world: classes, exams, administrative tasks, meetings, PhD defences, moved on to virtual space. It was a challenge but the majority of universities around the world were able to face it. The only downside nowadays, in my view, is the increasing bureaucracy that law schools have to support in the assessment of their courses, professors and students. I have no doubt that assessment is an essential step to increase the quality of law schools. The feedback provided allows schools to do better and improve their courses. But the assessment procedures should be easier and more simplified. The time consumed in those tasks reduces our availability to teach and research, and these are the main goals (and benefits) of becoming a law professor.

Article 11 TFEU mandates that "environmental protection requirements must be integrated into the definition and implementation of the Union's policies and activities, in particular with a view to promoting sustainable development". Competition law is not excluded from the current trend to make businesses also responsible from a sustainability point of view. This usually creates more costs and not less. I am thinking about the example of a collaboration of undertakings with the aim of decreasing emissions. Do you think the current framework is able to deal with such challenges? Or would you see the need to create a new sustainability justification/exemption?

Although environmental policy was not included in the EC Treaty, it is now an important EU law principle, explicitly mentioned in the Treaty on the Functioning of the European Union (TFEU), namely in articles 11 and 191, as well as in the EU Charter of Fundamental Rights (article 37), and may play a role in competition law enforcement. The current framework is adequate to deal with environmental interests and challenges, as article 101(3) TFEU allows the European Commission and national authorities to justify agreements that aim to protect the environment as long as they don't unnecessarily limit competition and fewer restraints on competition are not possible. In other words, competition may be restricted for environmental reasons, provided that those restrictions are necessary, adequate and proportionate. In fact, the European Commission in its assessment of anticompetitive practices does not accept unnecessary restrictions of competition (see the Notice – Guidelines on the application of article 81(3) of the EU Treaty, now article 101(3) TFEU).

In February 2017, for instance, the European Commission fined Campine (Belgium), Eco-Bat Technologies (UK) and Recylex (France) €68 million for fixing prices for purchasing scrap automotive batteries, in breach of EU competition law, and Commissioner Margrethe Vestager said: "Well-functioning markets can help us reduce waste and support the circular economy. Therefore, we do not tolerate behaviour that undermines competition." In other words, environmental effects of agreements between undertakings to achieve certain goals in specific sectors, such as a waste management or recycling scheme (namely agreements to reduce pollution) can be considered and justify those agreements, as long as competition is not unnecessarily limited.

At national level, several Member States and antitrust agencies are also considering benefits related to environmental policy objectives when assessing an agreement between competitiors or unilateral conducts by dominant firms. On 9 July 2020, for example, the Netherlands Authority for Consumers and Markets published its draft guidelines, *Sustainability Agreements*. These explain that sustainability agreements "are mostly aimed at a more economical (a more efficient) use of raw materials, at a reduction of pollutant emissions and waste streams, or at a reduction, in any other way, of the negative effects of production on humans, animals, the earth's climate, the environment, or nature" (paragraph 15). It proposes to take into account, in the competition law assessment, environmental sustainability initiatives that benefit society as a whole instead of only the user group buying the involved products: "benefits for society as a whole must be equal or greater than the disadvantages for users." Some doubts remain, however, whether this draft is in line with EU competition law.

Finally, it is also important to point out that competition law was also invoked by certain national governments to escape the obligation to adopt environmental measures. In fact, in the *Urgenda* judgment[1] the Dutch government argued that taking action to reduce greenhouse gas emissions in the Netherlands would distort the "level of playing field" for Dutch companies. This claim was rejected by the Dutch courts, and the Supreme Court decided on 20 December 2019 that the Dutch state would have to reduce gas emissions by the end of 2020. This controversial decision – considered by some a victory in the saga to limit climate change, and by others an example of judicial activism without legal support – was already followed by other courts (see, for instance, the judgment of 27 February 2020, in which the England and Wales Court of Appeal declared the government's plan to expand Heathrow unlawful) and is, nevertheless, a sign that environmental concerns are increasing and cannot be ignored in competition law assessment.

Digitalisation changes market structures in a fast pace. Margrethe Vestager said at a recent conference,[2] "On one hand, we're asked to do more, or act faster, to stop big tech companies driving out competition. On the other, we're told that by taking firm action in defence of European consumers

---

1   ECLI:NL:HR:2019:2007; see, https://www.urgenda.nl/wp-content/uploads/ENG-Dutch-Supreme-Court-Urgenda-v-Netherlands-20-12-2019.pdf

2   Chillin' Competition Conference (Brussels, 9 December 2019).

and businesses, we're stopping some companies in Europe from reaching the scale they need to be world leaders." How should competition policy in digital markets be shaped while preserving digital innovation?

To achieve the right balance between competition and digital innovation is not easy, especially because competition authorities have usually assessed competition cases focusing on consumer harm (identified with price increases). In addition, competition authorities tend to ignore the analysis of the positive innovation effects of the agreement or unilateral conduct and to accept Schumpeter's view of "creative destruction" (claiming that firms with a dominant position will be challenged by the entrance of new innovative companies). In this context, two issues seem particularly relevant. On the one hand, there it is the ongoing discussion about competition as a driver of innovation. For many Member States, competition law enforcement is limiting innovative businesses. The French and German governments, for instance, requested the review of merger control in order to allow national champions, arguing (apparently) that competition law enforcement prevents European companies from gaining relevance and becoming leaders in the world context. Particular illustrative was the *National Industrial Strategy 2030* presented by the German minister for economic affairs, which recommended the softening of antitrust laws and foresaw that Member States could use state funds to support certain industries, namely a European factory for car batteries. This proposal was considered unusual and diverged from the historical ordoliberal economic German approach. In addition, it contradicted the European Commission view (expressed in the merger decision Case M.7932 *Dow/DuPont*[3]) and supported by certain literature, that competition is a driver of innovation in concentrated markets.

Accepting this premise, we have to address the second dimension of the problem: how should competition authorities take into account

---

3   [2017] OJ C353/9.

the benefits of innovation and particularly of digital innovation in the assessment of competition cases? In fact, in the digital economy, with the new business models, firms provide users with access to services for free (such as search engines and social networking) in exchange for data and, therefore, innovation is an indicator more relevant than price. The problem is that the insights from industrial economics research related to innovation are not very clear and in the very limited cases in which competition authorities tried to consider innovation in the application of competition law, the results achieved have frequently been criticised. However, some efforts, at national, European and international levels, have been made to change the status quo. For example, a study published in 2016 by Kern, Dewenter and Kerber showed that American agencies (Department of Justice and Fair Trade Commission) used a "more innovation-specific" assessment concept in their merger reviews: innovation aspects were considered either in a broader concept of relevant market (which would include research and innovation) or by taking into account the plain number of competitors and, in addition, the concept of "innovation competition" was mentioned in the US Merger Guidelines in 2010. In the EU context, on the other hand, innovation concerns have also been considered in the *Horizontal Merger Guidelines*,[4] as well as in the TTBER[5] and in a few merger cases mainly involving pharmaceutical companies. Particularly relevant is the merger case *Dow/DuPont* in which the European Commission did not accept the argument of the parties that the merger would "stimulate the overall innovation rate" arguing that "even in the case where the reduction in the number of independent firms means that each firm invests more, overall innovation is slowed down due to the loss of an independent innovator."

---

4   [2004] OJ C31/5, para 38.

5   Commission Regulation (EU) 316/2014 on the application of Article 101(3) of the Treaty on the Functioning of the European Union to categories of technology transfer agreements [2014] OJ L93/17.

Moreover, several recent decisions of the European Commission also mentioned innovation as a condition to promote consumer choice while applying competition rules. In March 2019, in the *Google/AdSense* case, for instance, the European Commission decided that Google had abused its market dominance by preventing rivals from competing in the online search advertising intermediation market and found that Google's conduct harmed competition and consumers, and stifled innovation: "it denied other companies the chance to compete and innovate and reduced consumers' choice." In conclusion, the importance of digital innovation nowadays, namely with the new business models created by tech giants (such as Amazon, Facebook or Google), is undeniable and competition authorities will have to find ways to take those positive effects into account.

Platform competition is a new buzzword. Do you think that the traditional tools of competition agencies to define markets, market power and exclusionary conduct are sufficient to tackle cases concerning platform competition?

I believe we don't need to change competition law to face the new challenges of digital platforms (that is to say online applications that connect multiple groups of users and the value of each group increases with the presence of others). We just need to adapt the existing tools and complement them eventually with new regulatory measures (for instance, new tools on data privacy). This is, moreover, the main conclusion of several reports adopted by competition authorities and other entities in 2019, as the UK (*Unlocking Digital Competition: Report of the Digital Competition Expert Panel* – Furman Report), Germany (*A New Competition Framework for the Digital Economy – Report by the Commission "Competition Law 4.0"*), EU "Special Advisor's Report" (*Competition Policy for the Digital Era*) and the Stigler reports (*Stigler Committee on Digital Platforms* – Final Report) illustrate. In fact, despite presenting different solutions, these reports agree on several aspects. They all point out that digital platforms are different from traditional markets and competition agencies should adapt their tools.

Actually, online platforms (and the concept is used in a broad way in order to include a wide range of activities such as search engines, social media platforms and online digital content) with specific characteristics, such as network effects, economies of scale and the use of data to improve interactions between different group of users, can enhance competition (creating new and better products and services). On the other hand, digital platforms may also raise competition concerns, namely through the increase of market power of the firms, the gathering of data for target advertising and the creation of barriers to the market or other anticompetitive practices. To address these concerns, the competition reports don't propose the break-up of big digital platforms (as some American politicians did). They only point out the need to increase the speed and efficiency of competition tools to face the challenges of a changing digital environment. They all agree that the classic concept of market may be of less value in the digital economy, as it may not give information on innovation or on the competitors in the innovation market. In fact, it is difficult to define the relevant market and rely on a market share test due to the dynamic nature of digital markets, the fact that online platforms are multisided and also the fact that many digital services and products are free (and therefore non-price competition, based namely in innovation, is more relevant than competition based on the price of the services or products).

In this context, the European Commission has already decided (see the *Facebook/WhatsApp* merger decision, Case No COMP/M.7217) that market shares are not a good indicator of market power in digital markets. In the *Google Search (Shopping)* case (decision of 27 June 2017, Case AT.39740), however, the Commission took into account the market shares of the firm (and also other factors such as barriers to entry and expansion, the lack of multihoming users, brand effects and the lack of countervailing buyer power). In spite of the existing difficulties, the definition of the market allows the assessment of competitive constraints and it is the first step to assess market power. The 'Competition Law 4.0' Report[6] suggested, therefore, that the European Commission Notice on the definition of relevant market be revised. and that a separate Notice on market definition and the definition of market power with respect to digital platforms be published.

Some jurisdictions have already taken steps to adjust the concepts of relevant market and market power to the challenges in digital economy. The 2017 amendment to the German Competition Act, for instance, introduced a provision stating that in the assessment of market power in multisided markets and platforms the authorities should take into account (1) direct and indirect network effects, (2) the parallel use of services from different providers and the switching costs for users, (3) the undertaking's economies of scale arising in connection with network effects, (4) the undertaking's access to data relevant for competition, and (5) innovation-driven competitive pressure (GWB (Competition Act) s 18(3a)). In February 2019, the German Bundeskartellamt relied on this new provision to prohibit Facebook's data antitrust practices. Later, the German Ministry for Economic Affairs proposed new additional provisions: when assessing the market position of an undertaking that acts as an intermediary on a multisided market, the importance of those intermediary services for access to supply and sales markets needs to be taken into account; a company's access to data relevant for competition should also be considered a relevant factor to take into account when assessing market dominance.

---

6   This commission was set up by the Federal Minister for Economic Affairs and Energy in 2018 to address some of the challenges of competition law in the digital economy , see https://www.bmwi.de/Redaktion/EN/Publikationen/Wirtschaft/a-new-competition-framework-for-the-digital-economy.pdf?__blob=publication-File&v=3.

Finally, exclusionary abuses should also be rethought, as new abuses may be identified in digital markets. The EU *Special Advisor's Report* identified two abusive practices by digital platforms that required particular attention and should be under competition law scrutiny: (1) leveraging (online platforms, due to networks externalities and use of data, have advantages over new entrants) and (2) self-preferencing (a firm giving preferential treatment to its own products or services when it is in competition with products and services provided by other entities using the platform). At national level, the German Ministry of Economics and Energy published the draft Act on Digitalisation of German Competition Law (*GWB-Digitalisierungsgesetz*), which includes new rules to address digital markets abuses: s 19a prohibits abusive conduct by undertakings that have a paramount significance for competition across markets; s 20(3a) relates to conducts prohibited for companies with relative or superior market power who want to extend it to intermediaries on multisided markets. In conclusion, in a digital world, more vigorous enforcement of antitrust is required to re-establish a competitive environment.

Portuguese competition law provides the option to assess mergers based on market share and not on turnover. Do you think this is something that the Commission could also look at in order to tackle cases in the digital field?

There seems to be a problem of under-enforcement in merger control cases in the digital field according to the Stigler and Furman reports. And one of the main issues, in this context, are the killer acquisitions, that is to say, the acquisition of new and potential competitors in digital markets (innovative start-ups) as a measure to exclude competition. Although the EU report suggests that the existing solutions in the EU Merger Regulation are enough and adequate for now (avoiding administrative costs and legal uncertainty), in my view, the criteria for merger notification should be extended and merger analysis should incorporate the new theories of multisided markets. Portuguese competition law no 19/2012 provides that concentrations between undertakings have to be notified when they fulfil one of the following conditions:

a) As a consequence of the concentration, a market share equal to or greater than 50% of the domestic market in a specific product or service, or in a substantial part of it, is acquired, created or reinforced;

b) As a consequence of the concentration, a market share equal to or greater than 30% but smaller than 50% of the domestic market in a specific product or service, or in a substantial part of it, is acquired, created or reinforced in the case where the individual turnover in Portugal in the previous financial year, by at least two of the undertakings involved in the concentration are greater than €5 million, net of taxes directly related to such a turnover;

c) The undertakings that are involved in the concentration have reached an aggregate turnover in Portugal in the previous financial year greater than €100 million, net of taxes directly related to such a turnover, as long as the turnover in Portugal of at least two of these undertakings is above €5 million.

The Portuguese solution is broader than the EU one because it uses alternative criteria (market shares and the aggregate turnover), but it does not take into account the value of the transaction, which seems a particularly adequate criterion to apply in merger cases in the digital area. This solution has already been adopted in other jurisdictions. In fact, in 2017, Germany and Austria changed their merger regimes and introduced an additional threshold for the notification requirement: if the value of transaction reaches a certain threshold – €400 million under German law and €200 million under Austrian law – the proposed merger should be notified. The new provisions on transaction value thresholds are particularly adequate to mergers in digital economy, where companies or assets, which generate little or no turnover, are purchased at a high price (usually indicating innovative business ideas). This solution should also be considered at the EU level.

The Commission has recently invited three experts to prepare a special report on Competition Policy in the Digital Era. Do you think that researchers will be more and more involved in order to help enforcers and practitioners deal with complex issues like artificial intelligence?

In my view, to involve researchers to help enforcers and practitioners is an essential step towards achieving good, reasonable and effective regulations and decisions. This solution has been followed by many antitrust agencies when discussing how to apply competition rules in the digital era. This debate was also vigorous among academics and has played a fundamental role in the development of competition policy. It concerned the goals of competition policy in the digital era, the underlying economic theories and the need to adapt competition tools to dynamic and innovative markets.

In 2019 several competition reports, authored by researchers and experts, were adopted by European governments and antitrust agencies, making interesting suggestions on how to adapt competition rules to the new digital reality. Among them, we can point out as particularly relevant the Furman et al. report (*Unlocking Digital Competition: Report of the Digital Competition Expert Panel*, adopted by the UK government in May 2019), the Jacques Crémer, Yves-Alexandre de Montjoye, Heike Schweitzer report (*Competition Policy for the Digital Era*, commissioned by the European Commission in April 2019) and the Martin Schallbruch, Heike Schweitzer and Achim Wambach report (*A New Competition Framework for the Digital Economy – Report by the Commission "Competition Law 4.0"*, adopted by the German Federal Ministry for Economic Affairs and Energy in September 2019). Some of those recommendations have already been introduced in legislative proposals or announced as priorities by antitrust agencies. For instance, vice-president of the European Commission, Margrethe Vestager, announced at the end of 2019 that the Commission's market definition would be revised to address the challenges of digital markets.

At the same time the UK government is considering the creation of a technology regulator to police large tech companies such as Google or Facebook. And recently, in January 2020, the German Ministry for Economic Affairs presented the ministerial draft bill, the 10th amendment of the act, officially called "Act against Restraints of Competition Digitisation Act", which introduces several changes. Section 18(3) and (3b), concerning market dominance, adds, for example, that, in assessing the market position of an undertaking in relation to its competitors, account shall be taken namely of "its access to data relevant for competition"; in addition it explains that, " when assessing the market position of an undertaking acting as an intermediary on multisided markets, account should be taken in particular of the importance of the intermediary services it provides for access to supply and sales markets". In conclusion, the help of researchers and experts will be essential to the adequate enforcement of competition rules in the digital field by antitrust agencies.

Are you in favour of leniency programmes? The ECN+ Directive, which is currently in the phase of implementation in Portugal, provides some streamlining but it doesn't provide for a one-stop shop for leniency applicants. Do you see it crucial in the long run to have a one-stop shop in Europe in order to have more applications?

The leniency programme allows the company, whichever first provides relevant information to antitrust agencies, to avoid a fine (which can be significant, as the recent case *Cartel Trucks*, Case COMP/39824, shows). From the point of view of the competition authority the detection and investigation of cartels would be harder (or even impossible) without those programmes. Among the benefits of the leniency programme, the most relevant, as already mentioned, is immunity from an antitrust fine. At a European level, if all the requirements of the 2006 leniency notice are fulfilled the companies may obtain 100% of immunity. At national level, almost all Member States follow a similar solution. The problem is that there is a decline in the leniency programme enforcement in Europe. The lack of legal and jurisdictional certainty in leniency programmes are some of the reasons presented to that decline. In fact, if the immunity applicant is not certain whether the reported behaviour will qualify for immunity, or if other competition authorities will step in and apply administrative fines, or if the applicant still has to face private enforcement, the attractiveness of this programme will diminish and Commission reliance on immunity applications to investigate and sanction cartels will decrease. One-stop shop for leniency applications might be necessary to strengthen leniency programmes, even if this solution is not foreseen in the ECN+ Directive.

In most jurisdictions in Europe, it is common policy not to treat the existence of a compliance programme as a mitigating factor per se. Do you think compliance efforts by companies should be explicitly taken into account in some way in competition policy, for example when setting the fine?

If companies have a compliance strategy, that is to say if they proactively adopt measures to respect competition rules, they can minimise the risks and the costs of competition law infringement. The European Commission provides guidance on how a firm can ensure compliance in order to promote competition culture; however, it does not take into account compliance strategy when setting the fine. Other jurisdictions, on the other hand, such as the Hungarian, Italian or American jurisdictions, have already adopted measures in order to consider the existence of a compliance programme as a mitigation factor. In fact, Notice No 11/2017 of the president of the Hungarian Competition Authority (GVH) and the chair of the Competition Council of the Hungarian Competition

Authority mentions that in the course of imposing a fine "the GVH takes into account both the *ex ante* and *ex post* compliance efforts and programmes of undertakings" and can reduce the fine (up to 7% in *ex ante* compliance programmes or up to 5% in *ex post* compliance efforts). The mere existence of a compliance programme cannot in itself be assessed as a fine reducing factor, according to the Notice. In order to achieve that result the undertaking must: a) prove its sufficient compliance efforts; b) terminate the infringing conduct; c) prove that the termination of the infringement was due to the compliance programme and d) prove that no high-ranked corporate executive was involved in the infringement.

In 2018, the Italian competition authorities issued the *Guidelines on antitrust compliance programmes* that provided several criteria to assess whether the programme should count as a mitigating factor. The guidelines allow for a reduction of up to 15% of the fine in *ex ante* compliance programmes (adopted before the opening of the proceedings) and a reduction of up to 5% of the fine for compliance programmes implemented during the investigation (*ex post* compliance programmes), requiring proof of the adoption and of effective and concrete commitment to following a suitable programme. Finally, on 1 June 2020, the US Department of Justice updated its guidance on corporate compliance programmes and reoriented it around certain fundamental questions: Is the corporation's compliance programme well designed? Is it adequately resourced and empowered to function effectively? Is the programme review limited to a "snapshot in time" or is it based on "continuous access to operational data and information across functions"? In other words, a compliance programme that only exists on paper will not be rewarded; the programme needs to work in practice. To sum up, compliance programmes that function effectively may promote competition culture, raising awareness of businesses to antitrust infringements. So, as long as the programmes are suitable and effective they could be considered as a mitigation factor, namely at EU level.

What do you see as the most interesting challenge for competition law in the coming years?

I would say that competition policy should continue meeting the challenges of the *brave new* green and digital world. The issue is that, as in Aldous Huxley's novel, what might appear to be impressive and spectacular at first glance may in fact be harmful. Digital technologies changed our world, leading to new business models and promoting innovative societal and economic opportunities. Data and information are the basis of social and economic interaction nowadays and will bring a revolution in almost all sectors of our society. These benefits go, however, hand in hand with several risks and costs: loss of privacy, concentration of economic wealth, increase of inequality, growth of large platforms which become "gateways", locking users in there, and extending their influence on the market to social and political aspects.

A consensus has, therefore, emerged pointing out the need to reinforce the powers of competition authorities in digital markets and recommending new measures (which are slowly being introduced in competition laws). In fact, several proposals are now on the table in different jurisdictions concerning the concept of market and the assessment of market power in digital economy, the prohibition of new types of abuses the burden and standard of proof, and a deeper scrutiny of merger cases. 2020 will just be the beginning of new competition measures in this area. At the same time other regulatory measures, such as the Digital Services Act proposed by the European Commission, intended to increase liability and safety rules for digital platforms, services and products, will complement the scrutiny by antitrust agencies.

In addition to the challenges of the digital world, competition rules can also contribute to help making Europe climate neutral by 2050. The EU has already taken some steps towards a climate-neutral economy and in the context of competition law the European Commission has announced that in 2020–2021 new rules on state aid, concerning energy and environment, will appear in order to promote the "green transition". Companies will receive aid as long as they cut emissions and (certain) European regions will be supported to convert their economies to environment-friendly industries. Finally, traditional competition concerns, such as remedies (the debate about their effectiveness is still going on and *ex post* assessments concerning their application are needed) and leniency (the discussion about which measures should be introduced to keep this tool attractive is still relevant) will certainly be in antitrust agency agendas.

María Luisa (Marisa) Tierno Centella*

DG COMP, European Commission

Nicola Northway

María Luisa (Marisa) Tierno Centella leads cartel investigations at DG COMP, such as *Forex*, *European Government Bonds and SSA bonds*, *Gas Insulated Switchgear* and *Animal Feed Phosphates* (a record 35-year cartel). She drafted the legislative package introducing EU settlements and the 2006 Leniency Notice. She was previously an official of the Dutch Competition Authority for seven years, having practised law for five years at Gómez-Acebo & Pombo (Brussels office). Marisa has a law degree (Universidad Complutense de Madrid) and a Master's degree in European law (Université Libre de Bruxelles).

Nicola Northway is a highly respected senior adviser, who has developed a practical and commercial in-depth understanding of antitrust and regulation across a number of sectors. Nicola's experience is unique, combining public and private sector, in-house and private practice. As general counsel at the gas and electricity regulator, Ofgem, Nicola oversaw the first competition dawn raid by a regulator, as well as managing the legal aspects of the Enron and TXU insolvencies. Nicola was the global head of the competition team at Barclays Bank for 12 years, managing M&A and investigations cases, including the settlements of Libor and FX. Most recently Nicola was a partner at Baker McKenzie in London, leaving at the end of December 2019 to pursue a portfolio career.

---

*   The opinions expressed in this interview are personal and do not necessarily represent the position of the European Commission.

How did you first get involved in competition law, and was your focus always on the investigations side?

From the investigations side, I have been enforcing competition rules since I became an official of the Dutch competition authority (Nederlandse Mededingingsautoriteit – NMa) back in 1997, before joining the European Commission.

Years before that, competition law had been one of the subjects I had to study to get my Master's degree in European law (*Licence Spéciale en Droit Européen*) from the Université Libre de Bruxelles. It caught my attention immediately because I perceived it as a flexible, dynamic combination of law and economics, in which the last word had not been said. It had it all for a young lawyer genuinely committed to the European project and willing to work in an international environment: i) it is a cornerstone of the European integration in a single market, and ii) it is a field which is not so circumscribed to the one or the other legal order. Moreover, I had loved criminal law at university, and I perceived EU competition law as an opportunity to work in a quasi-criminal area without having to dwell into the darkest sides of human nature.

In my first job at the Brussels branch of Gómez-Acebo & Pombo, my practice extended for five years to a wider range of law fields, such as EU free movement rules and classic international law. Still, what I enjoyed most was the chance to plead an antitrust case before the (at the time) Court of First Instance: the *Eurovision I* case. I experienced then how it feels to win against the European Commission, in particular when you obtain the full annulment of a decision. It was the first time that an individual exemption was annulled by the court. I also enjoyed the privilege of participating in the legislative effort to render possible the accession of Slovenia and Latvia to the EU. More generally, I am grateful for the first-hand experience I gained putting in place compliance programmes, negotiating contracts, or dealing with state aid aspects of the rescue and re-privatisation of a bank.

You joined the Commission from private practice. How did you find your transition into the public sector and what was the thing that most surprised you?

Generally speaking, I am convinced that my previous work at the other side has enriched my perspective when I investigate cases, and helped my confidence when I enter into settlement talks or prepare a hearing, for instance. I try to put myself in the shoes of my counterparties, with a lot of respect, but no fear.

In reality, by the time I joined the Commission I had been enforcing antitrust rules for five years in the Netherlands at the NMa. That was a unique opportunity for me to do a few "first time ever cases" in that country, because we were applying a brand new national competition law, the *Mededingingswet* (e.g. cases in liberal professions or abuses of collective dominant positions in purchasing). The creative side of working on the first texts and trying the first methods was very inspiring and rewarding.

My transition from the private sector to the NMa involved learning Dutch in a few months, which was challenging. I was impressed by the flat structure of the NMa and I embraced the empowerment I experienced. I will never forget that they welcomed me and trusted me to represent the Netherlands in Brussels. I was very active in the discussions of the European Commission's proposals for the core EU antitrust regulations that are still in place (Regulations 1/2003 and 773/2004), as well as the block exemption regulations and the notices that introduced modernisation and a more economic approach to the assessment of vertical and horizontal cooperation.

Later on, what I liked most in the transition to the Commission was that all those new pieces of policy and legislation had to be applied and I worked on that from the directorate that oversaw policy and consistency. Of course, I also marvelled at the beauty of working in a team of colleagues from all over Europe, and I still do sometimes.

You have been involved in a number of long-running and complex cartel cases. Is there any particular area or industry sector that has been the most challenging to deal with and, if so, why?

The challenges I have encountered relate more to the complexity or novelty of the case, rather than the industries themselves. For instance, in *Gas Insulated Switchgear*, we managed to prove an unwritten agreement with indirect evidence and established for the first time the liability of parent companies for the conduct of a full-functioning joint venture. It may seem obvious now, but at the time they were big steps and required some courage.

Similarly, the *Animal Feed Phosphates* case[1] would have been a challenge anyway, because we managed to prove a record cartel of 35 years, but it was also the first time that the European Commission ran the settlement procedure. In that case, we created all the templates we still use, we got in the first settlement submissions ever and we paved the way for the settlement (and cooperation) cases that followed. At the last moment, one of the companies withdrew from the settlement, thereby reverting alone to the ordinary procedure. This required the adoption of two separate decisions applying two procedures (settlement and ordinary), which delayed the case resolution for a few months, and it turned out that we were overtaken by the second settlement case. Instead, we had to face the additional challenge of being pioneer as well in managing the first "hybrid procedure case".

There have been a number of hybrid cartel settlements by the European Commission, following the *Icap* judgement (Case T-180/15 *Icap plc and others v the European Commission* EU:T:2017:795), partially annulling the infringement decision of the Commission against Icap. Do you see

---

1   *Animal Feed Phosphates* (Case COMP/38.866), list of decisions available at <https://ec.europa.eu/competition/elojade/isef/case_details.cfm?proc_code=1_38866>.

the hybrid and staggered hybrid settlement process as being less attractive to the Commission going forward, given the procedural challenges you face? How do you reconcile that with the General Court's view siding with the Commission in *Pometon* (Case T-433/16 *Pometon v Commission* EU:T:2019:201)?

One could argue that the ordinary decisions against non-settling parties that you mention (and in Case T-105/17 *HSBC v Commission*) have been partially annulled by the General Court on substantive, case-specific reasons, rather than as a result of the so-called "staggered hybrid" procedure. On the point you make, it will be interesting to see how the ECJ approaches the relationship between the settlement and the ordinary decisions and procedures in staggered hybrids. Since they are *sub judice*, I will not comment further.

In any event, the ECJ has already ruled that parallel hybrids are an efficient, court-tested and safe option. As I mentioned before, I managed the first hybrid case, *Animal Feed Phosphates*, devising the "parallel hybrid" procedure. This implied the simultaneous adoption, first, of the statements of objections for settling and non-settling parties, and then of the respective decisions only five months later than foreseen in a full settlement scenario. Timab (the non-settling party) challenged the decision, but both the General Court and the ECJ confirmed that Timab's rights of defence and presumption of innocence had been respected.

Looking forward, the digital agenda is a key theme in the enforcement agenda and the collection and processing of data seems to be of concern to the Commission. Do you see this area as being the next frontier of cartel enforcement and where in your view are the main cartel issues likely to arise in terms of industry sector and behavioural issues?

Clearly most, if not all, industries have now a digital component (which has only increased with the COVID-19 crisis) in many dimensions (inputs, strategic positioning, market monitoring, online sales, etc). Cartel investigation tools extend to those environments and benefit from our capacity to introduce data-mining and machine learning methods, including deep learning algorithms. This is happening already thanks to our colleagues with that specific technical profile, who are able to see complex patterns within big data sets and predict relevance of data for the investigation. In the years to come, the court may be looking into cases where this knowledge has been translated into graphics and reports. The amount of data the inspectors need to review and collect during dawn raids has increased dramatically in the last years, which has generalised the so-called "continued inspections" to finalise the selection of data at Commission premises. My impression is that this trend will continue and that our selection instruments will be continuously refined to meet the pace of technical development.

From a cartel-centred perspective, one can theoretically think of forms of collusion, (including conscious signalling, using similar conditions and tools, etc) in platforms or by having competitors deliberately relying on the same re-pricing parameters in the algorithms they use, which would be able to generate decisions/adjustments affecting prices or other competition parameters. We may be confronted in the future with the need to specify when the interaction between algorithms can be considered explicit collusion, rather than simply tacit collusion, for instance, because they are actually mutually decoding and communicating with each other.

Should leniency be expanded to other areas – e.g. verticals?

As you know, some authorities have done this. The European Commission has not. The current leniency notice was conceived to apply only to "secret cartels", not to any cartel (although not every aspect needs to be secret) because insider information is sometimes crucial to detect or comprehend the features of those well-concealed infringements. Turning to vertical restraints, the question is (in my view) whether the difficulties in investigating vertical restraints justify an exemption of the penalty or a reduction of fines. Arguably, when vertical restraints are set out in contractual clauses or well known by their "victims", it is not indispensable to create those high incentives to self-report. Speaking only for myself, I think that granting full immunity for vertical restraints is controversial, because (unlike in multilateral infringements such as cartels) it can mean that nobody is liable for the infringement. However, a fine reduction is already possible for companies who do not only self-incriminate, but also enable a simplified procedure accepting liability (the so-called cooperation procedure, which emulates cartel settlements replicating its phases and the settlement submissions). Going forward, I personally would not exclude the possibility that digitalisation and learning algorithms may render the introduction and implementation of vertical restraints more subtle and difficult to detect and that in such a context the public interest could be well served by introducing some form of leniency, targeting the right incentives and circumstances.

Now the US Department of Justice has issued its guidance, is the European Commission an outlier when it comes to compliance credit?

I would say the Commission is consistent. It encourages compliance programmes, but complying with the law is normal behaviour and the reward for complying is a safe journey. In my view, if we find an infringement despite the compliance programme, there is little point in rewarding a failure, because we would reward window-dressing. Then, does a company that has been sanctioned for an infringement really need any additional incentive to introduce a compliance programme for the future to make sure it has terminated the infringement and to avoid recidivism?

What is the one feature of other antitrust regimes that makes you jealous? Criminal/individual sanctions?

I do not envy criminal sanctions because I personally think that the current public and judicial consensus in Europe generally considers that civil penalties are a proportionate way to address cartels and that it is possible to calculate amounts commensurate to the infringements without putting individuals in jail. This consensus enables our level of enforcement and of deterrence. As you know, if a punishment is perceived in a given jurisdiction as too heavy, it is not really enforced. On the other hand, civil sanctions on individuals, like debarment, are interesting extra deterrence devices for some behaviours.

What I would have loved is the possibility to plead with the legal service in my cases, and not only help them prepare their defence and attend the court hearings without taking the floor. In other systems this is possible and I guess you can say it makes me "jealous".

I am sure that in your experience there are behaviours by parties in a cartel case that do not help the party under investigation, do you have any advice for practitioners and their clients about the best way to deal with the Commission's case teams?

For parties who are cooperating with the investigation, it does not help to overstate the implications of evidence. Then, lawyers used to other legal systems would be well advised to remember that in our administrative oral hearings the case teams are part of the Commission staff hearing the arguments. It is misconceived to take the hearing officer for a judge or the case team for an opposing party. In my view, they are likely to be more persuasive and influential if they argue on objective grounds, avoiding sarcastic comments meant to antagonise rather than to convince.

From the many cases you have seen, are women involved in cartels?

No. They may have had fewer opportunities to be involved in them, and/or they may be less tempted to break the law. What I do see are many talented female lawyers across the table, some in the first line, many of them in the background and many female colleagues enforcing the law against cartels.

Anna Vernet
DG COMP, European Commission
Emma Trogen

Anna Vernet is head of the unit in DG Competition responsible for cooperation within the European Competition Network, National Courts and Private Enforcement. The role of the unit is to ensure coherent and effective public and private enforcement in the EU. From 2009 to 2015 Anna was working as policy analyst in Directorate A of DG COMP, dealing with antitrust policy. She started her career at the European Commission in 2004 by joining the DG COMP telecommunications unit. Prior to working for the Commission, she was in private practice, advising clients in various sectors on different aspects of competition law. Anna graduated from Uppsala University in 1998 and holds a Master's degree from the European University Institute in Fiesole, Italy.

Emma Trogen is Deputy Director General and Head of the Legal Department at Cosmetics Europe, the trade association representing the European cosmetics and personal care industry. She is responsible for all legal matters pertaining to the EU policy work of the association, and ensures association legal and statutory compliance, including on antitrust. A qualified attorney, Emma previously worked in the EU and competition law practices of Skadden, Arps, Slate, Meagher & Flom, and Swedish firm Vinge. She obtained her law degree from the University of Nantes, France and has complementary EU law degrees from the Universities of Cardiff (Wales) and Rennes (France).

Tell us about your educational and professional background.

I have a law degree from Uppsala University in Sweden and a Master's in European law from the European University Institute in Fiesole, Italy. Between the two I did a traineeship at a law firm in Brussels, which already gave me an appetite to work in a truly European environment. After my Master's degree I spent six months at the office of the French judge at the Court of Justice in Luxembourg, which was a very enriching experience for a young lawyer. My first real job was at one of the leading Swedish law firms where I stayed for around five years – first in Stockholm, but also for two years in Malmö in south of Sweden, commuting from Copenhagen in Denmark to Sweden every day like a true European using the right to free movement. Ever since my specialisation in Uppsala, the red thread throughout was European law with an emphasis on competition law.

How and when did you arrive at DG COMP and what positions have you occupied there?

After five years in private practice, I wanted to try working at the European Commission. My experience as trainee in Brussels and Luxembourg – and my year in Fiesole – had really given me an appetite for trying this out. So this led me to DG COMP, where I started early 2004. It is amazing to say that out loud – 2004! When I started I thought this was an adventure for a few years in the European institutions and now the clock is already at 16 years and counting.

I had the chance to start as a case handler in a very dynamic antitrust unit focusing on the telecommunications sector. In those days DG COMP and DG Connect (at the time DG Information Society) worked seamlessly in joint teams on the notifications by national telecom regulators imposing remedies on telecom companies. With its merger-like deadlines (one month for assessment if no second phase), that added an extra spice to the work on antitrust cases. Already at the time, though, I was very interested in the broader picture and also the cooperation within the European Competition Network (ECN). When I joined DG COMP, the modernisation of EU competition law through Regulation 1/2003 was just taking place and that was a very exciting moment. In 2009 I moved to the antitrust policy unit and changed perspective from individual cases to general policy. My first task in that new unit was to work on the revision of the rules for cooperation between competitors (the horizontal regime). One of the most interesting discussions at the time was around standard-setting and standard essential patents, which led to a new chapter in the guidelines on these issues. During my years in that unit I then led the revisions of, for example, the guidelines on *de minimis* and the Block Exemption Regulation on technology transfer agreements. It was a privilege to work with some of the best brains that DG COMP could offer and try to learn as much as possible. In autumn 2015, I then finally took the step to become a manager and moved to take up the responsibility as deputy head of unit for the unit responsible for cooperation within the ECN, National Courts and Private Enforcement. A bit more than a year later I took up the position as head of unit for the same unit.

How do you picture your mission within an antitrust enforcement agency?

The fact of working for the public good, to the benefit of the European consumer, is really something that still continues to motivate me every day. In this world where so much is about the big companies, the big money, the big politicians, it is a privilege to work to protect European consumers. Because that is what it is all about. We can frame it in different words, for example, Philip Lowe used to repeat the mantra of "make markets work", while Executive Vice President Vestager puts a lot of emphasis on fairness in the larger sense and a market that works for people. But for me it all boils down to the same – ensure that the capital plays fairly and that the market doesn't profit unduly on the cost of the consumer. Of course, competition policy is also about protecting companies – for example, ensuring that small companies have a fair chance to grow without being foreclosed by giants – which then indirectly benefits the consumer.

How have you seen DG COMP evolve during your time within the institution, both in terms of substantive assessments and in terms of procedures? And from a different angle, how do you perceive that the European Commission's stated objectives on gender balance have been taken up by DG COMP?

DG Competition was a fantastic work place in 2004 and is a fantastic work place today – not because everything is perfect but in particular because of the colleagues in house. I am still amazed by the level of professionalism and expertise of my colleagues, both lawyers and economists. Working with highly skilled and motivated colleagues from all over the union is for me a privilege. This has not changed during the 16 years I have been there.

In terms of substantive assessment, I arrived at DG Competition during a period where a lot of emphasis was put on the importance of effects-based assessments. Not only were all the Block Exemption Regulations and guidelines on 101 TFEU now based on that type of thinking, but also that of the Article 102 policy. Effects-based assessment still underlines a large part of antitrust cases, but maybe today the pendulum has swung somewhat back towards a more qualitative effects-based assessment as compared with the stronger position of belief in the need for quantitative assessments that prevailed at the time.

In the last mandate, the three goals of "speed, relevance and quality" were Commissioner Vestager's motto. And indeed for certain type of restrictions investigations can, and should, be speedy and that is why also enforcement of by-object infringements are needed. The objective of speed is also why the Commission has made efforts to streamline procedures and set up new procedures for this purpose. I am, in particular, thinking of the recently set up cooperation procedure which allows for a quick closure of cases where companies cooperate, for example on remedies or evidence, in return for a rebate on fines. In terms of procedures, I also just have to mention that when I started in DG COMP all documents where signed through paper "signataires" which, coming from the private sector, in the beginning made me completely mad. Of course, we still have the need, as in any public organisation, to have the hierarchy's sign-off on certain type of documents. But today at least it is done fully electronically!

The gender balance at management level has improved radically in DG COMP since I started. Looking at middle management (heads of unit) we are now very close to 50% of the posts being occupied by women. For senior management there is still some way to go (here women occupy around 30% of the posts today). This is a world of difference as compared to when I started in 2004. At the time women held less than 15% of both middle management and senior management posts.

I have never felt my gender as such to be any disadvantage for my career possibilities in COMP. For quite some years, when the children were smaller, however, I chose to work part-time and to consciously put aside the career track. I never listened to those who told me "it will be too late", "one only gets a certain number of chances", and that is an advice that I would like to share with younger colleagues – take your time and go for a management career (if that's what you want) when you feel it is the right moment in your life. In my experience the European Commission is a generous organisation in that sense – new chances will come for motivated and talented colleagues.

Now, being a manager it continues to be a challenge to have a good work – life balance. In particular with younger kids that is not always an easy equation – but the possibilities of working virtually obviously makes it easier today as compared with 2004.

Another big change when it comes to management culture in DG COMP is that today, as compared with when I started, much more emphasis is put on core management skills in the selection procedures as compared to expert skills. That is a very good development.

What is your advice to younger professionals who want to work with competition law? And, more particularly, do you have any specific thoughts to share with respect to a career as a civil servant, either within a European or a national agency?

The very best colleagues that I have met often have an understanding of both the legal and the economic side of competition law, and that is really an asset working in our field. My first advice is therefore for a lawyer to take some time to understand the economics and vice versa. My second advice would be to try both sides, i.e. both private practice and public enforcement, in one way or another. It could be courts, a national competition authority (NCA), a traineeship at the Commission. I still feel the advantage of having worked in private practice since it makes me understand the different viewpoints better. As regards trying out a career as a civil servant, the most hands-on advice I can give is: do a traineeship. There are many possibilities and this is what will allow you to see if the public side is interesting for a young professional. It is also in that context that one will start to learn how one could find a more permanent position within the institutions.

You have been heading the ECN unit for the last four years. What is the role of the European Commission in the ECN and what is your vision of the network?

The ECN is, in my view, really a role model for how Europe can work. As you know, since 2004 it has been a fully decentralised enforcement system where the NCAs apply EU competition law in parallel with the Commission. All the authorities in the network, Commission included, have full powers to apply the TFEU directly. The role of the Commission in the network is to help to achieve a coherent and effective application of EU competition law. There are a number of mechanisms set out in Regulation 1/2003 that help us to achieve that goal, for example, the obligation on NCAs to notify draft decisions to the Commission a month before they are adopted. Through such mechanisms the Commission gets a full overview of the decisional practice of NCAs and can ensure that all authorities go in the same direction. However, true coherence cannot, in my view, be achieved through such mechanisms alone, but necessitates the creation of a spirit of a common goal and mission. In the ECN we now really have an atmosphere of joint learning and advancement. We have a number of working groups, for example, the working group on digital markets, where we discuss policy issues and cases at a very early stage so that we can get each other's feedback on how best to go about a new issue. The strategic steer to the network is given by the biannual meeting of the heads of the authorities, the DGs meeting. In this forum the heads of authorities discuss topical issues and take decisions on ways to cooperate within the network.

My vision of the ECN for the future is that we will come to an even closer cooperation within the network, in particular after the implementation of the ECN+ Directive (we will come to that) when all authorities will be fully equipped with the tools and resources they need. Recent years have shown that the days when NCAs only dealt with national markets and national behaviour are gone. In this digital era we are now living in, more and more markets become European, or even global, and the Commission cannot do all the cases. Actually already today, NCAs do more than 90% of the cases enforcing articles 101 and 102 TFEU. The globalisation and digitalisation of markets may, in the future, possibly lead the ECN to also wishing to start discussing priority-setting in terms of which cases to pick up within the network as a whole. Today this is purely a matter of national competence.

The ECN was created in 2004. How has ECN developed since its beginnings? How do you work differently today after 15 years of experience?

The ECN is now already 16 years old. It has now developed into a mature, smooth and well-oiled machine where we process at least around 100 national cases applying the EU competition rules per year. Every day the colleagues in my unit email and talk to the colleagues in the NCAs. Every day the colleagues in one NCA call the colleagues in another NCA. There are discussions about case allocation, about jointly pursuing a certain type of case, about helping each other with investigatory measures, for example through doing an inspection for a sister authority. The biggest difference I can see it is that in the beginning, necessarily so, a lot of work was focused on setting up the processes for how the network would work, while in the last five years we have moved much more to in-depth discussions and joint learning on substance. Of course sometimes we have divergences of view, even if those occasions are more rare than is sometimes perceived. We try to solve divergences in an amical and constructive manner, and in real terms this mean that the leverage of the Commission's ability to take over a national case is very often enough. After the implementation of ECN+, there will, however, be a lot of improvements on the procedural side within the network in the sense that, for example, leniency procedures will be harmonised and cross-border enforcement of unpaid fines will be made possible.

The ECN is a mechanism to effectively deal with cross-border practices restricting competition and to enable an efficient and consistent application of competition law. A major step in this process was anchored with the adoption of the ECN+ Directive. What do you see as the major achievements with this directive and how do you see the network evolve after the end of the implementation period of the directive?

Working toward the ECN+ Directive together with the NCAs was a fantastic journey. Once again, this is a role model as to how Europe can work. There were years spent on preparing within the network, really examining in depth what the network would need to become fully effective – to tap the last potential. The NCAs were almost all present at the negotiations in Council and many of them are also now holding the pen when drafting national laws. There are many achievements in this directive, and I don't think I want to single out one in particular because what is most important will depend on what was most lacking in a specific Member State. In one Member State, the rules on independence may make most difference, while in another it may be the rules removing all obstacles for a deterrent fining policy.

Since March 2020 we are experiencing an unprecedented public health crisis. Our ways of working changed significantly overnight. How do you steer a Member States network digitally and what topics were in particular relevant for the ECN network during the initial crisis management period?

In the very beginning of the crisis, on 23 March 2020, the ECN issued a statement explaining how competition authorities can help companies deal with these unprecedented times. This joint statement aimed to both reassure companies that there would be no intervention under competition law against necessary and temporary measures aiming at tackling shortages of supply, but also to give a warning that companies could not use the crisis as an excuse for anticompetitive practices unrelated to COVID-19. The joint statement underlines the importance of access to essential goods such as face masks and sanitising gel at competitive prices. Following the joint statement, the Commission and NCAs have worked together to ensure early coordination of actions in order to avoid overlaps of any Covid-19-related investigations and to ensure coherence in any guidance provided to market participants in different Member States. Many NCAs have launched investigations concerning different types of situation where companies have been trying to use the crisis at the cost of the consumer. A large number of these cases concern the pricing of essential goods and refusal to supply such goods to competitors. The saddest examples are the investigations concerning excessive prices in the funeral services sector. Many NCAs have also provided informal guidance to companies on whether different types of cooperation were in line with the ECN statement and therefore not infringing EU competition law. The network has been faced with, for example, questions on cooperation on coordinated extension of moratoria of loans. I really do think that the network has risen to the challenge here!

Now, in practical terms, we were all facing the difficulty of adapting to working virtually. Not only the Commission, but the whole network quickly adapted and could continue business as usual. Dealing with requests for informal guidance, starting new investigations e.g. on essential goods and also (after a while) adopting decisions on ongoing cases. There are obviously particular challenges when it comes to inspections. In terms of meetings, we have now learned to have ECN meetings fully virtually. My experience is that it works well once one understands how to adapt – and how to chair a virtual meeting. But I think I speak for all of us if I say that we jointly miss the opportunity to meet and discuss face to face. Real contact cannot be replaced even by video calls. However, in the future I am sure that we will benefit from the experiences of the crisis and feed this experience into the future functioning of the network.

Now looking forward to when the worst period of the public health crisis is over, we are facing another enormous challenge. Does it ring a bell if I mention 1929? What in the beginning looked like a severe recession seems now to be turning into a possible depression at global level. I am personally convinced that enforcement of competition law is part of the answer of how to get Europe back on track. Through targeted and coordinated competition enforcement we, the ECN including the Commission, can contribute to the recovery of the European economy. However, I think that we can assume that there will come a period during the next decade where we will hear voices being raised against competition law, arguing that what can best help the European economy is to temporarily set aside competition law. So in the years to come we need to all join forces and be excellent advocates for the benefits of targeted use of competition enforcement.

You are also in charge of private enforcement. Does the current system work and how does private enforcement complement public enforcement?

It is now some time since the Damages Directive was implemented in all Member States – there was some delay in these. Overall, the implementation is very well done and we have now all reasons to believe that we have the base for effective private enforcement in the EU.

Since then we have also issued guidelines on passing on of cartel overcharges and, this summer, guidelines on how to protect confidential information before national courts to further the day-to-day effectiveness of the European private enforcement system. Depending on whether a Member State has a system with specialised courts or not, there are a lot of novelties that national judges may be facing and we hope that these guidelines will be of some assistance.

The last few years, the number of private enforcement actions in the EU has rocketed. Recent research (from 2019) shows that we have more than 250 judgments on the merits from 13 different countries. I insist on the latter figure since it is often presumed that private enforcement is limited to a few countries. That used to be the cases but now we see jurisprudence developing in more and more countries. These cases were judged by around 120 different courts and most of them were so-called follow-on cases (i.e. following a public enforcement decision by the Commission or an NCA).

The exponential curve that we have seen the last few years will continue. It is clear that both infringers and purchasers now start think about the possibility of being inflicted/awarded damages. In a few years' time, when we see the outcome of the many ongoing cases, for example following the Commission's *Trucks* case, it may also be easier to put a price tag on the financial risk of damages. But it is here, on the issue of quantification, where I see the challenges for the years to come. In particular in cases such as *Trucks*, where there are many actions ongoing in a number of countries (and sometimes before a number of regional courts in the same country), it is important that the courts strive to achieve similar results. It would be unfortunate if, for the same cartel, courts in country X quantify the harm as 5% while courts in country Y would quantify the harm as 15%. Within one country there are normally means of dealing with these matters, but between different countries this is more of a challenge.

For me, private enforcement is an important complement to public enforcement. It ensures the even further increase of fairness in the system – and even though the goal of private enforcement is compensation of the harmed, and not deterrence, the risk for damages will be part of what will make companies think twice before they infringe the law.

The work of DG COMP should also be seen in the larger context of the policy priorities of the European Commission, for example the digital transition and the Green Deal. How does the DG COMP action fit into these policy priorities and what does it in particular mean to your unit and to the ECN network?

The question of to what extent competition policy can take into account, and contribute to, other policy goals of society has always fascinated me. It was actually the topic of my Master's thesis in Fiesole in 1999/2000, which shows that some questions always remain topical.

So, let me touch briefly upon how our work can contribute to two of the most important goals of the EU – to the green transition and to the digital policy (I have already touched upon how what we are doing can also contribute to the important goal of economic recovery).

Let me start with the green transition and the Green Deal. It is clear that competition policy, as many policies, has a role to play in tackling climate change. Obviously state aid can play an important role in the green transition by steering companies incentives in the right direction. But also antitrust (and mergers, of course) has a role to play: it is only if we have truly competitive markets (with a proper public enforcement) that companies will achieve the green goals imposed on them by regulation in the most efficient way. It is competitive markets that drive innovation – also when it comes to new production methods that can help to achieve the green goals. Competition also means that when we, European consumers, ask for environmentally friendly products, then the companies will deliver. I do think that we have a very important role here as citizens and consumers – to drive the demand in the right direction. It is encouraging to listen to people around you talking more and more about the option of buying an electrical car next time, or about changing supplier of electricity to go for only hydropower (e.g. in Sweden, where that is possible).

So competition policy has a clear role to play here. But, in my view, this is an area where regulation will and should continue to play the first violin. Competition policy can support, but can never replace, regulation.

In most cases, unilateral actions by companies would seem enough for them to change a production method or start selling a new brand with a green label. But on certain occasions there may be a need for companies to act jointly. In this respect, there is for the moment an increasing debate in the antitrust field about how article 101 TFEU applies to agreements between competitors aiming, for example, at reducing greenhouse gases through agreeing to change their production methods.

In my view, there is already a lot competitors can do jointly, for example, competitors coming together to create a joint environmental label. As long as labels are open for other companies and are non-exclusive, many such schemes will not pose competition problems (obviously one needs to assess every case on the facts).

But the question of how to apply article 101 TFEU to sustainability agreements, in particular in not-so-clear-cut cases, is an issue that we discuss intensely within the network and that has, over many years, been particularly relevant in the Dutch context (with specific national guidelines on sustainability agreements).

Looking forward, the Commission is currently reviewing the two Horizontal Block Exemption Regulations and the Horizontal Co-operation Guidelines. In the recent public consultation we got comments by stakeholders on the need to provide guidance on agreements on sustainability issues (including environmental issues). So this revision is now a good opportunity to look into the need for clearer guidance on sustainability agreements, including agreements aiming to reduce greenhouse gas emissions, that would be compatible with competition law. This would help ensure that companies are not deterred from entering into such agreements which actually benefit the environment without, on balance, harming the consumer.

I want to also mention another project that I am currently working on that is also very close to my heart – in the interface of how competition policy can contribute to the wider Commission objectives. A project that can, in my view, also make a contribution to the socio-economic recovery of the EU economy.

This Commission continues, as the previous one, to put a strong emphasis on the social pillar and on a sustainable EU in social terms. Digitalisation and more generally the on-demand economy have an impact on working conditions in both new (e.g. platform work) and more traditional forms of labour. In particular, for the younger generation, work has become less bound to space and time, for both employees and self-employed, but also less certain in terms of income (and other social protections). One of the most obvious examples that we see on the streets are all the bike-riders doing deliveries of food.

In this fast-evolving labour market, it is now sometimes difficult to know whether a certain individual is really an employee or a self-employed. Many individuals in today's labour market may be in a vulnerable position even if, on paper, they are not employees. We all see that there are different incentives for companies to offer contracts as self-employed rather than as employees. Think about taxes, social security costs etc.

Now, the problem with competition law, as it stands today, is that all individuals who are qualified as self-employed risk being seen as undertakings and therefore risk infringing competition law if they collectively bargain to achieve better working conditions. This creates uncertainty for individuals and competition authorities, which in turn may be an obstacle for the improvement of working conditions of certain vulnerable parts of the workforce. In order to ensure that competition law doesn't stand in the way for vulnerable individuals coming together when justified, we are therefore now working on an initiative aiming to assess whether there is a need to adopt measures at EU level to ensure that collective bargaining is accessible not only to employees and false self-employed, but also to the genuine self-employed who need it.

Obviously this competition law-related initiative is only one piece of the puzzle to improve the situation of some platform workers and other genuine self-employed. But I do think it can be a good complement to other initiatives addressing specific employment and social aspects, such as DG EMPL's initiative on fair minimum wage.

Diane Wood
US Court of Appeals for the Seventh Circuit
Lina Khan

Diane Wood is a judge of the US Court of Appeals (7th Circuit) and a senior lecturer at the University of Chicago. She earned her BA (1971) and JD (1975) from the University of Texas at Austin, and then clerked for Judge Irving L Goldberg of the 5th Circuit US Court of Appeals and for Supreme Court Justice Harry A Blackmun. She then worked at the US State Department. In 1980 she began teaching law, primarily at the University of Chicago. From 1993 to 1995 she served in the Justice Department's Antitrust Division. In 1995 she joined the court, where she served as chief judge from 2013 to 2020.

Lina Khan is an associate professor of law at Columbia Law School, where she teaches and writes about antitrust law, the antimonopoly tradition, and law and political economy. Before joining Columbia, Khan served as counsel to the US House Judiciary Committee's Subcommittee on Antitrust, Commercial and Administrative Law, where she helped lead the Subcommittee's investigation into digital markets. Previously, she was a legal fellow in the office of Commissioner Rohit Chopra at the Federal Trade Commission and legal director at the Open Markets Institute. She is a graduate of Williams College and Yale Law School.

Prior to your appointment to the 7th Circuit, you were a legal academic specialising in antitrust (among other areas), and you worked for several years at the Antitrust Division. What drew you to antitrust?

My first exposure to antitrust law occurred during the summer after my second year in law school (at the University of Texas at Austin), when I was a summer associate in Washington, DC, at Covington & Burling. The first case to which I was assigned was *Purex v Clorox*. I came to appreciate the fact that this was the private spin-off from the Supreme Court's famous decision in *FTC v Proctor & Gamble Co*,[1] which had been issued so many years earlier. The partner called me into his office and said, "We need to have an analysis of everything in the record that P&G/Clorox did that might be understood to be an attempt to monopolise. And oh, by the way, no one really understands attempts to monopolise." I dutifully went off to the library, read everything I could find on attempts to monopolise (and antitrust more generally), and then spent the rest of my time at the firm wading through the record. I produced an extremely lengthy memorandum that I hoped responded to the partner's question. A few years later, after I had finished my clerkship at the Supreme Court and after a short time at the State Department, I returned to Covington and more or less picked up where I left off with the *Clorox* case (and obviously many others). But I enjoyed that summer experience immensely, and so I made sure to take the course in antitrust when I returned to law school in the fall. I was fortunate enough to have the late and much-missed Steve Susman as my professor, because Steve was taking some time off from his law practice. From that time to the present day, I've been hooked.

---

1   386 U.S. 568 (1967).

You entered legal practice and academia around the late 1970s and early 1980s, right around the time when the growing influence of the Chicago school was ushering in a profound shift in antitrust theory and practice. What was it like to begin working in antitrust at such a transformative moment?

Antitrust was definitely in a ferment at the time I was beginning my career as a lawyer. I would back things up to October term 1976, when I was clerking at the Supreme Court. That year, the Court issued five significant decisions in the area of antitrust: *Brunswick Corp v Pueblo Bowl-O-Mat, Inc,*[2] *United States Steel Corp v Fortner Enterprises, Inc,*[3] *Illinois Brick Co v Illinois,*[4] *Continental TV, Inc v GTE Sylvania Inc,*[5] and *Bates v State Bar of Arizona.*[6] Anyone who has been anywhere near antitrust for the last 40 to 50 years will recognise the significance of each one of these cases. Each one was influenced by classic Chicago-school thinking. When I was fortunate enough to begin teaching at the University of Chicago Law School a few years later (in 1981, to be exact), I looked forward to exploring these ideas further. I was never a card-carrying Chicago school adherent, but it was plain to me that any serious antitrust work would need to take those insights into account and give a good answer to why they should not be accepted. I had that opportunity at the law school, both when I taught the basic antitrust class (usually with an economist as a co-teacher, which was also enriching) and when I taught my seminar in international antitrust. I had developed my interest in the international aspects of antitrust law when I worked at the State Department, in the Economic, Business and Commerce section of the Office of the Legal Adviser. There I had the opportunity to glimpse the complex

2   429 U.S. 477 (1977).
3   429 U.S. 610 (1977).
4   431 U.S. 720 (1977).
5   433 U.S. 36 (1977).
6   433 U.S. 350 (1977).

interaction between a country's competition laws and its economic structure, its history and its policy goals. I became convinced then that scrupulous attention to underlying empirical assumptions and premises is critical, probably not just for antitrust but for all comparative-law studies. Something that appears to be a universal truth for the United States, with its 230-year history of open competition among all of the states and territories, may not work so well in the absence of that experience. Size of economy, international trade policy and the rest of the legal infrastructure (e.g. are laws forbidding discrimination on the basis of race, sex, religion and so forth vigorously enforced, thereby ensuring competitive labour markets; do the capital markets function competitively?) all matter, too.

Your scholarship has examined antitrust regimes beyond the US, and you have argued in favour of "soft harmonisation" of national competition laws.[7] Do you think soft harmonisation remains a worthy goal? And how effective do you think harmonisation efforts have been?

I am more convinced than ever that "soft harmonisation" is the right approach, when one asks how to ensure more competitive markets globally. Note that the underlying assumption of this question is that competition law is, in the abstract, a good thing. I believe that to be the case. It ensures that the competitive process can work without the distortions that cartels or firms with substantial market power can inflict. When competition law is firmly in place in countries that trade extensively with one another, as it has been between the United States and the European Union for many years now, it also helps to ensure that the much-vaunted "level playing field" exists. I alluded to one advantage of "soft" harmonisation in the previous answer: it allows an individual country to tailor its competition law to its own situation. In a more subtle

---

7   Diane P Wood, "International Harmonization of Antitrust Law: The Tortoise or the Hare?" (2002) 3 Chi J Int'l L 391.

sense, it ensures the dignity of each country, and its ability usefully to contribute to the broader conversation. The International Competition Network has served as an effective convening organisation, though by its very nature, it is not the only such forum. Many countries, for instance, have taken advantage of regional groups too, in which they can work to harmonise such things as merger review and cartel enforcement, to understand one another's positions better, and to facilitate cooperative efforts.

My final comment about "soft harmonisation" is a comparative one. There are only two other alternatives: no effort to harmonise at all, or "hard" (in the sense of treaty-based, mandatory, top-down) harmonisation. Because I believe that competition law is an important part of both national and global economic policy, I do not favour the abandonment of any efforts to harmonise. As for "hard" harmonisation, as I have pointed out in many articles, it is very hard to pin down rules that are both meaningful (that is, not just glittering generalities) and widely accepted. Many countries' laws have provisions that depend on the fact that enforcement is almost exclusively in the hands of a government agency. That both opens and closes doors that are available to a place such as the United States, which uses federal enforcement (Department of Justice, Federal Trade Commission (FTC)), state enforcement (state attorneys general, using either state law or federal law), and private enforcement. Finally, I would note that since the conclusion of the Uruguay round of World Trade Organization (WTO) negotiations, international efforts at "hard" harmonisation have not gone well. Efforts to draft competition rules that would fit within the WTO have failed. My own conclusion, thus, is that if we want to make progress, "soft" harmonisation is the way to go.

You have written favourably about harmonisation between the competition laws of United States and the European Union, stating that "the practical differences, as opposed to the hypothetical differences, that exist between the United States and the EU have become quite small".[8] Yet public commentary in recent years has focused extensively on the differences between these two regimes, especially with regard to their approaches to enforcement in digital markets and the European Commission's enforcement of its "abuse of dominance" standard. Do you think these differences are overstated?

The answer to this question depends on whether one is a "glass half-full" sort of person, or a "glass half-empty" believer. Day-to-day, case-to-case, there are very few differences between EU competition law and US antitrust law. But that does not mean that the differences are zero, or even that they are trending in that direction. When I opposed an international treaty on competition law, or even a side agreement on competition law that could be administered by the WTO, I frequently pointed out that the US view on large-firm behaviour is quite different from that of the EU. In the US, the tools for addressing large-firm behaviour are largely found in section 2 of the Sherman Act, though one might say that Clayton Act section 7 also plays a preventative role. In the EU, the primary tool is article 102 of the Treaty on the Functioning of the European Union. The first key difference is that the EU is not so reluctant to impose behavioural remedies. When it does so, it has all of the resources of the Competition Directorate of the European Commission at its command, to administer those remedies. In contrast, as we recall from the many years during which the modified final judgment existed in the *AT&T* case, behavioural remedies in the United States are administered and monitored by the courts. Yet the courts are ill-suited for that role, and so there is a strong preference in the US to avoid such remedies.

Another critical difference is what we might think of as the threshold of pain: the US does not intervene in monopolisation cases until the alleged

---

8   *ibid* 403.

monopolist appears to have a very substantial market share – maybe 70 or 80% – thereby permitting the inference that the firm in question also wields a high level of market power. That threshold is lower in Europe, and so it is more possible for the EU to intervene before markets have frozen altogether.

Finally, the EU has never sworn off the idea that competition law exists in part to enforce open access to markets and fair business practices. During its heyday, the Chicago school forswore those goals, in favour of a single-minded focus on lower prices and greater output. In my view, that policy difference helps to explain why the EU has taken stronger steps with respect to digital markets and their mega-firms (Alphabet, Amazon, Facebook etc.). Given path-dependence and the sheer market power of these firms, it may not be possible to preserve competition for the future without such preventative steps. There is now a rich literature developing in the United States that is re-examining the assumptions that had been made during the 1980s through the first decade of the 21st century. As I noted earlier, although many had thought that those assumptions were *a priori* truths, they may have turned out only to reflect the empirical characteristics of certain markets, at a certain point in time. Those empirical characteristics seem to be shifting, as markets become more digital, and so it is quite appropriate to take another look at the way in which we are enforcing these basic laws.

Over the last few years, antitrust has become a major topic of public discussion. Growing empirical research has shown that markets across the economy have become more concentrated and less competitive – resulting in higher prices, lower wages and declining rates of new business formation – and policymakers are now assessing whether existing antitrust laws and enforcement levels are adequate. In your view, are there particular aspects of the antitrust laws that invite legislative attention or clarification?

As I indicated in my last answer, the short answer is "yes", there are aspects of our antitrust laws that need re-examination in light of the modern digital world whose boundaries seem only to be the limits of planet Earth. I do not have a legislative wish-list, but I can suggest several topics that are worth careful study: (1) do we need more robust remedies that can be ordered by a court against a monopolist (or dominant firm), such as civil fines, so that we no longer face the unpleasant choice between behavioural micro-management and divestiture; (2) should we attempt to put some definition of market power in the Sherman Act, the Clayton Act and the Federal Trade Commission Act, and at the same time set that threshold closer to the one used in Europe, so that we can intervene before a market ossifies with only one or two firms, or before it turns into an impenetrable oligopoly; (3) should we re-examine the deregulation movement that began under the Carter administration and then accelerated under the Reagan administration, and create a way to regulate behavioural remedies that might be imposed both for monopolists and for oligopolists (perhaps within the FTC, or perhaps in an independent agency); and (4) should we put into place (or reinstate) a more robust form of line of business reporting, so that we can spot at an earlier time when a market is moving toward undue concentration and weaker competition? Given the way in which digital platforms allow firms to trace everything they touch, such reporting would be less difficult than it was in the past and would allow for smarter enforcement. Indeed, such reporting would also be a way to monitor the competitive consequences of earlier interventions, as some scholars have urged, to assess the competitive health of those markets.

In the United States, antitrust law now assesses the vast majority of conduct under the "rule of reason" standard, which is meant to facilitate a fact-specific inquiry that balances harms and benefits. Several scholars have argued that the rule of reason heavily favours antitrust defendants, contributes to soaring litigation costs, and renders antitrust law unpredictable and indeterminate.[9]

---

9   See, e.g., Michael A Carrier, "The Rule of Reason: An Empirical Update for the 21st Century" (2009) 16 Geo Mason L Rev 827 (finding that between 1999 and 2009, defendants won in 99% of antitrust cases where a court made a final determination under the rule of reason); Rebecca Allensworth, "Adversarial Economics in Antitrust Litigation" (2012) 106 NWUL Rev 1261, 1273; Maurice Stucke, "Does the Rule of Reason Violate the Rule of Law?" (2009) 42 UC Davis L Rev 1375, 1427.

Meanwhile Justice Stephen Breyer and Chief Justice John Roberts alike have criticised the standard for being highly unadministrable, stating that courts are ill-equipped to engage in the open-ended analysis that rule of reason invites.[10] Do you agree with any of these critiques?

The debate between the per se rule and the rule of reason has shifted over the years, in my opinion. With the narrow exception of hard-core cartels – the type that are often pursued criminally – we no longer have a per se rule that resembles the one the Supreme Court described in *Northern Pacific Ry v United States*.[11] Instead, we have the full-blown rule of reason, and the rule of reason "light", sometimes called "quick look". I agree with the Chief Justice and Justice Breyer that the full-blown rule of reason is a mess. It produces shockingly expensive litigation costs, in the form of expert fees, burdensome discovery and time. No one is certain what question all this data is supposed to answer. Do we want to know if the defendant has market power? Do we want to know if a certain practice hurt competitors in the market in the past? Do we want to know if it is likely to harm the market if continued into the future? Do we want to know who else (either from another country or from the US) might be able to enter the market and curb any anticompetitive excesses? And how is one supposed to decide whether the anticompetitive hypothesis is, on balance, more likely than the hypothesis of vigorous competition? I believe that the system would be better if we reinstated some clear rules that administrative agencies, lawyers and courts could follow. We all know that bright lines can be troublesome at the edges. But at what cost are we pursuing perfection?

---

10 See, e.g., Leegin Creative Leather Products, Inc v PSKS, Inc, 551 U.S. 877, 916 (2007) (Breyer dissenting) ("How easily can courts identify instances in which the benefits are likely to outweigh potential harms? My own answer is, not very easily."); FTC v Actavis, 570 U.S. 136, 173 (2013) (Roberts dissenting) ("The majority declares that such questions should henceforth be scrutinized by antitrust law's unruly rule of reason. Good luck to the district courts that must, when faced with a patent settlement, weigh the 'likely anticompetitive effects, redeeming virtues, market power, and potentially offsetting legal considerations present in the circumstances.'").

11 356 U.S. 1, 5 (1958).

In recent decades, antitrust analysis has been increasingly guided by microeconomics, and antitrust litigation today relies heavily on the testimony of economic experts. Some scholars have stated that generalist judges often lack the expertise to independently assess the economic arguments before them and have questioned whether the current approach to antitrust effectively delegates outsized authority to economists.[12] Given that the vast majority of federal judges do not arrive at the bench as experts in antitrust economics, do you think it is reasonable to expect that they would be equipped to adjudicate between battling economists? What do you see as the appropriate role of economics in antitrust?

It is certainly true that most generalist federal judges do not come to the bench with a sophisticated understanding of microeconomics. And despite the best efforts of the Federal Judicial Center to educate them on this topic (and the FJC has great materials), a judge will never approach the expertise of either the experienced antitrust lawyer or the expert that lawyer has hired. But that may not be as big a problem as it seems at first blush. Very often the judge needs only to assess whether the expert may offer her report. Judges work with Federal Rule of Evidence 702 every day, not just with economists, but with experts ranging from hydrogeologists, to chemists, to pharmacologists, to brain surgeons, to a host of others. I can assure you that there is nothing simple about a complex environmental pollution case, in which the experts are considering who polluted a body of water and how, and at the same time there is an overlay of bankruptcy law and battling insurance companies.

The judge thus can allow the experts' reports into the record, and let the parties fight things out. Recall that actual trials in federal courts occur in a vanishingly small number of cases – maybe 1.5%. So what the judge is doing is evaluating whether there is *some* evidence supporting a certain

---

12   See, e.g., Allensworth (n 9); Rebecca Haw, "Amicus Briefs and the Sherman Act: Why Antitrust Needs a New Deal" (2011) 89 Tex L Rev 1247.

viewpoint and then either ending the case there (if the answer is no on a critical element of the plaintiff's case) or moving it along to the next stage (which usually prompts a new round of settlement talks). The judge also has no problem serving as the procedural monitor, calling for discovery conferences, scheduling pre-trial conferences, drafting a pre-trial order, etc.

What our system does do, however, is place an enormous responsibility on the shoulders of the advocates. Counsel *must* be able to reduce their arguments to plain English. One would think that they need to do so in order to communicate effectively with their clients, but they certainly need to do so in order to educate the judge on the case. A generalist judge can follow those arguments, and indeed, such a judge is likely to keep a more open mind than someone who has been "captured" by the antitrust industry. (Think, for example, of the problems that the Federal Circuit has been experiencing for many years. It has had a near-monopoly on patent appeals, but the Supreme Court has frequently disagreed with its outcomes.) My own view, therefore, is that the advantages of generalist judges outweigh the purported disadvantages.

Courts have claimed that antitrust is akin to a common-law regime, where courts revise rules as new problems arise.[13] But antitrust doctrine is rife with descriptive claims that have been empirically rebutted, even as those now-refuted theories remain embedded in case law. For example, the Supreme Court's 1986 *Matsushita* ruling claimed that predatory pricing is an irrational business strategy, one that is "rarely tried, and even more rarely successful" – an assumption that led the Court later to introduce a recoupment requirement that has crippled predatory pricing claims.[14] But predatory pricing has been shown to be a rational business strategy in a host of industries, and scholars have shown that the practice can hurt

---

13   Leegin Creative Leather Prods, Inc v PSKS, Inc, 551 U.S. 877, 899–900 (2007) ("from the beginning the Court has treated the Sherman Act as a common-law statute.").

14   Matsushita Electric Industrial Co v Zenith Radio Cor., 475 U.S. 574, 589 (1986); Brooke Grp Ltd v Brown & Williamson Tobacco Corp, 509 U.S. 209, 222–24 (1993).

consumers and competition even when losses aren't recouped.[15] Despite this new learning, the doctrine has not evolved. Do you think the common-law approach to antitrust does, on the whole, enable the law to keep pace with new empirical realities? What are the challenges?

The advantage of the common-law approach is that it allows the judge to apply the law to new situations. Congress evidently did not want to write down an exclusive list of prohibited practices, because it knew that the minute it did so, creative businesses would find some other way to distort competition. And a list in the form "A, B, C, D and anything else likely to harm competition are forbidden" is just the common-law method with a few bells and whistles. Indeed, that is more or less what we have, if one thinks of Clayton Act, section 3.

The real problem you are flagging is one of inadequate appellate review. The courts of appeals do not have the power to reject a Supreme Court decision – even an old one – and the Supreme Court today has limited its plenary review of cases to the smallest number I can remember. For October term 2019, it issued only 55 merits opinions: 53 signed opinions, and 2 per curiam opinions.[16] The comparable number for October term 2018 was 67.[17] Roughly speaking, the Court accepts 1% of the cases brought before it by way of a petition for a writ of certiorari or (very rarely) appeal. That 1% comes from all 13 circuit courts, all 50 state supreme courts (or, more technically, the highest court of the state in which a decision may be had), all territorial courts, and a few specialised tribunals such as the Court of Appeals for the Armed Forces. It is hardly surprising that antitrust has a hard time elbowing its way onto the Court's docket.

---

15 Christopher R Leslie, "Predatory Pricing and Recoupment" (2013) 113 Colum L Rev 1695; Sandeep Vaheesan, "Reconsidering Brooke Group: Predatory Pricing in Light of the Empirical Learning" (2015) 12 Berkeley Bus LJ 81.

16 See <https://www.scotusblog.com/statistics/>.

17 See <https://www.scotusblog.com/wp-content/uploads/2019/07/StatPack_OT18-7_30_19.pdf>.

Various solutions have been suggested for this problem, but none yet commands strong support. Some have suggested a National Court of Appeals that would have mandatory jurisdiction over some set of cases (usually, those involving conflicts); some have suggested routing all antitrust appeals to a single tribunal, along the lines of the Federal Circuit in relation to patent law; some have suggested a certification procedure under which a court of appeals could ask the Supreme Court to revisit a question when the court of appeals is convinced that the old law is simply out of date. The last of those may work, but one should expect strong pushback from the Supreme Court, which considers it essential to be able to control its own docket. Perhaps that concern could be addressed if those certified questions (on some analogy to the certifications that courts of appeals receive from district courts under 28 U.S.C. § 1292(b)) went into the certiorari pool and were subject to the same screening as all other petitions. I have written elsewhere to explain why I oppose the Federal Circuit model, both for patents and certainly for other subjects such as antitrust.

I also believe that it would be quite difficult, without moving to a much more administrative system than we presently have, to work our way out of the problem of updating the law through either amendments to the statutes or rule-making. To be clear, I do not favour any changes in the US system of private enforcement of the antitrust laws. It is a system that has worked well for us. It avoids the politicisation of antitrust laws, to the extent that is possible, and allows the law to continue to develop even when a particular administration may have other priorities.

Courts and enforcers frequently discuss the need to balance type I and type II errors (also known as false positives and false negatives). Some enforcers and academics have criticised current case law for favouring false negatives over false positives, arguing that this tendency has contributed to significant under-enforcement by the antitrust agencies. In your view, does the existing law get this balance right? If not, what improvements would you recommend?

The argument in favour of erring on the side of type II errors (under-enforcement) is that, even if an anticompetitive practice is mistakenly allowed to continue, the market will eventually fix it. On the other hand, this argument goes, a type I error (over-enforcement) permanently removes from the menu a business practice that may be procompetitive, or at least neutral. This argument rests critically on the assumption that the market correction predicted for the type II error will occur within a meaningful time. But modern literature suggests that markets are more sluggish than this, and that the type II error may endure for decades. And on the other side, if the type I error is bad enough, nothing prevents Congress from enacting a law to fix it. Antitrust is a field of statutory law, after all, not constitutional law. Congress takes such steps from time to time, as the Lilly Ledbetter Fair Pay Act of 2009 illustrates.[18]

So if type II errors are worse than we thought, and type I errors more amenable to correction, there is a good argument for not putting our thumb on either side of the scale. Let the evidence speak for itself in every case, and don't worry that a prohibition of a new way to distort competition may in the end require tweaking.

What guidance would you offer to women embarking on careers in antitrust, be it as practitioners or academics?

Antitrust is an endlessly fascinating area. It invites its practitioners into every nook and cranny of both the US economy and increasingly that of the world. It involves not only hard-headed economic analysis of business practices, but also the social analysis of firm behaviour,

---

18   Pub. L. No. 111-2, 123 Stat. 5 (2009) (relating to equal pay for women).

individual motivations, strategic thinking and game-playing. I would encourage any woman to pursue a career in antitrust. This is a particularly interesting time, as antitrust is once again adapting to profound changes in the way economic activity takes place. Women have a great deal to contribute to this area, and so I hope they will consider it seriously.

Stéphanie Yon-Courtin
European Parliament

Angélique de Brousse

Stéphanie Yon-Courtin became a lawyer at the Paris Bar in 2004, specialising in competition law, and worked in international law firms. She then joined the office of the president of the French Competition Authority (Bruno Lasserre) as an adviser on international affairs. Prior to that, she worked as a legal expert for the European Commission. Since 2019, Stéphanie is a Member of the European Parliament (Renew Group). She is vice-president of the Committee on Economic and Monetary Affairs (ECON) and substitute of the Committee on the Internal Market and Consumer Protection (IMCO). She was rapporteur for the 2019 annual competition policy report.

Angélique de Brousse is senior legal counsel, competition law EMEA, at Johnson & Johnson, responsible for all aspects of competition law and all business sectors. Prior to joining Johnson & Johnson, she was in private practice for nearly 20 years, and worked as counsel at Freshfields Bruckhaus Deringer, where she worked extensively on a number of merger, cartel and abuse of dominance cases, as well as compliance and training for French, Belgian and international clients. Angélique is a founding member and vice-president of l'Entente (ASBL), the association of French competition practitioners based in Brussels, as well as a founding member and board member of W@ CompetitionFR, a platform for female competition practitioners in France. She completed her legal education in Paris (Nanterre and the Sorbonne) and received an LLM from Queen Mary University of London.

On digital

You are calling on the European Commission to adapt its rules to tackle the challenges in the digital sector, in particular platforms and privacy issues. Can you summarise your position and what is your proposal in this respect?

In fast-moving digital markets, competition policy could in some cases be excessively slow, and therefore be at risk of being ineffective when it comes to remedying systemic market failures and reinstating competition. Data has definitely become the new oil of the economy; digital platforms have gained such a central position that it puts them in a position to become even more powerful than Member States: they can collect vital data that others cannot. Mandating companies to stop their harmful behaviour is not sufficient in order to bring competition back to these markets. There is an obvious need to align EU rules to the digital age, but there is no one simple solution. It will require better enforcement of our toolbox, new (or renewed) competition rules and additional regulation.

On one hand, we should make a better use of the current EU toolbox. Although fines can have an impact on the reputation of those companies that are penalised, they often are not an effective disincentive as the financial impact is ultimately passed on to the consumers. The European Commission should make use of targeted and effective behavioural remedies previously validated with the relevant stakeholders. From that perspective, a cease-and-desist order should be much more prescriptive in upcoming remedies.

Back in October 2019, the Commission used interim measures for the first time in almost 20 years, which forced Broadcom to remove exclusivity requirements put on purchasers of their chipsets. They are a pragmatic option to act timely in order to avoid any irreversible damage to competition. We should consider relaxing the criteria for these measures so that the European Commission has the opportunity to apply these more frequently – we all know how long and costly antitrust procedures can be.

In addition, we need to maximise the use of our soft law. It is time to review the notion of abuse of a dominant position and the "essential facilities" doctrine to ensure that they are fit for purpose in the digital age.

Furthermore, we should review EU merger and acquisition rules. In a digital world, consumers are offered more and more services for free. The Commission should consider revising the thresholds for a merger in order to include factors such as the number of consumers affected and the value of the related transactions. It should also consider the effects of market and network power associated with data.

Finally, as the economy is evolving, innovative solutions must be promoted, as they will play a crucial role. Competition rules are enshrined in the EU Treaties, and I am not calling for a change. However, there is still a lot of room for improvement in the current situation. Broadly speaking, and to state the obvious, the main challenge for the European Commission in terms of digital competition lies with the speed of antitrust procedures. The European Commission should make use of fast-track antitrust procedures. The new competition tool, along with the upcoming *ex ante* regulation, might be an option to avoid another ten-year antitrust case. The European Commission is thinking about an *ex ante* regulation that would consist of listing the prohibited practices. This is required in the digital sector where things are evolving so rapidly and where medium and small players need to have a chance to compete against large online platforms.

Talking about mergers in the digital space, France has recently adopted new rules introducing an *ex ante* review of any acquisition – even below the French merger thresholds – for companies of a systemic nature ("*companies structurantes*"). You were yourself calling for a "prior informal declaration" at EU level for any acquisition involving data. What do you think of the French measure and do you think the EC should consider such an option at EU-level as well? Or should it follow the tracks of Germany and Austria with a transaction-value threshold; or introduce, in Phase II, a reversal of the burden of proof that the transaction doesn't raise concerns, as Germany is proposing?

I strongly believe that it is a good move and it is going in the right direction. However, it is key that this does not lead to each nation taking its own measures as this would lead to a fragmented approach to merger review; instead we should be looking at a global solution, as otherwise targeted companies will always try to exploit tax or any type of loophole resulting from a non-cohesive measure at EU level. That is why I am advocating for an *ex ante* review at EU level. I think it would be useful for the Commission to introduce a centralised *ex ante* market-monitoring system to provide EU, and national competition and regulatory authorities with the necessary means to gather data anonymously, so that early detection of market failures becomes a reality. Then, we should introduce a targeted regulation when practices become systemic, as it is foreseen with the *ex ante* regulation, which is part of the Digital Services Act.

To do so, we need to come up with a harmonised definition of what we call "systemic platforms" or "*companies structurantes*". The Commission must identify the key digital players and establish a set of indicators that define their systemic nature. It is easier said than done. Not only should it take the market share into consideration but also indicators such as the abuse of practices of certain large scale networks, the control of a significant volume of non-replicable data, and any ability for players to define market rules themselves in such a multifaceted market.

In an ideal world, I would have advocated for an upstream declaration when it comes to acquisitions involving data, so we could also look at operations that do not meet the current EU merger control thresholds. I understand that DG COMP has its own limits and does not have the means to do so. If we want to be serious about data, the Commission needs to allocate adequate resources and ensure specific expertise, in order to tackle growing issues such as dominant positions of online platforms or artificial intelligence.

The European Competition Network is one of the best networks in competition law and it allows us to share best practices. I think that the initiatives carried out by Austria and Germany regarding transaction value are good ones, and should be introduced at EU level. As mentioned above, the European Commission should consider revising the thresholds for its merger review in order to include factors such as the number of consumers affected and the value of the related transactions. The Commission will be able to capture more transactions in digital. Price does matter to consumers but privacy and freedom of choice do. The Commission has still a long way to go in assessing a reliable set of demanding regimes for data access, including data interoperability, which can be imposed in particular when data access opens up secondary markets for complementary services or when data is confined to dominant firms.

In order to avoid any merger or acquisition related to data that would be detrimental to competition, I am in favour of the reversal of the burden of proof in Phase II. Although I acknowledge that a number of start-ups are created in the hope of an acquisition by a larger firm, it is quite clear that the buy-out of start-ups by dominant players, such as big technology companies and platforms, might stifle innovation and threaten sovereignty. The majority of our European start-ups end up as a part of larger non-European stakeholders.

You call on the potential structural separation of search engine activities in the Google Shopping case. Don't you think this goes quite far, and can you tell us more about how this would work?

I see it as a last resort solution that we should not put aside and that becomes more and more obvious. It is interesting to see that this solution is always seen as too radical or going too far while, in the meantime, Big Tech platforms keep making the most of the current framework. Let me stress the fact that during the COVID-19 crisis, Apple has become a US$2 trillion company and Google still has 92% of market share in Europe. I think they have already gone quite far and not the other way around.

In the *Google Shopping* case, the remedies offered have clearly been ineffective at restoring competition in the market. Yet, technical solutions exist to stop some abuses, but they would need to be tested in advance with the relevant stakeholders A successful solution would be one where online consumers can easily find a range of comparison shopping services, where they are offered independent choice and not a system such as Google that provides a "default" comparison shopping service on the general search results page, diverting users from other services.

What we need is a level playing field. Users should always get the best answers to their question. So far, there are risks associated with the current model as the gatekeeper can put their own services forward, making it difficult for others to compete The *ex ante* regulation and the new competition tool might put an end to this issue of self-preferencing, and give control back to consumers.

The Commission has opened an in-depth investigation into the *Google/ Fitbit* case. Do you think that data should be key to the assessment and how should the Commission take it into account in merger control?

As discussed above, EU merger and acquisition rules to assess their anticompetitive nature are not adapted to the digital sector. In general, they are based on the impact of the transaction on prices. When the small but significant and non-transitory increase in price (SSNIP) test is carried out, price is at the core of the relevant market definition. However, in the digital world, services are usually free of charge (or paid for by your personal data).

The European Commission should consider whether price is the main element that encourages people to switch from one service provider to another. The Commission must review the impact of the transaction on more stringent criteria, taking into account whether there is less qualitative choice for the consumer after the transaction, or the impact that the transaction will have on the use of the data. It means considering the effects of the power of the market and network associated with both personal and financial data.

To do so, the Commission must monitor closely this data as an indicator of the existence of market power and consider related data as a crucial element of its analyses and test. The Commission should adjudge the control of such data as a proxy for the existence of market power under its guidance on article 102 TFEU (Treaty on the Functioning of the European Union) and ensure that data collection will not further entrench the market power of a few dominant players.

The data of Fitbit's 28 million users will increase Google's powerful position in online advertising and might further exclude potential competitors. If Google acquires consumer data generated by the use of Fitbit devices, including now COVID-19 – related data, it would be able to use that data, such as users' daily steps, calories burned and distance travelled, for its own benefit, and could undermine the ability of other companies to bring new products to consumers. What if Google later acquires an insurance company which could then have easy access to a massive amount of private data from millions of Google customers? Are we ready to see all this ultraconfidential health data publicly released on the Internet, and to pay more expensive insurance bills to cover health problems?

In my opinion, this will be a landmark decision and the European Commission should use that case to illustrate the change of paradigm and show how serious we are with data, competition and consumer protection. That is why I think it is very important for the Commission to organise multisectoral and inter-institutional forums involving industry, national regulators such as data protection authorities, consumer groups and other relevant stakeholders to remove silos from our competition policy and have the broadest picture.

On the Commission-proposed new competition tool

You raised in the EU Parliament *2019 Report on Competition Policy* the inappropriateness of competition tools in fast-moving digital markets – the European Commission has in the meantime made a proposal to introduce a new competition tool. Although the UK gives a clear and concrete example of how this could work, a lot of voices believe that this may give very extensive powers to the Commission, and that there may not be enough checks and balances?

We are still at an early stage of this new competition tool, as the Commission has just released its impact assessment and is assessing the results of the online consultation. It is no surprise that law firms are quite sceptical regarding this new tool that would, according to them, increase legal uncertainty.

If it is too early to assess the pros and cons of the tool, I see it as an opportunity to speed up processes in antitrust. When you look at what is happening in the US, we feel like the EU is lagging behind. I am in favour of giving the means to the European Commission to act in a timely manner and preserve fair competition in digital markets. However, with more freedom and flexibility come transparency and accountability. These conditions can be met by involving the European Parliament more. I also think that the European Parliament should be involved, like Member States, when the European Commission proposes draft papers on competition. We, as representatives of the EU citizens, have to be in the driving seat.

It will give the European Commission the authority required to enforce rules and impose bold decisions.

As a former lawyer, I would hate seeing politics interfering in DG COMP decisions, but this is a question of finding the right balance. Although I very much appreciate the cooperation of European Vice-President Vestager when it comes to the structural dialogue with the European Parliament, I think there is room to do more. There should be regular exchanges with the Commission, in line with the inter-institutional agreement with Parliament and, in that respect, the Competition Working Group could be an appropriate place for establishing regular dialogue.

Competition ultimately benefits consumers and companies and their representatives should therefore be involved in designing competition policies. Look at the US Congress, which even has the power to initiate investigations.

On foreign direct investment and industrial policy

You invite the Commission to adopt a more favourable approach for a strong EU industrial policy to ensure and maintain competitiveness in global markets, as well as put into place effective tools to ensure a level playing field with foreign state-owned companies that may benefit from state support, in contrast with EU companies (due to EU state aid rules). Don't you think that this may reduce the incentive to foreign companies – including US companies – to invest in EU businesses, and may also unduly support businesses that are not sufficiently competitive on the global scene? What do you suggest to strike the right balance?

Our world has dramatically changed, and we must respond to new realities. The EU has for too long been too shy and naive. On one hand, the EU has never been bold in terms of industrial policy, which seems to be a politically incorrect word in the EU bubble. Yet, national approaches are not the way to go and will not be as efficient as a European approach in a globalised world. On the other hand, the EU has not yet managed to have an offensive trade policy as have some of its trade partners.

As a Renew Member of the European Parliament, and chair of the EU – Canada delegation, I am convinced that the EU should remain open and that any tools proposed should not undermine the principle of free trade. At the same time, we must realise that our internal market, with almost 450 million consumers, is one of our biggest achievements and a big opportunity not only for European companies but also for non-European ones. Neither do I want double standards for "European champions" as opposed to other EU companies, nor do I want double standards for European companies v non-European ones. I want a level playing field.

The rule is quite simple: companies that want to operate in our internal market must play by our rules. The European Commission is right to strengthen competition policy in the context of globalisation and to ensure reciprocity with third countries in the field of public procurement and state aid. We must adapt our rules to the current situation whereby state aid rules, which allow the proper functioning of our Single Market, do not apply to non-European operators who have access to that very Single Market.

A football match where the rules of the foreign team are more lenient than those of the home team would be totally unfair! The COVID-19 crisis has also alerted us of the need to preserve our key sectors in order to achieve the resilient Europe we all want.

Critics suggest that if the framework is too restrictive, then this might lead to fewer investments in Europe. Similarly, European companies operating abroad might be impacted by similar foreign investment regimes applicable in these jurisdictions. But aren't they already victims of unfair competition? I agree that being more offensive will upset our protectionist trade partners, but if we do too little, we risk losing market share.

This is more than a competition or trade issue. The issue of level playing field is a cross-sectoral issue and that is why I am calling to remove silos from European competition policy to better address the issue with trade, industrial and environmental policies, and consumer protection.

We need to ensure reciprocity with third countries on public procurement, state aid and investment policy in order to avoid distortion of competition and asymmetry between European and non-European operators. We should ensure binding implementation of the foreign direct investment screening mechanism. In the COVID-19 period, we should also prevent hostile takeover operations by large dominant players, to protect EU companies and essential goods. I hope we can have a dialogue on more protection of our companies against unfair international competition without being called protectionist. I would rather call us realistic.

On sustainability

How do you see the interaction between competition law and the Commission's "Green Deal"? Do you think that competition authorities, and DG COMP in particular, should take more into account considerations such as social and environmental issues, in particular efforts to reduce emissions or other sustainable efforts in their assessment under article 101 TFEU and in efficiencies under merger review? You also mention that DG COMP should take account data privacy as an element in its merger assessment – how would you balance-out privacy and competition considerations and do you think it is the responsibility of a competition regulator to assess privacy issues?

In the wake of the Commission's Green Deal, DG COMP is currently examining sustainability agreements as part of its review of two block exemption regulations. It is very timely since the Dutch Competition Authority published its draft sustainability guidelines, paving the way for more flexibility. Until now, some sustainability initiatives carried out by companies were found to be in violation of competition rules and did not managed to meet the exemption criteria.

I strongly believe that competition rules have a role to play to support the Green Deal objectives. It is true about state aid and IPCEIs (important projects of common European interest), but also mergers and horizontal cooperation agreements. For the latter, I assume it will require the European Commission to change its views on what would benefit society. As for data, price should not be the only criteria and the analysis should be broader and encompass EU objectives set out in the TFEU such as social and environmental issues.

Do not get me wrong, competition policy should not aim to serve political objectives, but it should contribute to the EU objectives as defined by Member States and representatives of citizens. As for environmental objectives such as carbon emissions reduction, companies could use more room to enter into sustainability agreements. However, the main obstacle is generally that the procompetitive effects of an agreement must outweigh its anticompetitive effects, which is not easy to prove.

Some would say that the European Commission would have to decide whether competition policy should be altered to make EU sustainable goals attainable. However, this is not exactly how I see things.

I am convinced that competition policy must be adapted to tackle digital, ecological, geopolitical, industrial and social challenges, and must be in line with the priorities outlined in the European Green Deal and the objectives of the Paris Agreement. In addition, I think that the green transition does not only concern companies or policymakers but consumers. If you look at the example of the fashion industry, you will find a growing trend questioning the merits of "fast fashion" and people willing to pay more to get a sustainable product. So maybe it is time to look at quality and consumer welfare, not only through price criteria?

I think that we should promote investments in green transition and not blame or threaten companies to do so. In this regard, I find it interesting that the Dutch Competition Authority will not impose fines with respect to published sustainability agreements for which the guidelines have been followed in good faith, but which have in the end proven to be incompatible with competition rules. In the meantime, the Commission will have to prevent any potential negative side-effects where larger companies use public aid or horizontal agreements intended "to green" their business models for other objectives such as reinforcing its dominant position in a given sector. We need to ensure healthy and fair competition to ensure that companies will be incentivised to innovate and meet consumer needs. It will be crucial in the context of the Green Deal and recovery plan.

The same goes for privacy. We have a strong legislative framework in Europe with the General Data Protection Regulation, as well as the European Data Protection Supervisor but it should not be a silo outside the competition arena. Competition policy is a tool that should make sure that businesses feel the need to innovate. Future European leaders will not just be the biggest companies but businesses that are the best in the world at what they do and share that success with Europeans, by creating jobs, contributing to the transformation of the economy and paying taxes here.

On COVID-19

The European Commission has been really quick to adopt measures to help companies deal with the public health and economic crisis, in particular state aid measures. Although such measures are essential to relaunching the economy, some say that they will also create significant disparities among Member States, especially between richer ones that can heavily support their companies and those that were already in financial difficulties before the COVID-19 crisis. What is your view on competition policy post-COVID?

I particularly welcome the quick response and tremendous work carried out by the European Commission concerning state aid measures to help countries fighting the pandemic. This flexibility was very much needed to help companies affected by the crisis. I support the application of the Temporary State Aid Framework for as long as necessary during the recovery period and believe it should be extended beyond the end of 2020, if necessary.

The risk of market distortions and increased divergences between countries exists, as not all Member States are able to provide the same level of support to their firms. However, we should avoid blaming one or another country for providing more financial assistance to their companies, in line with their fiscal capacity.

It is up to Member States to decide on their budgetary policy. However, state aid rules could harmonise and clarify what kind of financial assistance could be given to companies within the Temporary Framework. Besides the amendments to the Temporary Framework, I called on the Commission to set a common ground for minimum standards in order to specify that the requirement for companies receiving financial assistance is in line with ESG (environmental, social and corporate governance) criteria and taxation transparency, so as to avoid different national criteria giving rise to further discrepancies.

In this perspective, the European Commission made clear that aid should only be granted to cover the losses incurred due to COVID-19 and to companies facing the immediate effects of the crisis, and not those that were already financially unhealthy pre-crisis. However, I regret that the proposal for a Solvency Support Instrument has not been incorporated in the recovery plan. This proposal will enable equity support to businesses all over Europe by focusing on the hardest hit Member States and on the Member States that are least able to offer equity support to businesses. This is a proposal to ensure the integrity of our internal market, which acknowledges the fact that different Member States' financial markets and different-sized companies need different solutions. The European Parliament is working on this proposal, alongside the recovery plan, and we should make sure that this instrument is created. Although the recovery plan will allow Member States to get some fresh money to invest for recovery and come back to growth, this instrument is intended foremost for Member States that cannot afford to intervene. The Single Market must benefit all of us, since there is nothing to win to have one Member State lagging behind.

In the short-term, the pandemic has reminded us of the challenges lying in front of us. These are EU strategic sovereignty, digital and green transition as well as the recovery of our economy that would allow us to build tomorrow's world. To achieve these objectives, competition policy has a crucial role to play, both in protecting consumers from abusive practices, and in ensuring enforcement does not stand in the way of necessary business cooperation. The European Commission made the right decisions with its temporary guidelines or framework. The question is: what's next?

In the long-term, the COVID-19 crisis will have some major implications on competition law. We cannot go back to "business as usual". First, because the pandemic will make the economy less competitive and consumers more vulnerable for a while. Whereas competition authorities implemented the necessary measures and flexibility to mitigate the consequences of the pandemic, they will have to contribute to making economies competitive again while protecting consumers. European and national competition authorities will play a crucial role in providing decision-makers the advice and road map to overcome the current situation. The COVID-19 crisis has caused changes to consumer behaviour, businesses and the regulatory environment. If some changes are welcome, they may also aggravate existing issues such as rising market concentration and the growing power of digital platforms. One of the most important challenges is to learn from this crisis. I don't think we should aim at getting back to normal as soon as possible without adapting our regulatory environment, including EU competition rules. The temporary contribution of competition to other policy objectives in the context of the pandemic will have to be discussed in a wider debate, and that is why I called on the Commission to present to the Council and Parliament a Communication on the consequences of COVID-19 on competition. Consumers will remain at the centre of competition policy, and I hope they realise how much competition policy matters in their daily lives.

On state aid

On the *Apple* judgment: do you think the Commission went too far in intervening in national tax rules and are the EU competition tools appropriate to deal with Member States' tax regimes?

The Apple judgement was quite a huge setback for Vice-President Vestager. During the previous term, she made tax a priority and took some bold decision such as the *Apple* one.

The decision of the tribunal shows the limits of competition rules in taxation and I am afraid that the Commission will not try again anytime soon. This decision made clear that state aid rules are insufficient to address the problem of tax dumping in Europe and that issue is more a question of political will from Member States rather than interpretation of law. It is not the end of the game since the Commission may still decide to appeal the tribunal decision.

If we want to tackle unfair tax competition in Europe, it will not be enough; we would need to go further than reviewing the criteria for defining state aid. We cannot expect everything from the Commission. Either we continue the internal competition in tax matters, or we establish a kind of harmonised EU tax where corporate taxes would be roughly comparable and could not fall below a minimum rate.

In these difficult times, the incomes that Member States could collect from companies that do not pay their fair share of taxes could be more than useful. If we take the example of Ireland, the EU's recovery plan provides only a small grant for Dublin (€1.2 billion), more than ten times less than what the Apple dispute could bring. In the Renew Group, we are committed to ensuring new resources for the next Multiannual Financial Framework, to avoid citizens paying for the recovery plan but make sure that big tech pays their fair share of taxes in Europe. More than a financial issue, it is a question or fairness and accountability. We cannot ask citizens and SMEs to pay taxes and make efforts while listed companies that hit $2 trillion during the COVID-19 crisis do not pay taxes, it is unfair.

It is true that the Commission could use some additional tools to tackle tax issues without changing the EU Treaties but with no guarantee. First, the Commission could use the bridging clause, which allows derogations from the legislative procedure. Specifically, and under certain conditions, they allow a "switch" from unanimity to qualified majority voting for the adoption of an act in a given area. However, the activation of a bridging clause always depends on a decision adopted unanimously by the Council. Thus, in any case, all EU countries must agree before such a clause can be activated, which will not be the case in taxation. Alternatively, the Commission could present a proposal on how to tackle certain harmful tax structures that create distortion in the Single Market through article 116 TFEU. To do so, it must be established that there is a disparity between the provisions of the Member States, which distorts conditions of competition in the internal market that must be eliminated. However, as the article has never been used before, it is reasonable to say that the Commission will be cautious.

The genuine solution to this long-term issue is a treaty change and the end of unanimity in tax matters, but it is not on the table. However, political pressure keeps growing since the first big scandal "LuxLeaks".

General

You have met several times with Margrethe Vestager, are there any specific topics of interest that you share and would like to work on more closely with her?

We do share the need to adapt our rules to our globalised and digital world. When I first met her, I told her two of my priorities: the revision of the relevant market definition and the need for *ex ante* rules for systemic platforms. I am happy to see that, few months later, we have two ongoing consultations on these issues and that the Commission is seriously moving forward.

I am very grateful to have the opportunity to have a Renew vice-president such as Margrethe Vestager as Commissioner for Competition. She is already doing a great job. I would like to discuss with her the way to reconcile competition policy with other EU objectives, whether environmental, social or sovereignty issues. This is a debate that is very old in Brussels and has still not found a lasting solution. The COVID crisis has also reminded us of the challenges that we must face and to which we must respond. All means will be needed to achieve this, including competition policy. I hope to have the opportunity to work on this with Margrethe and with the Commissioner for the internal market, Thierry Breton.

Lastly, although I think she is doing a great job in terms of the structural dialogue with the European Parliament, I think there is more to be done. Exchanges with the representatives of European consumers should be more frequent. We should be updated more regularly on what is going on and be involved in a special working group at the European Commission, for instance. As an example, when we were in a middle of the pandemic, the Commission consulted Member States on the amendment to the Temporary State Aid Framework. The European Parliament was neither notified nor informed. I ask that the European Parliament be informed, and I don't think there is any regulation that forbids that.

I do think that, in addition to its role as co-legislator, the European Parliament has a real advocacy role to play in raising public awareness of the benefits of competition. In fulfilling such task, we have to strengthen its relationship with other governmental entities or institutions. Do not get me wrong, it's a way to preserve the administrative and independent role of the European Commission in competition law and policy, which must be kept apart from any political interference. More than ever, people need to be part of the European process to better understand and measure its benefits. We, as representatives of European citizens, are the democratic arm of the European Union.

You have a unique position with your experience as competition law practitioner, member of the French Competition Authority and now, MEP in charge of the European Parliament competition report. Do you have any advice to give to young practitioners, now that you can look back at your early days in private practice?

I feel very lucky for having the opportunity to live three different experiences dedicated to competition law and policy.

It did help me a lot to understand each party's constraints and functioning. My humble advice would be: be curious and do not stick to legal and technical issues to make up your mind. For those who know me in the competition world, you know that it is crucial to understand others' mindsets before making your own judgment. Be attentive to your clients, your colleagues and best international practices. Competition law goes beyond lawyers, it also requires you to listen to economists and economic reality.

The soft law is very important to me and I value the work of the European Competition Network (ECN). I had the opportunity to meet outstanding people there and I wish you the same opportunity. I also want you to keep in mind that competition law has an impact on European citizens' everyday lives.

I would conclude with this famous quote from Oscar Wilde: "Be yourself, everyone else is already taken".

Angela Huyue Zhang

The University of Hong Kong

Lilla Csorgo

Angela Huyue Zhang is an associate professor of law and director of the Centre for Chinese Law at the University of Hong Kong. Her research focuses on Chinese law, antitrust and trade and law and economics. She is a four-time recipient of the Concurrences Antitrust Writing Award, which honours the best antitrust papers published each year. Zhang earned her JSD (2011), JD (2008) and LLM (2005) degrees from the University of Chicago and LLB (2004) degree from Peking University. She previously taught at King's College, London, and practised with leading international law firms in the United States, Europe and Asia.

Lilla Csorgo is a senior consultant to Charles River Associates. She was most recently head of economics and policy for the Hong Kong Competition Commission. Her previous roles include chief economist for the New Zealand Commerce Commission, vice president with Charles River Associates, an economic adviser to the Commissioner of the Canadian Competition Bureau and economist member at the Canadian Competition Tribunal. Dr Csorgo has comprehensive knowledge of the theory and application of microeconomics, particularly industrial organisation, including competition, antitrust, and regulation. Dr Csorgo obtained her PhD in economics from the University of Toronto.

Do you believe that local market conditions should inform competition law? If yes, how? If not, why not?

Yes, I have always believed that the law should be read in context, and competition law enforcement should be responsive to the local market conditions. Competition agencies need to adopt careful case-by-case analysis by looking into the local market conditions in order to decide how to achieve the optimal enforcement outcome.

What do you see as the biggest difference between the US and EU approach to competition law, and the biggest difference between these two jurisdictions and the approach taken in China?

In my opinion, the biggest difference lies in the different judicial approach in cases relating to abuse of dominance. EU judges take a more deferential approach to agencies' decisions (although small adjustments have been made in light of *Intel*), while US courts require antitrust authorities to satisfy a much higher burden of proof. As for China, I would have to say that the key difference here is the near absence of judicial scrutiny over agency decisions and, as a result, we lack information as to whether the administrative agency has taken a decision with good reason.

What role do the underlying economic principles of competition economics play in Chinese antitrust/competition enforcement?

Chinese competition law enforcement can be divided into two major spheres: public enforcement, which is mainly handled by administrative agencies; and private enforcement, which is administered by the courts. Chinese courts have been more willing to employ economic principles in civil antitrust cases compared with the administrative agencies, and to this end underlying economic principles have played a crucial role in driving the decisions of some landmark civil cases.

Given the opaque nature of the administrative decision-making process, it is quite difficult to observe the role that economics has played in public enforcement. Based on the final decisions released by agencies, some former agencies appear to be more willing to engage in economic reasoning than others. The *Tetra Pak* case is an example in which the State Administration for Industry and Commerce conducted extensive economic assessment and consultations before arriving at a decision.

What factors other than underlying economic principles inform antitrust/ competition enforcement in China?

Chinese antitrust enforcement is largely driven by administrative agencies, and because agencies decisions are rarely subject to appeal, they possess significant discretion in handling cases. As I elaborate in my forthcoming book *Chinese Antitrust Exceptionalism* (OUP, forthcoming early 2021), the bureaucratic mission, culture and structure of Chinese agencies play an important role in shaping their enforcement priority and outcome. And the formal and informal bureaucratic constraints will continue to influence Chinese antitrust enforcement in the years to come.

Do you see the approach taken in China to antitrust/competition enforcement to be wholly incompatible with that taken by Western competition authorities?

The approach taken by Chinese agencies is not always compatible with that taken by Western competition authorities. And such incompatibilities are deep-seated in China's unique political and economic institutions. For instance, the law is generally perceived as a regulatory tool in a communist country. So it is not surprising that Chinese competition law has also been used to reduce and stabilise prices at times of inflation.

What are the most salient distinguishing features of Chinese firms, and are Western competition authorities up to addressing those features in their enforcement actions?

The most conspicuous feature that distinguishes Chinese firms from their counterparts is the degree of independence that such businesses have from the government. This feature again is deeply rooted in the Chinese political economy, where the state continues to play a pervasive role in directing and influencing the national economy. This has left foreign competition authorities with lingering thoughts about the extent of state control and many have found it difficult to delineate the boundary of the so-called "China, Inc" appropriately. Antitrust law was not designed with Chinese state capitalism in mind and so both the EU antitrust regulators and US judges have struggled to address and engage Chinese firms in a way that is compatible with their own principles and laws.

What do you see as Western competition authorities' best course of action to enforcing competition law against Chinese firms?

I think that Western authorities' best course of action in enforcing antitrust involves two factors: the first is remaining calm and not panicking. There is this common misconception in the West that all Chinese firms are managed and controlled by the Party. Although all Chinese firms appear to have the same owner – the Chinese state, they actually belong to different levels of governments in different regions with competing and divergent interests. This explains why we often observe cut-throat competition between Chinese firms at home and abroad. The second is, be consistent. It is perfectly understandable for Western authorities to be concerned about Chinese firms acquiring dominance in critically vital sectors, but Western competition authorities need to avoid applying a double standard to Chinese firms. Otherwise it will be difficult to convince their Chinese counterparts that antitrust enforcement should be free from political influence.

Given varied competition laws and approaches to enforcement across nations, how can a multinational firm best ensure it stays on the side of the law?

I think it is important for multinational firms to take a more holistic approach to legal compliance and understand the limits of law. Often the differences between law enforcement across nations is driven by the varied institutional environments, which are in effect shaped by the pertinent local political and economic factors. Lawyers advising multinational companies should be sensitive to the contemporary context in which law is being enforced.

How do you see the COVID-19 pandemic and deterioration in US and Chinese relations impacting the enforcement of competition law in regard to multinational firms operating within China and Chinese firms outside China?

There is a heightened risk that antitrust law will be politicised in light of growing Sino-US tensions and the COVID-19 pandemic. As I elaborate in *Chinese Antitrust Exceptionalism*, Chinese antitrust law has been employed as an economic weapon that forms part of China's tit-for-tat strategy against aggressive US sanctions. Similarly, Western regulators have begun employing their competition laws to address issues of trade and national security. For example, in June 2020, the EU released a White Paper proposing a new form of merger control related to state-back acquisitions; this seems to directly target acquisitions initiated by Chinese firms in Europe.

Setting aside these relatively recent developments, considering incompatibilities between Western and Chinese political and market systems, can one expect an eventual decrease in conflicts in approaches and uses of competition law?

Yes, I think so. Despite the conflicts we see in the way China regulates and is regulated, I still remain hopeful that a peaceful outcome will prevail. As I argue in *Chinese Antitrust Exceptionalism*, the solution to such conflicts lies in the exchange of hostages, that is, as Chinese authorities hold foreign firms hostage through aggressive application of antitrust law, foreign regulators can do the same to Chinese firms, not necessarily through antitrust law but also through trade and foreign investment rules. These dual outcomes will be conducive to compromise and cooperation.

Part II
In-House Counsel & Consultants

Sarah Biontino
Biontino Europe
Leonor Cordovil

Sarah Biontino is a French-qualified lawyer and worked for over six years in the European Commission's DG Competition, where she was involved in investigating and processing cases. She founded Biontino Europe in 2005 and it is the only boutique competition public affairs consultancy in Brussels. She was also the director of Blueprint's competition practice and, before that, Sarah created and then headed the EU public affairs team at Allen & Overy in Brussels. Sarah's native tongues are English and French and she is fluent in Russian and German.

Leonor Cordovil has PhDs in economic law and in international law (University of São Paulo and Université Paris 1 – Panthéon Sorbonne), Master's in international and economic law. She is antitrust, anticorruption and international trade law partner at Grinberg Cordovil, in São Paulo, professor of competition law at Fundação Getúlio Vargas, and antitrust officer at the International Bar Association. Leonor is co-founder of the Women in Antitrust network, author of three books and coordinator of four others. She has written several articles and is a frequent speaker at conferences.

You founded your public affairs consulting boutique firm focused on competition issues in 2005, still the only one in Brussels. How did you become a public affairs consultant? Could you tell us about your background?

I studied law in Paris and qualified as an avocat. I had been one of a small handful and the only woman in my year to specialise both in civil law and EU competition law. I then took the EU Commission concours and joined what was then called DG IV. I was 26 and by the time I was promoted into the legal service, I felt that I needed a change, so I rashly resigned! I was then lucky enough to work as a consultant at Allen & Overy, a forward-thinking firm that understood my wanderlust. After some years, I finally settled for good in Brussels and started the EU competition policy unit at A&O's Brussels office. By 2005, I was fidgety again and I thought that it would be great to broaden my horizons and jump straight into entrepreneurship. What could possibly go wrong – the concept seemed great? Fourteen years later, I still love the concept that I created and so do the clients!

There are many skills demanded from a public affairs consultant in competition cases, such as dealing with different interests in complex and complicated cases from different parties and authorities; managing the media; managing expectations; being aware of the regulators' backgrounds; ensuring a great atmosphere with authorities – among many others. You have been holding top positions with high visibility for a long time now. Could you talk about the upsides and downsides you have faced in your career as a woman?

You perfectly summarised the challenges of my job in your question, and women are ideally suited to these tasks! We are good listeners and mediators, skills that are rarer in men. I have often found that long and tortuous antitrust procedures can do with a shot of strategic and imaginative thinking, yet another trait that shines out in women. However complex the topic – and it helps to have a legal background – untangling it and then undertaking the "shuttle diplomacy" to get it sorted is all a matter of patience and I have lots of that.

In the past, in the competition field, politics and lobbying were seen as unimportant at worst and quirky at best, but recent events and cases have shone a light on their importance both in antitrust and in mergers – it took a woman commissioner to make that leap of faith, more by accident than by design! The current trend seems to be for more and more law firms to try their hand at lobbying, but it must be said that it's not a "knack" – it's a profession in its own right.

More unusual is my work in cartel cases. This is often more akin to "palliative care" where outside counsel might find it tough to pass on difficult messages to clients and get them to swallow the medicine. My work in this field has been much altered by all the recent settlement processes that are now available in the EU toolkit.

I have never faced any real downsides in my career because I am a woman. Indeed, I have found it an advantage in a world of men. I value the small but strong female network that I have always had, particularly at the Commission. We stick together through thick and thin!

In addition, could you give some tips to women working in this field?

My top tip is not to try too hard. I have noticed that many women have fought so hard to achieve a top position that they go into overdrive when they get there. This goes for politicians, officials, and practitioners. Slow down, ladies, would be my advice! Another mainstay for women, as I noted above, is that we are good mediators, not inclined to bully but rather to persuade – tenaciously, of course. This is essential when putting together and then executing a competition public affairs campaign. There will be many egos, both male and female, at play but the art of diplomacy is a uniquely feminine attribute.

There have been many women participating in important decisions in Europe, as you, years ago, in the European Commission's DG Competition, Angela Merkel, Margrethe Vestager... There are not many women in this level in other countries or regions, such as the US, China and Latin America. What in your opinion can explain the absence of women in such public leadership positions in these places?

I'm afraid that you are a tad too optimistic about Europe and about the Commission, there were no more than five women officials in DG IV when I joined and none in top jobs! Even today, there is only a small handful of women in power – the fact that we have only just seen the first woman president of the European Commission after 61 years is nothing to be proud of.

In the US, there are quite a few senior women in power, for example as judges and congresswomen and things seem to be changing fast, even if the Trumpian backlash is stinging! The DC antitrust agencies, in particular, have had an excellent record in appointing women leaders. I am not so familiar with China and Latin America. One of the best corporate general counsels that I ever worked with in a case is a woman heading up a massive legal department in Shanghai! I can only surmise that the lack of women in power anywhere in the world is due to the traditional structures of society that act as strong barriers to entry.

You have faced different competition authorities worldwide. Could you give us an example of global cases where you had to deal with different jurisdictions in the world? What advice would you give on how to deal with different competition authorities and regulations, especially considering the upcoming antitrust enforcement in countries as India and China?

I have only dealt with competition authorities in other jurisdictions in a round-about way because my consultancy is very small by design and concentrates essentially on Brussels and other EU jurisdictions. I have of course often factored in the ways in which other jurisdictions tackle procedures, in particular in merger enforcement. Timetables are becoming more and more strategic in the frequent face-off between competition authorities around the world.

Being a public affairs consultant in competition in the EU for major Tech companies denotes your expertise in the big tech field. Antitrust authorities are adopting different approaches and handing down different decisions in the new markets, especially the big tech ones. How can a company with a worldwide presence, in big tech, deal with these differences? How can a competition professional be prepared to face all these conflicting decisions?

The divergences that we all witnessed in the past are now falling away and this is largely due to the changing perception we all have of dominant tech companies known collectively as the GAFAMs. There are now parallel investigations going on around the world and, although this is a controversial way of putting it, these companies have often become the scapegoats highlighting broader worries about coping with the new industrial and technological revolution. For example, it is common knowledge that after eight years of asking itself whether Google's behaviour constituted antitrust infringements, the EU Commission in the end adopted tough infringement decisions which may or may not stand on appeal. Whatever the outcome, these decisions are now precursors to proceedings in other jurisdictions and might act as benchmarks.

More and more, competition cases are connected to data protection law. A recent example of this: the charges against Facebook in Germany. In your opinion, what are the challenges to a public affairs consultant in dealing with cases involving different fields with different authorities, sometimes in different jurisdictions?

I have mostly touched upon this type of issue in mergers, where complainants sometimes try and bring in ancillary issues to "muddy" the waters when it comes to looking at theories of harm. It is becoming increasingly clear, for example, that there is now a temptation to bring in issues relating to the value of data into merger analysis – it simply seems to be a question of finding the right case.

In antitrust there is a "bleed" of ancillary issues in some jurisdictions but there are also divergences of approach – competition law is different in Germany, for example, than it is in the EU system. There has recently been a louder and louder call to take account of the broader picture when assessing antitrust cases, but this has as yet not happened in practice.

I would personally find it hard conceptually to drive a campaign which would seek to broaden the topics involved in a competition investigation unless and until there is clear guidance from the EU court, I do not believe that Commission decisions should be regarded as settled case law. An inflation of settlements can mean that the legal basis of competition enforcement becomes shakier and, although politics has a role to play, nothing should replace a strong legal framework. I think that the court in Luxembourg's recent reaffirmation of certain legal ground rules is a useful wake-up call for those wanting to cut corners when it comes to the application of competition law.

We are facing growing enormous changes worldwide in economic, political and environmental spheres. In your opinion, broadly, what is the role of a professional women in these different changes?

I do not think that there is anything specific about the role of women in this context; the current political turmoil is for all of us to tackle in society. I am lucky that I have been analysing the effects of politics on competition for a very long time, so I am not so bewildered by what is happening in the world. First the trickledown effect of the financial crisis and then of course the cataclysm that is the COVID-19 pandemic have put our economic and legal systems' resilience under the spotlight, and the current trend towards "block" politics and protectionism is a direct consequence of all this. I do not think that competition policy can escape a broader economic and political reassessment, it must be fit for purpose to remain relevant.

In your opinion, women should invest in other women. Why?

I am lucky enough to work in a female environment and, as I noted above, I have always valued my women's network in the EU institutions. However, for me, the most important thing is to invest in young professionals, whether they are women or men. Being a public affairs consultant in my field is not an easy job, it requires skill and talent – it is often thought that you can sort of "fall into" it after another career or that it is a soft option. This is certainly not the case and when I can contribute to nurturing young talent when they choose my profession it fills me with pleasure and pride!

Grania Holzwarth
Deutsche Telekom
Ingrid Vandenborre

Grania Holzwarth is head of EU competition policy at Deutsche Telekom, responsible for EU competition affairs in Brussels, with a focus on ongoing competition cases in the field of telecoms mergers and antitrust cases in the ICT sector, as well as the development of competition policy in the context of digitalisation. She is chair of ETNO's (European Telecommunications Network Operators' Association) Competition Policy Taskforce and vice-chair of the ICLA (International Commercial Law Alliance) European chapter.

Ingrid Vandenborre is the partner in charge of the Brussels office of Skadden, Arps, Slate, Meagher & Flom, and focuses on EU and international merger control and competition law. She was recently named "Competition Lawyer of the Year" at the Benchmark Litigation Europe Awards, based on her representation of Aspen, and she represented Kuoni and Thomas Cook in an investigation by the European Commission into geo-blocking clauses that was suspended without penalty for both companies. Her recent merger control experience includes the representation of PayPal, Visa and Stryker in relation to the acquisitions of Honey, Plaid and Wright respectively, and ABB in its transaction with Hitachi.

Grania, thank you very much for accepting this interview. You are responsible for European competition affairs at Deutsche Telekom, a company you joined in 2001. This is a very long time in such a fast-developing sector. What key trends have you observed over this timeline?

Probably we are observing one of the most significant developments right now: the digital transformation. Also referred to as the 4th industrial revolution, it will lead to fundamental changes in how businesses, markets, communities and even our whole lives will be structured and function. Digital technologies, in particular AI (artificial intelligence), immense computing power and storage capacity, will bring unprecedented opportunities – for which, by the way, the telecom industry's next generation infrastructure will be one of the key drivers.

The telecoms sector has seen many exciting developments on the technical as well as on the corporate side over recent years. One of the first projects I was working on when I started at Deutsche Telekom group was the IPO of T-Mobile International, its holding company for all mobile subsidiaries. Although this did not materialise in the end, at the time it resonated the industry trend of clearly separating mobile and fixed operators. They were regarded as two very different animals with quite distinct needs, the one being young and dynamic, the other a former state-run incumbent. This trend reversed to the exact opposite in less than 10 years, when the mobile and fixed business were merged to one entity in 2010.

Obviously, these restructurings were mainly driven by the technological evolutions. At the outset, mobile technologies and services were very distinct, a fast-growing business with rapid changes: 2G, GPRS, EDGE, 3G, 4G, LTE-A – sometimes bringing drastic changes to the ways we communicate or even to our overall lives, if you think about the impact the introduction of the smartphone has had on our daily routine. Now with fixed – mobile convergence, technologies have grown together and we see more integrated services, like multiplay offers. With the full virtualisation of future networks (such as 5G) fixed and mobile access networks will be unified in one core network, and the devices and services will be agnostic to access technology.

These trends can also be observed on the M&A side. While in-market consolidation remains critical you now see a clear increase in fixed – mobile convergent mergers or even broader mergers to offer more diversified service, e.g. mergers with media companies. In the context of the digitalisation, the trend of convergence extends way beyond the telecoms industry. We can observe cross-sectoral convergence, where connectivity, content and other OTT (over-the-top) services are growing together and directly competing with each other. Also on the network side, there will be wider convergence beyond just telecoms and cable operators. Other vertical players, such as platforms or the automotive industry, will enter at all levels of the value chain, including in networks.

Deutsche Telekom is ever-increasingly active in a broad variety of digital markets including the Internet of Things (IoT), big data, AI, cyber security, cloud computing and storage, digital solutions and consultancy, etc. What, in your view, are the biggest competition law challenges of the digital revolution for the telecoms industry?

The digital revolution opens up an array of opportunities, but undeniably also some serious challenges for the telecoms industry. Like most other traditional industries, we need to adapt to new business models, changing competitive dynamics and different consumer needs. This raises different competition law issues and questions along the value chain.

Let's take the retail level, for example: operators' SMS services are being substituted by messaging apps and traditional voice telephony is being replaced by VoIP (voice over Internet protocol) services offered by the platforms. These services can be used without having to rely on our networks and actually, this is quite frequently done by using WiFi hotspots as alternative infrastructure. This raises multiple questions, starting with what is the right market definition. Which services beyond the traditional telecommunication services are part of the same market? Beyond that it has implications on the assessment of market power and how to factor in the competitive constraints exerted by the platforms.

In relation to the large online platforms there is also a bigger picture challenge that the telecoms sector faces in competing with the disruptive technologies and services. European telecoms markets are very fragmented, heavily regulated and given less flexibility by investors, which naturally leads to a competitive disadvantage. Looking at Deutsche Telekom's subsidiary in the US we already see that the different structures and regulatory approach in the US market lead to a more favourable investment climate. How drastic this difference plays out in relation to large platforms can be seen if you take a look at their market caps, which are the highest worldwide. This lack of level playing field in combination with missing scale makes it difficult to compete with the platform industry. In particular, this applies to innovative technologies, such as AI or cloud computing, where scale is crucial and the only way to achieve such competitive scale is consolidation or cooperation. In order to enable more competitiveness in these digital ecosystems it is essential to at least lower the hurdles for industry cooperation, which is something that could be tackled in the ongoing review of the Horizontal Guidelines and the Horizontal Block Exemption Regulations. At the same time, the significance of efficiencies in the context of consolidation needs to be acknowledged and the role they play in merger analysis must be strengthened.

Looking at our networks, there is a more fundamental challenge for the telecoms industry when it comes to scale and the roll-out of digital infrastructure. The roll-out of next generation networks, such as 5G, will be even more capital intensive than previous generations, while at the same time revenues in Europe are shrinking. On the fixed network side, the large-scale investment needed for the fibre build-out are generally recognised by promoting co-investment schemes in the new European Electronic Communications Code, but in practice still face some difficulties. On the mobile network side, the need for network-sharing, in particular in the context of 5G, should be equally acknowledged by the authorities. Network-sharing among operators is critical in order to ensure a fast rollout and efficient investments, and to avoid building redundant access networks. It creates significant cost-savings for network deployment by freeing up resources for other investments in innovation, while at the same time preserving the independence of – and differentiation between – operators at retail level.

For the last months, competition agencies and experts in Europe have been reflecting on the direction that EU competition policy should take to address new challenges posed by the digital economy, yet promoting innovation. Reports authored and presented by these agencies anticipated more antitrust enforcement within the existing antitrust legal framework they deemed fit for purpose with some "adjustments". However, recent trends show a shift in the scope of EU antitrust enforcement with increasingly more interventionist proposals to regulate the digital industry and platforms more specifically. What is your take on the ongoing digital debate?

What we can clearly see from the various reports around the world contributing to the policy debate with regard to the digital economy is that there is an agreement on the different characteristics of these markets that lead to more structural problems such as gatekeeping and tipping. Most of the reports also suggest that the solution to keeping these markets innovative and contestable would be twofold, on one hand an adjustment of competition law enforcement and on the other hand additional regulation of digital players would be necessary. The question of which role competition law and regulation should play with regard to digital markets is also reflected in the most recent DG Comp initiative to make competition law fit for the digital economy. The Commission has launched two parallel consultations on the potential Digital Service Act on the regulatory side and on the possibility of a new competition tool on the competition law side, both at least partially aimed at addressing the same issues. Here the orchestration of the interplay between the suggested competition law enlargement and new regulation will be a delicate task. Given the identified enforcement gap, arguably the scope for a new competition tool may be very limited, if a case by case ex ante regulation will be introduced and the existing competition toolbox is adapted. In reality, given the fundamental changes driven by digitisation an even broader view may need to be taken looking at the interaction of various policy areas together, for example data regulation and consumer protection laws.

Looking more closely at competition enforcement, multiple reports have identified the need for adaption to the challenges of the digital economy which is characterised by strong network effects, increasing return to scale and strong economies of scope which result in more concentrated markets. Another important particularity are indeed the business models in these markets, where services are often zero-priced for consumers and one of the most valuable assets – data – is obtained at very low cost. Clearly here there are still some shortcomings in adequately capturing the characteristics and effects that arise in the context of the digital economy, which then as a consequence produce more type 2 errors, arguably in some instances at a higher error cost. To correct such imbalance of false negatives and false positives requires the authorities at least to be more agile and innovative regarding the enforcement of competition law with regard to the digital economy.

There are also areas where more concrete adjustments could be made to existing competition law rules. One instance here could be the ongoing review of the Market Definition Notice. Some very obvious changes that need to be addressed here are the adaption of price-based tools, such as SSNIP test, to other criteria like quality. Another one is the role of data which could be captured with more focus on the supply-side substitutability. The Commission's Special Adviser Report argues that in digital markets, there should be less emphasis on market definition and more attention to the theories of harm and anticompetitive strategies. While market definition is a very helpful tool to set the frame for the following analysis in traditional markets, it actually may be less informative in digital markets, especially against the background that in the digital economy we are often looking at more conglomerate structures or ecosystems with multiple interlinked markets, and it is more difficult to identify potential competitors in markets that are more dynamic and in flux, in particular, where we are more likely to have competition for markets and not competition in markets. In any event, regardless of the role you assign to market definition, it is necessary to have a more dynamic, forward-looking approach with more attention to potential competition.

At the same time, it is not only the abovementioned characteristics and substantive analysis, but also, on the procedural side, enforcers will need to adapt, given the pace of these markets. It is important for them to keep up with the digital markets, which can be prone to irreversibly tipping, leaving intervention then no longer able to restore competitiveness. Timely intervention is crucial and beneficial to all market participants as it creates legal certainty in this, for the time being, somewhat uncharted territory. With a view to reacting promptly in these fast-moving markets, closer monitoring of these markets, early intervention and streamlining procedures should be envisaged. Another option to prevent digital markets from irreversibly tipping could be a wider use of interim measures, a revival of which we have seen in the Commission's ongoing *Broadcom* case.

The rollout of 5G is destined to revolutionise mobile communications and data transmission. Real-time data transmission, in particular, will play a key role in the data economy. The advisers to Margrethe Vestager noted in their 4 April 2019 report that there are cases where an obligation to ensure data access, and possibly data interoperability, may need to be imposed, and this would be the case for data needed to serve complementary markets or aftermarkets, i.e. markets that are part of the broader ecosystem served by the data controller. Do you have a view on data access or data interoperability remedies and the implications of such remedies for the telecoms sector in particular?

Driven by new technologies, like AI, blockchain and IoT, the role of data has dramatically changed. In the digital economy data is an indispensable asset for virtually all industry sectors. Data and data analytics will be key to remaining competitive, allowing businesses to become faster, more efficient, more accurate and ultimately deliver better output for consumers. In light of this importance, data access could be an effective remedy against distortion of competition emanating from information asymmetries.

The challenges with a data access and interoperability remedy arise with practical implementation. There remains a lack of clarity around the concrete design of such a remedy. For instance, one unsolved question is what actually is the threshold that triggers intervention in the context of data. What amount or which kind of data actually leads to an anti-competitive advantage that justifies mandated access? Should this only be the case if the criteria of the essential facilities doctrine are met or do the different characteristics of data, e.g. being a low cost, non-rivalrous good, call for a different standard? These open questions are not limited to intervention thresholds, but also the level of execution. To what kind of data should access be granted: personal or non-personal, raw or aggregated, one-off or continuous real-time? How can you deal with data protection issues in the context of personal data, to effectively safeguard a user's rights under the GDPR? And last but not least, to whom should access be granted? Identifying markets and competitors can be more difficult in the digital economy. Not least because of the conglomerate structures with competition for markets instead of competition within markets. Beyond that, the dynamics of these markets make it more complicated to detect new entrants.

However, data access remedies are just one side of the coin in order to achieve a competitive data economy and keep markets contestable where the facilitation of data pooling/sharing may be even more important. Data pooling/sharing enables companies to exchange data on a commercial basis in order to achieve scale and maximise the potential of data assets. One example of a tool to enable such data sharing/pooling are data marketplaces, such as Deutsche Telekom's Data Intelligence Hub, which allows providers and users of data to exchange information across sectors via a secure interface. In general, such data sharing/pooling will be of procompetitive nature, given the efficiencies created by the combination of the data. Beyond that data sharing/pooling is critical for the more fragmented European economy to maximise the value and economic benefits of the data for society and to drive innovation. Therefore, it is necessary to eliminate barriers to such cooperation and create the right conditions for industry-led initiatives to develop.

In this context, interoperability and standardisation will play an important role for both data access as mandated remedy on the one hand and industry-led data sharing/pooling on the other. Beyond EU competition law mandating interoperability requirements to address market concentration on a case-by-case basis, it is crucial to develop common standards to further facilitate data-sharing across different applications, specifically for non-personal industrial data.

In the aftermath of the European Commission's decision to block the *Alstom/Siemens* merger in 2019, and in light of the ongoing debate around "killer acquisitions", there is a call for increasing vigour in competition enforcement. How do you see the current debate?

In my opinion, these are two very distinct debates: (i) the blocking of the *Siemens/Alstom* merger has sparked a discussion around too vigorous enforcement and the role of industrial policy in competition law ; and (ii) the "killer acquisitions" debate, is about underenforcement in the digital economy.

Looking at *Siemens/Alstom*, certainly blocking a merger is a very drastic decision, but the Commission rarely resorts to this measure. I cannot speak in detail on the merits of the case, but one valid question following this decision seems to be how the competitive assessment should factor in the future developments of the analysed markets, for instance with a more dynamic market definition recognising the increasing role of global competition. On the industry policy angle, I would concur that competition law cases should not be decided on political grounds, despite this being very valid debate, and undoubtedly the concerns will have to be addressed with other policy tools. I also do not think that we need political intervention in European merger control, such as a ministerial intervention.

Similarly, the debate around "killer acquisitions" in the context of digital markets has intensified lately based on the concern that the large online platforms are buying up potential competitors. According to the Commission's Special Adviser's Report, this is all the more worrying when it is done systematically as part of their strategy. While you can clearly observe the increasing acquisitions by the large platforms, it is less clear which competitive effects these acquisitions have. So far, we are lacking in-depth assessment in a systematic and substantive manner that would give us a good understanding of what impact the acquisition of start-ups has on innovation.

Besides the substantial questions revolving around these "killer acquisitions" there are also some procedural issues, since such acquisitions are currently not captured by the European merger control notification thresholds. One of the main questions is whether a transaction value – based threshold needs to be introduced, similar to that in Germany and Austria. In my opinion, such a transaction value – based threshold would not be a very efficient tool to capture these "killer acquisitions". The transaction value would have to be set very low in order to actually capture the acquisition of these start-ups, but a low threshold would in turn produce a very high amount of unwanted notifications, thereby overburdening industry and authorities. Alternatively, if the transaction value is set high, e.g. for instance in Germany it was set at €400 million, only very exceptional cases would be captured. Other options also under discussion regarding "killer acquisitions" could be to change the burden of proof once a buyer has a certain position or to look at the acquisition of start-ups by dominant platforms under the regime of article 102 TFEU going back to *Continental Can*.

Deutsche Telekom is one of Europe's largest telecoms providers. The group also operates a number of subsidiaries across the world, including under the well-known brand name T-Mobile. Can you share a few words as to how you manage Deutsche Telekom's exposure in an increasingly global, complex and robust antitrust enforcement environment? What are the principles and guardrails that you apply in your practice?

The business of Deutsche Telekom is based on integrity, respect and compliance with the law. Deutsche Telekom's ambition to be Europe's leading telecoms operator is not limited to the telecommunication network but extends to all units, including leadership in compliance. Compliance is crucial for Deutsche Telekom and its trustworthiness. One recent example is that Deutsche Telekom was among one of the first companies to self-impose digital ethics guidelines in relation to AI, before the EC High Level Expert Group on AI was even discussing this.

More concretely, at Deutsche Telekom compliance means adhering to legal provisions, the company's internal policies and ethical principles. In the area of antitrust this translates to a mix of policy-setting, constant risk analysis, continuous communication, repeated training and advice. This can range from individual advice on a case-by-case basis to on-the-spot training for whole departments. Beyond the central unit at Deutsche Telekom headquarters, there are also decentralised units within the subsidiaries to deal with specific national antitrust compliance elements. The antirust compliance management system has been carefully designed in cooperation with the compliance department, and the correct implementation on a day-to-day basis is performed by the entire antitrust team of Deutsche Telekom, which, by the way, won the ACC Global Competition Team Award in 2019.

The antitrust compliance management system is implemented throughout the whole Deutsche Telekom group. In fact, Deutsche Telekom was one of the first companies to get a certification from external auditors confirming that the Deutsche Telekom group has an effective compliance management system to avoid antitrust violations and to recognise them in time.

What in your view, should be the Commission's focal point for competition policy?

One of the current priorities for the competition policy of the Commission rightly is the digital economy, as the follow-up to the Commission's Special Adviser Report. Here, the ongoing initiatives of the consumer IoT sector enquiry, the review on the Market Definition Notice and the DSA & NCT consultation are an important step. The necessary exercise, in my opinion, is twofold. One, analysing what changes can be already be directly adopted and put into practice immediately. Two, where open questions remain, work towards a better understanding of the competitive forces in these markets, which the Commission can do quite efficiently with sector enquiries.

The overall aim here should be on how to ensure that digital markets are competitive and innovative, and to prevent high concentration and tipping of these markets. In my view, that means that the focus needs to shift from a more static assessment to a more dynamic perspective. The assessment should not only look at the current market structure, but also factor in future developments and potential competitors. When it comes to looking at the theories of harm in a more dynamic approach, barriers to entry, innovation capabilities and incentives will play a more important role. With regard to remedies, interoperability, portability and access will be crucial to ensure competitiveness in digital markets.

The focal point of the competitive assessment of digital markets should be on innovation and not on prices. To that end, a priority should be the further development of methodologies to better analyse the ability and incentives to innovate. Likewise, advancing competition law analytics regarding data should be a preeminent concern for the Commission.

Another issue that should be a key priority for the Commission, in my opinion, is how to deal with the growing importance of scale in a global economy. From a competition policy perspective this translates to consolidation on one hand and cooperation on the other. While consolidation will remain an important strategy to reach a level playing field required to globally compete, I believe that in future we will see more collaboration between companies in order to achieve greater scale. Cooperation, whether on a horizontal or vertical level, will allow European players to overcome the structural and regulatory disadvantages and gain the necessary scale and efficiencies. Industry collaborations will be one of the vehicles that will drive competitiveness and innovation in the European markets. Therefore, it should be one of the priorities of EU competition policy to reduce the burden and hurdles for collaboration initiatives in order to enable growth and not stifle industry dynamics. This can be achieved by establishing more guidance for the industry and legal clarity in the Vertical and Horizontal Guidelines and by creating more freedom by adapting the Vertical and Horizontal Block Exemption Regulation.

Finally, the Commission should as a priority further ensure a harmonised approach to competition policy in Europe. Avoiding fragmentation of competition law across Europe is crucial, this is particularly important with regard to digital markets, which often operate beyond national boundaries and where we see increasing initiatives to address concerns on a national level. In this context the speed of enforcement by DG Competition will be one of the pivotal factors in securing a unified approach across Europe.

You started your career at Deutsche Telekom as a Mergers and Acquisitions (M&A) lawyer. What drew you into competition law and what fascinates you most about being a competition lawyer in the telecoms industry?

Actually, although both are very different, in the telecoms sector M&A and competition law go hand in hand. Most telecoms M&A transactions will trigger an in-depth merger control procedure, and competition law will be factored into the M&A analysis right from the very start and will be the determining factor for the closing of a transaction.

Starting in the corporate law department of a multinational company seemed like a very compelling opportunity, coming from university with a specialisation in international private and corporate law. Undeniably, the diversity of transactions and experience gained on Deutsche Telekom's M&A activities was exceptional and continues to be so, only that now I have authorities and not another company sitting at the other side of the table.

Besides this being a whole new challenge, having had very little knowledge of competition law before I started, one of the compelling aspects in telecoms antitrust is the constant evolution. Each advancement in technology, new trend and the dynamics of the telecoms sector brings new challenges for the competition assessment. In addition to the "classic" issues you can now observe a new M&A landscape with the convergence trend, the investment needs of next-generation networks triggering a wave of co-investment and network-sharing cooperation.

Last, but certainly not least, the current policy debates at European level triggered by digitisation, globalisation and climate change are very stimulating. These challenges are enhanced by the current crisis and may lead to some more fundamental rethinking of policy approaches.

Finally, what advice would you share with others who are thinking about embarking on a similar career path?

I would say the career path as in-house lawyer is not as straightforward as it may be in a law firm. There are multiple options, from a very linear career as specialist in a particular legal field to a more disruptive career path by moving around within the organisation outside the legal department. Actually, over time I saw many colleagues discover their passion for the business side, leaving the law behind.

Another difference is that being an in-house lawyer you are naturally closer to the business, so you are not merely advising a client but are part of it. For one this means that you will need a better understanding of the financial, commercial and strategic needs and constraints, but this also means you are closely involved in business decisions and their implementation, as a member of the team responsible for the solutions from start to finish.

Xiaojin (Jenny) Huang

Tencent

Elizabeth Xiao-Ru Wang

Xiaojin (Jenny) Huang is the director of the competition policy office of Tencent, in charge of legal and policy research, as well as internal compliance on competition law. She joined Tencent in March 2012. Before that, she worked with a leading Chinese law firm for four years, mainly advising multinationals on merger control, administrative investigations and legal compliance. Ms Huang obtained a doctorate in law from Chinese Academy of Social Sciences and a Juris Master degree from the University of International Business and Economics. She has conducted extensive research on various competition law issues in the online world and has broad experience in relevant practice.

Elizabeth Xiao-Ru Wang is an executive vice-president with Compass Lexecon and specializes in antitrust and intellectual property (IP) issues. She has provided economic analyses in merger review, commercial disputes and regulatory hearings, especially in cross-border matters. Dr Wang has been involved in casework in a variety of industries, including technology platforms, life sciences, agriculture, financial markets, transportation and consumer products. She has submitted reports to authorities in China and the United States and has testified in Chinese courts. Dr Wang has been part of the leadership of the American Bar Association. She was also named multiple times to the *International Who's Who Legal: Competition Economists* list. In addition, she has published and spoken frequently on antitrust and IP issues. Dr Wang has a PhD in economics from the University of Chicago and a BA in Economics from Peking University in China.

What inspired you to choose the legal field over others?

I had no idea about my future career path until I faced this issue when nearing graduation from university. I was majoring in marketing when I was studying for my bachelor's degree. During the four-years of campus life, I gradually realised that a marketing major and career may not be a good fit for me, as they requires high-level creativity, which to be honest, I thought I lacked. Then I decided to get a master's degree for a different major.

In December 2001, China became a WTO member. I saw a lot of media coverage saying that there would be a massive demand for talent in international trade and international law. When I read that there were only 200 lawyers who had a good command of both the English language and the relevant legal knowledge, and therefore could handle foreign-related legal matters at that time in China, I was quite impressed and was motivated to become one of them. I tried very hard and fortunately, was admitted by the Law School of the University of International Business and Economics (UIBE) in 2004. I believe I made the right choice, as I met knowledgeable professors and talented classmates and schoolmates who inspired and helped me a lot in my career development after graduation.

Entering into the WTO significantly sped up China's legislation process in antitrust law. On 30 August 2007, China's Anti-Monopoly Law (AML) was enacted after 13 years of deliberation, and the law entered into force on 1 August 2008. Several months before that, upon recommendation of a classmate of UIBE, I joined T&D Associates, a boutique law firm constantly recognised as a *Chambers* band-1 law firm on competition law in China.

Although the law was new in China at that time, it already had a long history in the US, EU and other jurisdictions. Multinationals operating business in China paid high attention to this law, and many of them came to T&D for assistance, but I was far from equipped with abundant knowledge to assist the clients. Every coin is two-sided. One side is that

I had to start from the ground up, and always felt inferior due to my inexperience; the other side is that, thanks to my boss John Yong Ren's trust, I had a good chance to be involved in very complicated cases, even though I was a freshman (for example, I was fortunate to work, from day one to the finishing line, on a merger filing made in 2008 which turned out to be the second conditionally cleared one in China). That urged me to quickly acquire new knowledge and expertise.

In order to enhance my knowledge on antitrust theory, I began to pursue my doctoral degree at the Chinese Academy of Social Sciences in 2011. Under the supervision of Professor Wang Xiaoye, I had the chance to learn the antitrust law comprehensively and communicated with more antitrust experts. In 2012, (when Tencent was in an antitrust dispute with Qihoo360), I joined Tencent.

Looking back, the inspiration for my legal career choice comes from the opportunity created by the economic development and the improvement of the legal environment in China. I owe a lot to the experts who participated in the legislative process of the AML, and wish the practitioners around the world could have more opportunity to communicate and work with each other to have the relevant research and practice further improved, so that the younger generation can benefit from the new opportunities created by us.

How does working in-house compare with working in a law firm?

Companies need both types of legal support, as they have their different advantages and limitations. Generally speaking, in-house lawyers have better knowledge and understanding of their companies' business models and work requirement, while they may not be able to provide advice for each internal legal enquiry due to lack of time, resource or experience. On the other hand, external lawyers can organise a dedicated legal team and leverage their experience accumulated from serving various clients, while they may not be able to provide thorough advice due to lack of sufficient understanding of the clients' businesses and industry knowledge.

These advantages and limitations require both in-house and outside lawyers to improve their capabilities constantly to maintain the advantages and overcome as many limitations as possible. The difference between the two lies in where they give higher priority in terms of improvement.

For in-house counsels, their first priority may be to understand their companies' businesses, while maintaining professionalism. They need to keep close watch on the industry development, and keep good communication with their business teams, understand what the business teams are going to do, how the products or services will function and what the logic behind is. Only with a comprehensive understanding of the above can in-house counsels identify the legal issues and then consider whether such issues can be solved internally or if outside counsels need to be involved.

For outside counsel, their first priority is to improve professionalism. They need to keep a close eye on the development of legislation, enforcement and judicial practices, gaining insight on where the legal issues are and how they can be solved properly. Acquiring such insight also needs adequate practice, and thus outside counsels may have to try their best to win some clients and accumulate entry-level experience first.

Another important difference I want to mention is that, compared with outside counsel, aside from identifying legal risks, in-house counsels need to try to find a workable solution. This is the biggest challenge. However, the legal issues encountered by Internet companies are often novel ones. There are neither specific provisions in the statutes nor relevant precedents for them to refer to. However, given the dynamic market competition, the business teams always have to move fast, so in-house counsels need to respond in a short turnaround. But external lawyers may not always have abundant personnel or adequate experience to provide timely support. This requires in-house counsels to have a good knowledge of both the law and the business, so that a balance can be struck.

Furthermore, working in-house may require better communication skills and a more comprehensive perspective. My personal experience is that, when working in a law firm, the people I needed to communicate with were limited, including the boss, colleagues, clients and officials. However, while working in a company, especially a large-sized company, I not only need to work with colleagues from the legal and business departments, but also to coordinate with the colleagues from the departments of government affairs (GA), public relations (PR), etc. This requires us to understand each other and think from more different perspectives.

What are your main responsibilities at Tencent?

I lead a team focusing on the antitrust compliance practice, with the aim of mitigating antitrust risk. The specific responsibilities are:

– Strategically designing an effective antitrust compliance programme, aiming for enhancing legal awareness on antitrust (from senior management to our co-workers) and mitigating relevant legal risks;

– Monitoring the latest antitrust developments on legislation, enforcement activities, and litigation in China and other major jurisdictions, providing legal analysis and giving timely alerts to interested parties;

– Identifying potential antitrust risks arising from business operations, assessing the risks, alerting the business teams and providing workable solutions;

– Providing legal assistance to the litigation team on antitrust cases;

– Giving training sessions to colleagues from different departments relevant to general legal compliance practice, business operations, GA, PR, etc;

– Supporting GA departments on communicating with the authorities, including both antitrust enforcement agencies and industry regulatory bodies;

– Working with PR departments on antitrust-related PR risk management;

– Responding to the antitrust legislative bodies with suggestions on the exposure to the draft antitrust law and relevant regulations;

– Conducting research on competition polices, especially on the Internet industry;

– Supporting companies in the Tencent investment portfolio on antitrust risk management.

What challenges do you think are unique to China in the digital era?

According to the Digital Economy Report 2019 released by UNCTAD, the geography of the digital economy is highly concentrated in the US and China: 68% of the market capitalisation value of the world's 70 largest digital platforms comes from the US, and 22% from China. In recent years, the digital economy maintained rapid growth momentum in China and has become the key driver of China's economy. As reported by the China Academy of Information and Communications Technology, digital economy accounted for 36.2% of GDP in 2019.

Although we see an encouraging digital economy development trend in China, the digital gap between the urban and rural areas is one of the biggest challenges faced by China. China has the largest population in the world – 1.4 billion. While China's GDP ranks number 2 worldwide, its GDP per capita is just slightly over USD 10,000, which ranks around number 70 worldwide. By comparison, US GDP per capita is over USD 60,000, and in another 24 countries such as Germany, France, the UK and Japan, it is over USD 40,000.

While access to the Internet seems ubiquitous, according to the statistical report on China's Internet development published by China Internet Network Information Centre, Internet penetration rate in China reached only 61.2% in 2019. Due to the COVID-19 pandemic, students have to attend online classes, making us we realise that even a smartphone is unaffordable for many low-income families. Access to the Internet means access to information and knowledge.

The digital gap has far-reaching consequences when it comes to education. Education is the best way to create equality for the children living in low-income families. However, in 2019, the enrolment rate of students in higher education institutions only reached 51.6%. So, China has a long way to go to bridge the digital gap and that will help make a level playing field on education.

Many Chinese Internet companies joined this campaign. For example, Tencent's "WeCounty" programme is an initiative striving to eliminate poverty and revitalise China's rural areas through the power of the Internet. By customising a WeChat official account, villages can build their own online service centre. Every villager can then access over 70 types of services at their fingertips using mobile devices.

The second challenge I want to mention is personal data protection. Specifically, Internet users may encounter unauthorised collection of personal data, excessive requests for authorisation, unlawful trading of personal data, and business operators' failure to comply with personal data protection obligations under the cybersecurity regulations, which leads to data leakage.

To solve this problem, we need to improve the legal framework. Currently, there is no single comprehensive data protection law in China. Statutory provisions are fragmented and scattered, lacking consistency and coherence. Moreover, most of the statutes in force are drafted in a doctrinal manner and require further explanation by specific regulations, which are not yet in place, probably making enterprises confused in daily compliance practice.

Another issue is that law enforcement measures lack deterrence and seeking remedies through litigation is difficult for those harmed by data breaches.

In recent years, several noteworthy campaigns have been launched to curb numerous apps' infringement of consumer data – related rights. Nonetheless, the apps involved were only required to make rectification and are rarely sanctioned in a real sense. Meanwhile, the absence of class action system in China makes it difficult for consumers to seek remedies through litigation: there have only been very limited public interest litigations against personal data infringers brought by consumer associations or prosecutors.

How do you balance work and family, and what advice do you have for female working professionals who struggle to balance their commitment to both?

There are multiple roles for us to take, e.g. child, spouse, employee, friend. For each role, we shoulder certain responsibilities and need to meet the expectations of our counterparty. However, the time we get for every day is limited, so there comes the task of "balance" – balance between the time we spend on each role, weighing the benefits and potential risks arising from the time allocation.

As regards the balance between work and family, I am sorry to say that I don't think I have achieved a good balance there – every day, I regret being unable to spend enough time with my kids, and at the same time, I feel upset for my lower work commitment compared with what I fulfilled before the kids were born. So, maybe I don't have much good advice, but let me share what I am doing in trying to achieve the balance.

First, at the workplace, being a trustworthy person and also trusting and supporting our colleagues. For professional women, when we get into a career, we try to show our commitment, professionalism and trustworthiness by responding quickly and professionally to requests from clients and colleagues, offering strong support to them in a team when and where needed, so that if (for example, during pregnancy and maternity leave), we need to tilt the scale more in the direction of families, they will give trust and support in return.

Second, at home, making the husband a real partner. Chairman Mao, the founding father of the PRC, said women hold up half of the sky. With the promotion of gender equality and the development of higher education, women in China have made strides in career development. However, most of them take up a vast majority of domestic work, especially taking care of and educating kids. This makes work – family balance more challenging for women. So, how to improve the performance of the partner at home is a big question. If the partner can spend more time in family obligations, that is a blessing for us.

Finding and cooperating well with a good nanny means a lot. A lot of parents feel uneasy if kids are taken care of by nannies, rather than by grandparents or relatives, as no trust has been established between them. However, my experience has showed me that a good nanny will be a strong helper. So, don't give up on this solution. Devise good questions to find a good one and be trustful, respectful and kind with them: you will get a capable assistant.

Finally, which one (family or work) should be put in priority is a hard question to answer. We need to take a fluid approach, which means that tilting the scale according to the urgency of various needs. While keeping up efforts to meet different needs, we also need to understand and accept the limits of the time and the capabilities of our partners as well as ourselves, so that an inner peace can be achieved in this high-spaced world.

Does antitrust have a role to play in regulating big data?

In the era of digital economy, data has become a new subject of competition. Without doubt, as an important source for generating profits, companies, especially big tech companies, are fighting for greater control over data. With the advent of big data, there are heated debates over whether it would pose harm to competition and, if so, whether and how antitrust laws should intervene to restore a level playing field. Some commentators claim that big data and technological algorithms may be used by companies to facilitate collusion, erect barriers to entry or maintain dominance by restricting their competitors' access to data. I believe that antitrust laws have a role to play in regulating such misuses of data, but it should be applied within an appropriate framework to refrain from curbing innovation.

To begin with, antitrust laws can be used to prohibit cartels disguised in technological algorithms. It is universally accepted that price-fixing is the most severe antitrust violation. Therefore, no matter what form it takes, price-fixing should be treated as cartel conduct. There are no relevant cases in China yet, but I have seen cases in other jurisdictions. For example, in 2015, the US Department of Justice (DOJ) fined a poster-seller for facilitating a cartel through a pricing algorithm with its competitors on Amazon. Assistant Attorney General Bill Baer emphasised that the DOJ "will not tolerate anticompetitive conduct, whether it occurs in a smoke-filled room or over the Internet using complex pricing algorithms". However, I believe in-parallel but independent use of pricing algorithms without an agreement on price-fixing should not give rise to competitive concerns.

In addition, there are discussions as to whether abuse of data would constitute an abuse of dominance. According to the Provisional Regulations on Prohibiting Abuse of Dominance, together with the business model, number of users, network effects, lock-in effects, technical characteristics, market innovation and others, the data possessed by enterprises and the ability to process data are among the factors to be considered in assessing the market power in the Internet industry.

Although an Internet company with valuable data may be treated as a dominant market player, it is difficult to find a dominant market player only based on its possession of big data. First, valuable data is scattered on various kinds of platforms, for example, the traffic data of a city can be found not only on navigation software, but also on taxi-hailing apps. Second, drawing an analogy with a manufacturing process, data is just like raw materials and cannot alone convert to market power on artificial intelligence, without algorithms and computing power, which equate to manufacturing techniques and capabilities.

Even if a company rich in data is deemed as holding a dominant position, abuse of data doesn't necessarily constitute an abuse of dominance, if only consumers' interest is harmed, but no competition harm could be demonstrated. There is some disagreement on this issue, but antitrust law regulates competitive behaviours, and is not directly aiming to protect consumers' interest. Therefore, when no competitive harm exists, consumers' interest protection law is in a good position to intervene compared with the antitrust law.

To sum up, although "pricing algorithm" is a new technical term, analysing it from an antitrust perspective is just pouring new wine into old bottles, and the competition authorities' enforcement toolbox suffices.

What do you think is the most significant barrier to female leadership?

I would say the most significant barrier to female leadership are gender stereotypes. This stereotype may be perceived by us from our childhoods – dad worked outside and earned more money, while mum was more committed to domestic work, taking care of kids and grandparents, cooking meals, washing clothes and cleaning the home... When we entered the career playing field, we saw more males in senior positions, and there was some belief that, in comparison with men, women tend to put family above their careers, they are less ambitious, determined and sociable, and therefore less capable.

Externally, this stereotype discourages employers from considering female candidates for certain positions and from offering leadership opportunities to female employees. But this is not the biggest obstacle, as the inner perception of the stereotype even matters more. It holds females back from reaching for opportunities and aspiring to lead.

Actually, when Tencent approached me years ago, I spent a lot time before making the final decision, because I didn't believe I was capable enough to handle complex legal issues in the fast-changing industry, and I also worried that during pregnancy and maternity leave, I was unable to be fully committed to this new challenging job. Thanks to encouragement from my friends and husband, I accepted the offer in the end. It turned out that after joining Tencent, as expected, I encountered a lot of challenges, due to the lack of knowledge not only on antitrust law, but also on the business and the industry (at that time, the AML was less than four years old, and there were few cases which could provide meaningful guidance on practice). But after several years of effort, I gained much experience and confidence both on professionalism and team management. If I had given up at the very beginning out of inner fear, I would have taken a totally different career path.

In China, in recent years, we have seen great developments in gender equality. According to a survey report published by a major talent recruitment website in 2019, 92.1% of female respondents and 92% of male respondents agreed on gender equality and that females had equal opportunity to develop their career. And the percentage for the recognition of the need for women to go to work instead of staying home was 92% (female) and 80.1% (male). This reflects an awakening of female consciousness. However, we still see more men in the career pipeline, especially for senior positions.

To break the gender stereotype, most importantly, we need to believe in ourselves. Actually, female leaders possess the same traits as their male counterparts in curiosity, vision and passion, and they even do better in empathy, perseverance and collaboration. As a slogan goes, "fortune favours the bold". When opportunities come, just strive for them and, in the face of inequality, speak out loudly so that our voices can be heard and our efforts can be seen.

As a woman in a senior position in one of the China's largest tech firms, do you feel that tech companies are particularly tough for women to succeed?

Working in tech companies is a tough challenge. According to the Smart Transportation Report released years ago by Didi, the largest car-hailing platform in China, employees in China's Internet firms worked much longer hours compared with their counterparts in other industries, indicating the heavy pressure in China's booming Internet industry. Aside from long working hours, a number of Chinese Internet companies have adopted the 996-working-hour system as their official work schedule. And 24-hour standby is a standard service we provide to bosses and colleagues. The Internet world is changing too fast, technologies and business models are involving rapidly, and we face more and more fierce competition. Nobody can survive without making best endeavours.

It is a tough challenge equally faced by the whole industry, regardless of the gender difference. However, to succeed, women have to put more effort into their career, while fulfilling the family obligations at the same time (they always take on more responsibilities at home). But it is the same case with non-tech companies. And I think the tech industry even provides better chances for women to succeed. Taking working in an Internet company as an example, with the strong IT system and high-quality technological support, as well as the digital nature of the business, it is quite easy for employees to work remotely from home. In this way, women have a better chance to keep the work – family balance. In addition, working for industries of the future makes women always equipped with new cool technologies and techniques and are therefore able to keep pace with trends. This will pay off by helping women continually advance their professional capabilities, which will be very valuable even if they want to transfer to a non-tech company one day.

Which women inspire you and why?

The woman who inspires me the most is my mum. She is the best mother I have ever known. She received limited education at school, but she possesses quite a lot of traits which make a good mum.

She loves her children unconditionally and makes me live in a stress-free family. Modern parenthood philosophy advocates unconditional love of children, but I believe this is a very difficult target for most mothers. My mum is great in this. When I failed in the college entrance examination more than 20 years ago, I felt depressed and ashamed, and lived in self-contempt. I asked my mum, "Do you think your daughter is inferior to other children?" She smiled and answered without any hesitation that, "You have tried hard, even if you cannot be admitted by a prestigious university, mum is content and proud of you…" I will never forget the smile on her face and her soft tone that day. Whenever I am in difficult time, what my mum said that day inspires me. It also reminds me of the lyrics of "I am your angel" – "It makes no difference who you are, I am your angel".

My mum is an optimist with strong mind. When she was in her middle age, she lived under great pressure, acting as president of a kindergarten, while taking up a majority of the domestic work of a family of six (my dad was fully committed to his career at that time). I cannot image how tired she was every day, but all the family members got good care from her. After retirement, her health declined just like most seniors, but she is still enjoying her life.

This is the woman who inspires me most. She is the sunshine in my life. I wish to be a good mum like her.

Where will we find you on a Saturday morning at 10 am?

At 10 am on a Saturday morning, mostly likely I will be with the kids for outdoor activities, if I don't have to work. For employees in an Internet company, working days are not easy to get through, so I try to spend some time with the kids during the weekend. I read an article alerting that there are only 940 Saturdays between a child's birth and her leaving for college, which can be spent with parents, deducting the time they need to spend in sleep, at school, with friends and otherwise occupied with activities where parents are not involved. So, as they grow old, the remaining moments for parents become especially precious. In addition, according to my daughter, the most memorable moments for her are the time we spend together outdoors. This is the reason for how I spend my Saturday mornings.

Giving birth is a big challenge for female employees. They have to take a break of several months. Here comes the concern on whether they can catch up with the fast-changing business after the break. Therefore, some of them postpone or even give up the baby plan. I fully understand the choice, and believe life without kids can also be meaningful. At the same time, I would say that if we don't give up, the children will embark on a fantastic life journey, hand in hand with us. From that journey, we will experience the mystery of life, and the power of growth.

Deborah Majoras
Procter & Gamble

Hanna Anttilainen

Deborah Majoras has been the chief legal officer and secretary of The Procter & Gamble Company for a decade. She serves on the boards of directors of Valero Energy Corporation and several non-profits, including the United States Golf Association. She served as chairman of the US Federal Trade Commission (2004–2008), as principal deputy assistant attorney general at the US Department of Justice Antitrust Division (2001–2003), and as an antitrust partner at Jones Day. She recently received the Burton Award for "Legends in Law".

Hanna Anttilainen has 20 years of experience in competition law. She has worked for the European Commission since 2011 and is currently a head of unit at DG COMP, dealing with merger control. Prior to her head of unit position she was deputy head of unit and case manager in the area of merger control. In her current position, she manages the unit responsible for analysing mergers in the energy and environment sector, manages teams in roughly 40–50 merger cases per year and contributes to competition policy development. Prior to joining DG COMP, she worked for nearly 13 years in private practice in Brussels, in the area of competition law. She graduated from the Faculty of Law of Helsinki University in 1998 with a Master's degree.

You started your career at a law firm where you stayed for 10 years. You then switched to work for the Department of Justice as the deputy assistant attorney general, followed by a move to the Federal Trade Commission (FTC), where you served as chairman. After seven years of public service, you moved to Procter & Gamble (P&G). Overall, you have therefore pretty much "done" the three core areas of an antitrust lawyer, law firm, government and in-house. What was the best part of each job?

Without question, in all three roles, the best part has been the opportunity to work, learn from, and help develop some of the finest professionals in the world, all of whom wanted to make a positive difference. But to add the best parts uniquely of each: at the law firm, it was delving deeply into a wide variety substantive antitrust issues, which always included learning about a new market, and helping an array of clients solve problems. Working in the government, I loved making policy that empowered consumers, which was like solving a puzzle as we worked to incentivise certain market behaviour while minimising unintended consequences in the market. And at P&G, the best part is helping to build a sustainable business that serves consumers, while doing it in a way that is ethical, compliant and socially responsible.

In your 30 years of antitrust experience, what has been the biggest change in the antitrust industry in your view?

Ok, it has not yet been 30 years! But in my career, the biggest change has to be the expansion of competition laws around the world. And the significance lies not only in the number of new laws and enforcement agencies, but in the resulting mix of economic and social experiences that impact how those laws are applied and developed. When the laws lead to stronger economic development of markets that benefit consumers' lives, they are positive forces; but if they are used for economic engineering that prevents markets from optimally working for consumers, that is not positive.

What do you see as the biggest challenge for antitrust (whether mergers, cartels, abuse of dominant position, agreements) going forward? Both from a company perspective as well as a regulator perspective?

At a high level, the biggest challenge for antitrust enforcers will always be deciding when to intervene and when to keep hands off. Markets characterised by transparency work pretty darn well, and today, more than ever, consumers have vast sources of information about products and services in markets, including information shared with one another. Antitrust enforcers have an important role to play in ensuring that competition can thrive and thus provide what consumers need. Sometimes that means stepping back and letting the market work, rather than rushing to intervene. And it is a challenge to know which will be best for consumers in the short and long terms.

For both government enforcers and those of us counselling global businesses, responding to the evolution of markets significantly impacted by digital commerce and new consumer-facing platforms is currently the biggest challenge. The digital marketplace is only going to become more complex as technologies develop, and enforcers and advisers alike need to find practical solutions that allow competition to thrive.

If you had one wish for the regulators (in other words, what you would like regulators to do more or less of, or how you would like regulators to change), what would that be?

Aside from calling themselves "law enforcers", rather than "regulators" (which connotes steering rather than protecting competition), I would hope that competition enforcers see their roles as protecting competition, rather than just looking for cases to bring. Of course, part of enforcing competition law leads to bringing actions, but that is only part of it. Enforcers also need to stand up for competition through advocacy with legislative bodies, other government agencies and the private sector. To cite an example, at P&G,

we work hard to comply with all laws wherever we do business, including antitrust and advertising laws. As a large consumer products company, we advertise extensively and, when appropriate, we may use comparative advertising as a highly effective way to compete. But in some countries, certain regulators (often not the antitrust enforcers) view comparative advertising very negatively, despite the fact that truthful, comparative advertising can be very healthy for competition. Why should we have to make the choice of trying to compete over here (to satisfy the antitrust enforcer) and then dilute our competitive tools over here (to satisfy an advertising regulator)? External forces will always urge "more case, more cases", but protecting competition in whatever form necessary should be the goal.

Do you miss anything about working for the regulator?

I do. While I love serving consumers in my current job, I also loved public service. I miss having the opportunity to make policy that has the intent and potential to benefit so many. It was a unique opportunity to work alongside so many dedicated antitrust professionals in the US agencies, in many agencies around the world and in the private sector, and I learned a great deal from them all.

What is the toughest antitrust problem you have had to deal with while at P&G?

Within my first week at work at P&G, I was on a plane to Europe facing a multi-country antitrust investigation into historic laundry industry pricing practices, which had been kicked off by simultaneous dawn raids across Europe. In a very short period of time, I had to work with a large team inside and outside to get up to speed on one of P&G's largest businesses; garner the facts from over a long period, and respond to government requests. The currency inside P&G is relationships, which I did not have, and so, in addition, I had to quickly build relationships and earn credibility (something that my roles at DOJ and FTC, fortunately, had taught me a lot about). It was a challenging time, but I am proud that we did the right things to put the investigations behind us and move ahead. And as with all challenges, we learned a lot and are stronger today as a result.

Since then, fortunately, the major challenge has been ensuring not only that we comply with all competition laws around the world, but also that we "build strong competition law muscles" in our business partners in a fast-moving, volatile environment. We sell products into 180 jurisdictions around the globe and, while many have well-established competition law jurisprudence, many do not but may still have expectations regarding competitive behaviour. The key is to develop balanced, base competitive practices that can be used around the world, while adapting to local jurisdictions' unique or more specific requirements. While major antitrust matters may be more exciting to talk about, my favourite matters are the ones that never happened!

If you had to give one piece of advice to other women in the antitrust world, what would that be?

Go to work every day willing to lose your job – not *wanting* to lose it, but *willing* to lose it. That will liberate you to be who you are, not who you think others want you to be (and, in turn, to be open to collaborating with others who are different); to speak up and do the things that you believe are right; and to have the courage and humility to use your creativity, be willing to make mistakes and take smart risks.

P&G has not made an acquisition that would raise competition concerns for a long time. So it is not mergers that keeps you busy. P&G is also not the focus (at least publicly) of any recent major antitrust investigation (excluding the recent rejection by the French Supreme Court of the cleaning and personal hygiene product cartel). What keeps you awake at night?

Fortunately, I have been working long enough with volatility and uncertainty that I have learned to (most of the time) put it aside for the night, knowing that tomorrow will be another day to tackle our challenges. What I most worry about is whether there is something major lurking around the corner that I can't see but that could have a huge negative impact on our company and its reputation – it could be an antitrust issue, but it also could be any one of a large number of issues we have to deal with. Businesses today must move at the speed of light but must do so while retaining consumer and other stakeholder trust in our ethics, legal compliance, and world citizenship. I view myself as working on a team of temporary caretakers of a company that has been improving consumers' lives for 180 years, and we have to make sure it can do the same for another 180, and beyond.

(By the way, we do have merger work, too! For example:

- 2018: approx €3.4 billion acquisition of the consumer health business of Merck KGaA, Darmstadt, Germany;

- 2017: divestiture to Coty, Inc., valued at US$11.4 billion, of 41 speciality beauty brands including CoverGirl, Clairol and Wella;

- 2016: divestiture to Berkshire Hathaway, valued at more than US$4 billion, of P&G's Duracell batteries business;

- 2012: US$2.7 billion divestiture of the Pringles snack business to The Kellogg Company.)

With your experience dealing with competition law matters on both sides of the Atlantic, what is the major difference between US agencies and the European Commission (EC)?

While there are a lot of similarities, there are differences that stem from the two different legal systems (common law v civil code law) and different historic experiences. For example, when dealing with the professionals at the respective agencies, e.g. in negotiating a settlement, the EC tends to have more rules-prescribed practices, while US agency practices vary depending on the circumstances. The two jurisdictions also differ a bit in their treatment of competitor complaints. The EC addresses some distribution practices differently from the US agencies, because of the interest in maintaining a single market. And I think there is no question that a significant difference is the fact that the US agencies may not block a merger without first seeking court approval, which is not required by the EC.

When you hire in-house counsel for your team, what are the key characteristics or experience that you look for?

The proven ability to think clearly, effectively and creatively, paired with the desire to solve problems. Diversity of experiences and backgrounds. Effectiveness in working on teams, with openness to consider diverse viewpoints and find the "third and better way". Lifelong learners and self-developers. Proven resiliency in the face of challenge. Passion for serving the world's consumers. Potential for leadership.

What, in your view, makes a good regulator?

Balance in all things, but particularly between confidence and humility. It is important to have confidence that the mission is an important one and that the agency can fulfil that mission. And it is important to build capability and set a tone of excellence in execution, so that one can confidently support and advocate for the agency's work, in general and with respect to specific actions. Confidence in direction is important to preventing the agency from surrendering its agenda to media and the political pressure *du jour*. But ultimately, the role is one of service, and serving requires humility – it opens one up to recognising that you don't have all of the answers, to listening, to working hard at getting the right answers, to the willingness to own up to mistakes and to always working to improve. Humility keeps all of us focused on the mission, which is larger than any one of us.

What has been the most memorable moment of your career to date?

Oh my goodness, I am fortunate to have so many! Indeed, last year, I was cleaning out our basement, and I sifted through boxes and boxes of mementoes from my career, many that made me laugh and some that made me cry, all involving the wonderful people on the journey.

But to try to choose, it's a tie between (1) when at DOJ, I rose in the ceremonial courtroom of the US Court of Appeals for the DC Circuit to defend the settlement we had reached with Microsoft, with Robert Bork arguing the other side, and I said, "May it please the Court. My name is Deborah Majoras, and I represent the United States of America". I still get emotional when I think about it. And (2) After my ceremonial swearing-in at the FTC where then-Attorney General John Ashcroft had spoken, my mother, in a bit of a daze, kept repeating, "the attorney general said this is good for America, and he was talking about my daughter!" Emotion around that one, too!

Is there anything in your career that you would still like to experience (after having worked on all three sides of the fence)?

Yes! There most definitely are things out there that I would like to experience – I just don't know yet what they are!

Johanne Peyre

Pearson

Edurne Navarro

Johanne Peyre's extended experience encompasses both private practice (Cleary Gottlieb, Brussels, Paris and Washington DC) and in-house positions (practice lead with a global remit for the Michelin Group and subsequently Pearson Plc in New York). She is recognised among *40 in their 40s: Notable Women Competition Professionals*. Featured as an influential lawyer by several expert publications and think tanks (*Concurrences, Modern Legal Practice, GCR, BIICL, OECD etc.*), her expertise ranges from all aspects of competition law, private damages actions and innovative compliance solutions. Johanne is also dedicated to improving diversity in the legal sphere by her strong involvement in various mentoring initiatives (US National Federation of the Blind; Saks Institute for Mental Health Law, Policy and Ethics of USC Gould School of Law).

Edurne Navarro joined Uría Menéndez in 1992 and has been a partner since 2002. She is currently the partner in charge of managing the firm's Brussels office. Edurne has over 25 years' experience advising Spanish, European, North American and Asian undertakings in sectors such as telecommunications, energy, transport, pharmaceuticals, defence and banking. Her practice focuses on EU and Spanish competition law (principally merger control, state aids and cartels), trade law (mainly anti-dumping and rules of origin) as well as customs law and the application of EU regulations concerning international investments.

Having worked both in law firms and as in-house lawyer, could you describe what you have enjoyed most from each type of practice?

Rise of technical skillset and adrenaline excitement characterised my experience in private practice. I started my career in house and got the chance to work for close to 10 years in the Brussels office of Cleary Gottlieb. That office was already composed of approximately 100 lawyers from across the EU, specialising in competition law. It was a vibrant and young environment which enabled me to gain and strengthen my technical skills. I was lucky to work on fun, highly mediated cases with challenging competition law issues. In such a galaxy, the experience you forge in how to work hard on difficult issues with a multicultural environment is priceless. I like to say that it "makes" you a good lawyer, not only increasing your technical skills, but also raising your soft skills and stamina!

Later in my career, when I got to work in house with counsel not previously "stamped" with outside counsel experience, I realised that starting in private practice makes you a better in-house counsel.

In-house experience is a must-have to gain a business-open mindset and the satisfaction of professional development expansion. When you are in house, the business world opens. I very much enjoy interacting closely with the business, feeling part of the core motor of the company. As a competition and business lawyer you are associated upstream with strategic decisions and you witness the practical results of your advice. I personally find it extremely satisfactory. I also value the continuous learning opportunities you can find in house on topics related to company structure and functioning. Even with non-law-related topics, I always found that they enable us lawyers to better understand and hence serve our internal clients and colleagues. Such learning experiences also complement increased technical and soft skills (or emotional intelligence).

Could you share with us what made you decide to move in house?

It was not the result of a process I initiated. Although I always had in mind to go in house at some point later in my career, I was not actively looking for a position when I received the opportunity. I was a senior associate and had started to face difficulties as a woman who wanted a career in an environment which at that time was even more male-dominated than now. I recall that when the head-hunter contacted me, my initial reaction was to turn it down, telling him I was not looking for a change. He convinced me that I should at least give it a thought and start looking at what is next for me in my career development. He was right and I also took it as an interesting exercise. But then the concrete proposal came very quickly, and the position at stake turned out to be an incredible opportunity. Becoming the head of competition law for the Michelin Group, so early in my career, was unexpected and to be considered. It turned out for me to be the right choice and a fabulous experience.

Now, why did I always had in the back of my head that I would go in house? Why is that that I never even considered staying in private practice and leaning in to run for partnership? Why is that that even when considering taking the position at Michelin, part of me could not help thinking that I was not experienced enough yet, that the bar raised too high for me?

The reason is because of what I became conscious much later, i.e. society's syndrome of turning down women or pushing them to turn themselves down (well described in Sheryl Sandberg's book *Lean In*).

Times have not yet come to a satisfying level of change. I take it from a discussion I had recently with a partner of one of those big highly reputed firms. Being more forward-thinking than his partners, he had undertaken to take measures aimed at increasing diversity at his firm, mostly including the retention of talented women and millennials.

He appeared quite demotivated by his partners' reaction not to consider modern solutions that could encourage part-time or remote working solutions.

I remain grateful to my husband and other professional role models who convinced me at that time that I was no less capable than my counterparts and that I was fit and up for the challenge. They supported me and advised me to dare. Because what was called "to be expected" for men, for women it was "daring".

Were your expectations met in your position as in-house lawyer?

Distinct learning path and pace. As I mentioned earlier, in private practice I gained an invaluable experience and expertise on technical in-depth legal issues. It is precisely that expertise that is benefiting my in-house position and the company's interests in general.

What struck me at first is that from the moment you are in house, your practice and learning path shifts from a "vertical" expansion (i.e., going deeper into the technicalities and details of the specific practice area) to a "horizontal" one (i.e., focusing on practice development in the company's sector of activity; and expanding your skills in side area related to company-managing skills, such as communication, negotiation, management, audit, accounting, etc.).

I recall having felt "private-practice sick" in the early stage of my in-house journey. I missed working on high-profile complicated cases, searching for the detail or exception in the regulation or case law to feed an argument, writing long memos and spending hours brainstorming with other antitrust practitioners. I also had to overcome the classic change in status: in private practice the lawyer is a centre of profit, everything in the firm's organisation revolves around it and its needs; in house, the lawyer is a centre of cost and an "enabling function" supporting the profit-making ones (such as the business).

Past that "landing" stage, I must say that my experience in house has been an incredible, fast and diverse learning one, since the beginning. It has also been one filled with empowerment, challenges and self-expansion opportunities.

Being an associate in a law firm you are part of, and drowned into, a large team composed of associates, like you, practicing competition law, like you, at the same level as you. Usually the partners get to travel and meet with the client general counsel (GCs), write articles and speak at conferences. As soon as you get in house you are promoted to be that company's antitrust expert, highly ranked within the legal department. At Michelin I was hired to fill a newly created position and I became their first in-house competition law counsel. You suddenly are in the spotlight and by yourself.

It is very challenging, intimidating and exciting at the same time. It offers huge learning possibilities on very diverse areas and this may be what I love the most about being in house.

Business skills. The first skillset you must quickly expand and add on to your professional qualifications is understanding business. Understanding and anticipating the needs of the business you support is key to becoming a good in-house counsel in general and a good antitrust in-house counsel, in particular. Unlike outside counsel, you must gain the trust of your business colleagues and you win when they consider you as part of their team. You are associated with risk-taking decisions, be it daring borderline positions or more conservative approach than case law, taking into account various parameters pursuant to your insight of the activity, competition or client-relationship, and internal structure and people involved.

Negotiating skills. I notably found very valuable and rewarding to be directly involved in high stake negotiation meetings, to the point where the company valued my contribution enough to offer me the advanced training on negotiation techniques, which was open to the company's top managers.

Communication skills. Philippe Legrez (former Michelin Group GC) uses to say that the difference between outside and in-house counsel is that a good in-house counsel must have strong communication skills. He mainly refers to the ability to transform and convey a technical legal advice into a concise, intelligible and helpful input for the business, to enlighten decisions.

I would add that communication abilities extend to more than interacting with the business. It encompasses internal politics capabilities. A good in-house lawyer must be agile on strategy to be able to get traction internally (identifying the right supports and how to get them on board – e.g. involving more people upstream, even to the detriment of speed, in order to preclude opponents and hence avoid fighting time-consuming opposition downstream). Agility in communication is also the ability to adapt the content and tone of your message to the audience, from the sales force on the ground to board members at the top. I was lucky enough that antitrust risk was highly valued by Michelin when I moved in house, and the GC quickly facilitated my visibility within the organisation starting with quarterly face-to-face meetings with Jean-Dominique Senard, Michelin Group CEO.

Communication prerequisites also include the ability to communicate externally, outside the company, in situation such as benchmarking with other similar-sized companies, representing the company in lobbying actions, or speaking at public conferences (requiring public-speaking skills as well).

Self-expansion. Another difference I quickly noted in moving from private practice is the freedom you get to shape and expand your function. The aim of the function is to put the antitrust risk under control, not only by assessing on matters but also, and maybe more importantly, by proactively identifying areas of potential risk and designing adapted solutions. Then you have to advocate and articulate the necessity to be granted resources for implementation.

For example, when designing an antitrust compliance programme from scratch, I rapidly came to the conclusion that the most efficient way to raise awareness and disseminate compliance measures with a global remit was to set up an internal network composed of in-house lawyers whom I would train on antitrust and who would become my compliance local relays. I got these lawyers' managers and the human resources department on board to make this happen.

Of course, such freedom to be proactive comes with the duty to be proactive when needed to better perform your task, but it is a pathway to professional development (giving you opportunities to show what you are capable of).

Leadership and management. I believe that practicing in house gave me more opportunities to test and develop leadership and management skills than I could have in private practice. When it comes to development opportunities, private practice is more like a one-dimension ladder, whereas in-house opportunities lie on a 3D kind of web. In a law firm the career promotion is seniority and pay-scale. In-house counsel are added to other elements, such as becoming the legal support for additional functions (business, HR, communication, R&D etc.) within the organisation, managing a team, leaving legal to occupy other positions (sales, audit, HR, communication etc.). Although I started in house being the sole antitrust expert in the company, I rapidly set up and managed a network of over 30 lawyers in 15 countries and five continents. Not to mention the budget-management aspect of the in-house function, which comes with the interaction with accounting.

Diversity and humility. I started in house for Michelin, a leading tyre manufacturer, with a three-month integration phase which included a three-week factory internship on night shifts. The headquarters were also located on a plant site. Encounters with blue-collar workers were common. Even in non-industry sector of activity, working in house offers interactions with people from diverse horizons and social backgrounds. I value this diverse exposure. This makes a big difference from private practice, where you evolve in a preserved high-end world.

It is often said that women are less likely to network, and you have shown an interest in innovative networking. Could you tell us what your views are in that respect and what could be learnt to develop different networking formulas?

I am not sure about women being less likely to network. It might well be the case that there are fewer women in professional spheres with high propensity to network, and why that is is definitely a question to be asked.

I am a strong believer in thriving via networking, be it for an individual at a personal or professional level, or for a team or a company to reach goals. I rapidly found networking a key element to a successful compliance programme, especially in large companies.

Internal networking. As head of competition law my role is twofold: on the one hand it consists of assessing and managing competition law matters, and on the other it also encompasses putting risk under control. With my private practice background, I was armed for the first aspect. I just needed to better understand the business I was supporting, its goals, structure and how it operated, to be quickly fully on board. As regards the second component of my duties, compliance, I had to start from scratch. Not only from my professional background standpoint, but also from the internal organisation of the company. Indeed, the position has just been created and no antitrust compliance programme as such had ever been implemented. The challenge was massive. The company had already faced condemnation in the EU, was active in nearly all countries in the world, and emerging countries had already started to enact and aggressively implement competition regulations. Getting close to the business I managed to identify potentially risky contracts, structures, situations and behaviours. Similarly, was I able to design appropriate preventive or corrective actions and measures. How to adapt and implement those measures country by country, in a timely manner and with appropriate consistency, was the biggest challenge.

With the support of my management and top managers, I sat up a network composed of in-house business lawyers already employed in the different countries. When contacted, they all joined in the project, seizing this opportunity to connect with their international counterparts, exchange good practices, gain visibility within the organisation, gain or increase their knowledge of an area of law under scrutiny. The diverse component of the network, encompassing several nationalities and business cultures, was no stranger to that self-rewarding success.

With proper coordination and animation, the network grew and became very successful in various ways, to the benefit of the entire organisation:

i. Better-controlled risk. It proved extremely efficient to increase awareness levels via local training, implementing compliance measures and performing spot assessments as needed.

ii. Keys performance indicators for audit purposes. Yearly performance reports from the lawyers (on compliance measures and awareness level, such as number of persons trained, quiz results, mentions in employment contracts, mentions in personal goals etc.) enable me to provide accurate reporting on key performance indicators to my management.

iii. Human resources and professional development opportunity. Human resources and local managers used proper communication which helped promote the network by rewarding its members with more visibility and considering participation as a professional development opportunity.

iv. Data privacy, anti-bribery and corruption and other compliance units later used the structure to spread out consistent and fast compliance in their areas, reinforcing the "aura" and importance of the network.

External networking is also key to one's personal and professional development. Professionally it enables me to connect with my counterparts from similar-sized companies, benchmark on compliance efforts and stay informed of latest trends in the sector. Making your position and the name of the company you represent more visible in your area of practice helps it gain credibility and legitimacy. This feeds the interests of the company for purposes like lobbying. It also feeds your own professional development interests by remaining visible and informed of possible openings.

Networking can sometimes prove difficult because it requires you to dedicate additional time and efforts to show proactiveness in network initiatives. Some managers can be reluctant to allocate spending (e.g. for travel costs), but it is worth advocating for it.

What are your views on compliance solutions?

You are right to put it plural. Efficient compliance is a series of solutions put in place across the organisation with shared accountability.

What compliance efforts? Solutions must cover the three must-have "pillars" of a compliance programme: (i) prevention (how to prevent a breach or a risky situation from occurring?); (ii) detection (how to monitor the efficiency of your programme and how to detect deviant behaviour or breach?); and reaction (in case of possible breach, what follow-up actions must be taken?).

First, the company's organisation must identify possible gaps or risky situations every step of the way. Then it must design and implement adapted solutions to address those and thus mitigate the risk. Both assessment and implementation sides entail working closely with other divisions or departments within the company. This prevention "pillar" encompasses various and diverse aspects such as: review of structure and reporting lines, policies and internal communication, mandatory prior validations, instructions from management, certification, training and monitoring employees' awareness. Second, detection tools include internal reporting; employee interviews or more formal audit processes; a complaint-handling system and whistle-blowing mechanism. Third, the reaction part consists of ceasing any wrongdoing and getting the company ready for any potential litigation: taking immediate action to stop the infringement or correct the risky behaviour, considering disciplinary action, considering filing for leniency whenever relevant, documenting all corrective efforts, taking appropriate action to improve or add compliance measures.

How to implement compliance efforts? As already touched upon earlier, setting up a network of antitrust in-house lawyers is key to ensure global consistency, constant follow-up and key performance indicators. But none of the abovementioned efforts would prove efficient without strong support from the top. Commitment from top management is a necessary component and must be communicated internally to all employees. Now, if you keep on unfolding the rationale, you inevitably come to the conclusion that in order to secure such strong commitment from managers and employees it logically takes a shared accountability towards compliance.

How could new learning strategies, such as gaming learning solutions, be used? What have been your experiences in relation to these in the legal world?

Learning is essential to compliance. Antitrust risk is mostly of a behavioural nature. Because the organisation relies on employees to adopt compliant behaviour, you cannot ask employees to comply with principles or regulation they do not know or understand.

To that effect, training and the quality of the training tools are a vital component of efficient compliance. Internal communication and policies are necessary but not sufficient. To reach an acceptable level of awareness, employees must not only be communicated "dos and don'ts", they must also be properly trained. I cannot resist quoting Benjamin Franklin's "tell me and I forget, teach me and I may remember, involve me and I learn".

The quality of the training tools is a determining factor of the learner's involvement. It must be accurate (i.e., as close as possible to situation experienced by the learner in its daily activity) and interactive. We live in a technological era, which offers many possibilities in that regard and innovation is inviting itself into those compliance tools. I experience the best learning results and positive feedback with gaming solutions (or "serious" video game). Part of the success is due to the fun format (video games are appealing to current generation of learners), but also and mostly because it was designed for and with the help of the business. Involving business colleagues helped designing "real life" scenarios in which the player can picture itself, using real-life imaging and wording. Getting as close as possible to reality enables the player to take a more proactive approach. It also makes it more appealing to the player because the player does not only learn about what is right and what is not, it also provides for useful takeaways on how to react, what to answer etc. The first antitrust serious game I designed was such a success that it was being used not only by legal but also by the business division as a business training tool to train the sales force on visiting clients. Business appropriating a legal training tool is an indicator of high efficiency. This also helped dust off the legal department's image and propel it into an innovation/forward-thinking one.

Mentoring initiatives have proven useful when developed to support women in the legal profession. Have you benefited therefrom in any way?

"Mentoring" is a vast concept. It takes various faces. To me, mentoring should be about helping someone navigate and thrive into the professional sphere.

It shall not be about acquiring or expanding technical skills (this is training, not mentoring). This is a common pitfall to avoid but that you unfortunately find in many so-called "mentoring" initiatives. When launching an initiative, the organisation must be mindful of this, to avoid mentoring slipping and fading into training. Matching persons shall be carefully considered and mentors as well as mentees must receive guidance on how to mentor and what to expect as a mentee.

Mentoring is about providing guidance and support while expanding and focusing on soft skills (or emotional skills). To take full advantage of the mentoring opportunity, mentees should be prepared to expose themselves (expressing freely their frustrations and expectations) and receive criticism and advice in return. Advice given by a mentor shall be driven by their past experience. I consider that the added value of professional mentoring is to also benefit from the mentor's networking and experienced knowledge on "how to get there", "what pitfalls to identify and avoid", etc.

I have never benefited from any kind of formal mentoring programme, as such, but I always proactively seek advice from persons I find inspiring or that I admire. I guess it is a natural thing to do, and I am extremely grateful to those who took the time to listen, advise and tell me when they thought I was not taking the right path. These people are the role models you get a chance to meet and interact with in your life. I am not talking there about famous inspiring leaders (the Obamas, Ruth Bader Ginsburg, and the like), I am referring to persons close to you who also demonstrate a willingness to give you some useful support.

For example, I fell into competition law thanks to the great and strong personality of my professor in third year at university, whom I continue to admire. She was also active in private practice. I literally chased and harassed her to convince her to take me as a trainee. In the end she taught me more than competition law. I had no one into law in my family or family friends. I had strong technical skills, but I lacked knowledge on how law practices operate, what to expect, how to express it and to whom etc. She opened up this world to me. Later, I took advice from people I admired and who would show they believed in me. When I was a young associate at Cleary, partners Romano Subiotto and Maurits Dolmans gave me helpful advice beyond the matters I worked on for them. They provided me guidance on which matters I should work on and which partners I should work for in order to expand my area of expertise. Romano would encourage me to be proactive in writing articles and building up my profile/ Later they would think of and contact me for interesting openings. They helped me tremendously in gaining confidence in myself.

During my years at Michelin I was blessed to meet with Florence Vincent (chief audit & risks officer) who spontaneously offered to give me some kind of informal mentoring support. Despite her crazy schedule, overloaded with business trips overseas, she would find the time to catch up regularly with me over lunch. Her experience and precious advice helped me navigate into the politics of the organisation at top management level. I valued her judgment and nowadays I continue to value her friendship and recommendations. I still continue seeking guidance from inspiring people I trust. During the time I reported to Graeme Baldwin (deputy GC) at Pearson, he would take the time to very kindly offer me his support and guidance to help build my profile as a newcomer into the organisation and as a "Frenchie" in a pure Anglo-Saxon professional environment. When I stopped reporting to him as my manager, I asked if we could still set up regular mentoring catch-ups, and this way I managed to continue benefiting from his very valuable inputs and views. Bjarne Tellemann, former Pearson Chief Legal Officer, and current GC for GSK also kept close contact with me and I continue benefiting from is advice and innovative ideas. I am very grateful.

How relevant do you consider role models in professional life, and has there been any person in particular you have been inspired by?

As shared above, I consider role models to be fantastic people you get the chance to closely interact with in your life, and there are a few of them. You get more than just inspired by role models, you are guided by them.

Inspiring people is a broader and more distant concept that encompasses famous personalities, e.g. political, moral or corporate leaders. You can nevertheless get direct impact from the inspiring people you interact with more closely. They help you shape your own views on professional organisations and management.

Although I cannot say they have inspired my daily activity, I cannot resist mentioning two personalities I came across who impressed me. The first one is Jean-Dominique Senard, former Michelin Group CEO and current president of Renault – Nissan – Mitsubishi. I had regular meetings with him during my time at Michelin. I always thought highly of him and I have been impressed by his leadership style. One anecdote speaks for itself: we had an appointment to get him video-recorded for antitrust compliance training purposes. I was sitting in the waiting room of his office and his assistant had already warned me of the delay due to crisis management in the wake of the Fukushima disaster (the group had employees and plants in Japan). He came himself to apologise and explain the situation to me, while confirming he was still taking my compliance efforts seriously and still on for the video if I did not mind waiting. A mix of rigour, fairness, humility and respect, without any need to show authority off: the ingredients of natural and legitimate leadership.

The second person to really impress me is Haben Girma (her book: *Haben: The Deafblind Woman Who Conquered Harvard Law*). Female, black, deaf and blind, she graduated from Harvard Law School. I got the chance to speak with her (via a keyboard linked to her braille keyboard, she could listen to me via her fingers). She holds an impressively positive mindset and dedicates a lot of her time to advocating for a better inclusive access to persons with disabilities. She is model of tenacity and hope that should inspire us all.

I also cannot resist mentioning that I first started in private practice under the direct supervision of Christine Lagarde, before she became chair of Baker McKenzie, then French minister of economy and subsequently head of the International Monetary Fund. That proximity influenced the way I paid attention to her career rise and, although I would never compare myself to her high bar, I guess it played an indirect positive influence on my "daring" side, encouraging my taking risks.

Do you consider there are any differences between the US and EU mentoring methods you may have come across during your career?

In my experience, mentoring is more developed in the US. Companies use it seriously as professional development tool for their employees. It is more formalised in its implementation, with mentoring programmes you can register for online, and identifying a specific mentor or asked to be assigned one. This increases tremendously mentoring opportunities for potential mentees and employees seeking advice. It increases opportunities to connect people.

When mentoring is informal, not institutionalised, there are a lot of barriers to overcome (e.g. identifying the right mentor, daring to request mentoring, managing efficient mentoring exchanges). Formal mentoring programmes spare you the energy and sometimes embarrassment of having to proactively ask for it. It also offers mentoring opportunities to people who would not have even considered it otherwise.

Would you consider female mentoring helpful to reduce the gender gap?

Let me first state that, whether informal or formal, mentoring has proven useful to, and has always been used by, all genders. Studies have shown that women tend to be less proactive in seeking mentoring support and networking support for various reasons. Among those reasons are: the fact that professional environments, at higher levels of management, are still male-dominated; the gender difference in being raised, the "not-to-be-bossy-girl" syndrome; the tendency to wait and reward women on their merits, what they have accomplished, rather than promoting men on their potential and what they could achieve, etc. So I believe that formal mentoring programmes increase professional development opportunities for women.

Now, to the question on whether women should be mentored by other women to help reduce the gender gap, I am not sure. Even though I understand and agree with Sheryl Sandberg that women should "lean in", I am convinced that to get things to evolve, it similarly takes initiatives to change the male vision and facilitate women "leaning in". For that reason, it could be useful to get more men mentoring women, so that they get to be confronted with the bias and struggle women face in the workplace and get used to taking an active role in finding solutions. Similarly, it could also prove helpful to have more men mentored by women, to get them familiar with women occupying higher management positions. This could help transform mentalities in the long run.

What has been the most challenging experience in your career?

I found my debut in house very challenging. The position of head of global competition law had just been created, in the wake of the group's condemnation for abuse of dominance at EU level. Expectations were very high and so was the pressure I felt. In addition, I was the only one with a competition law background. Hence, I had no framework in place that I could rely on with respect to competition law issues and compliance, and I had no one to turn to for brainstorming to test my opinions, compliance design and implementation moves.

Starting from scratch was very challenging but it has also been a great learning and rewarding experience. I was lucky to receive strong support from my management, always open to my ideas and my proactive behaviour. From the difficult situations and push-backs I had to go through, I learnt a lot, especially on management and strategy, key skills for a good in-house lawyer.

Another challenging experience worth mentioning is my move to Pearson in New York and the cultural shock that came with it. Not so much about the EU/US differences in the workplace (although one cannot assume how big they could be before experiencing it: having been raised in both French and Canadian cultures I assumed I would not be surprised; the move proved me wrong). There was a big corporate cultural difference. Where I had assumed the biggest challenge would come from the activity and related law issues (with a new focus on digital and interacting with the big tech platforms), it came more from the corporate cultural differences: from a very traditional French industry to a very agile and innovating digital one. Very challenging in the positive sense, testing and improving my agility and adaptation skills.

What has been the most rewarding experience in your career?

Recognition from my peers and officials on my accomplishments felt very rewarding. The UK and the French competition authorities invited me along to give their teams a presentation on my compliance programme in the context of their drafting of compliance guidance. At Michelin I benefited from a one-year training on innovation which included a Silicon Valley tour (visiting and meeting with representatives of Google, Pixar, Tesla, Orangelab etc., to discuss innovation). I was the only legal expert selected, along with mostly R&D experts. This was a terrific learning and rewarding experience.

But where I felt the most rewarded was during my mentoring of a wonderful young and talented woman, Avesta Alani. She is a Kurdish refugee who immigrated to Canada and she is blind. Avesta managed to overcome her personal challenges, gained self-confidence, entered the Toronto Law School with scholarships, and is studying while remaining actively engaged in volunteering for blind people. She even found the time to write a book that I recommend reading (*Diffability: The Liberation of Potential*). Even though I still feel that she taught me more than the support I gave her, if there is a chance that I modestly contributed to help her thrive, this makes me utterly proud.

What would be your piece of advice to women who are starting their career in the legal world? What would you have done differently in retrospective?

To evolve and thrive you must continuously raise your expectations. So, always set your goals higher than you think you can reach, because you can do it. I wish I had applied that recommendation to myself. In retrospect, this might be something I would have done differently.

Anything else you would like to share with us that we have not asked about?

I would like to mention a challenge faced by the position itself as in-house legal expert. From my experience and that of many of my counterparts, the position of expert in general, and even more the case for legal experts, hardly fit into the corporate organisation's career evolution grid. That grid is usually tailored for the business-related positions and tend to be based on level of management or how many employees one supervises. This usually favours general practitioners (hence, they usually manage a team) to the detriment of experts (because usually the organisation is at the same time depriving them to manage a team so that they can fulfil their expert role). This has become a real issue in many organisations. I think their structures should invest more on the expert positions, especially in times where legal departments are constantly asked to be more agile and provide the same high-quality services with fewer resources. So, while you can always turn good experts into good managers, turning good managers into good experts is less straightforward.

Anne Riley
Independent Antitrust Compliance Consultant

Mariana Tavares de Araujo

Anne Riley retired in March 2019 as head of Royal Dutch Shell's global antitrust group, which she had led since September 1992 (having practiced as an antitrust lawyer since 1985) and was a member of Shell's Group Ethics and Compliance Office leadership team until her retirement. She is currently chair of the International Chamber of Commerce Task Force on Antitrust Compliance and Advocacy and a non-governmental adviser to the European Union (DG COMP) for the International Competition Network. She has been awarded a number of legal and compliance awards, including "Women in Compliance, Innovator of the Year".

Mariana Tavares de Araujo is a partner with Levy & Salomão Advogados. Prior to joining the firm, Ms Araujo worked with the Brazilian government, where she served as head of the government agency in charge of antitrust enforcement and consumer protection policy. She provides counsel for the World Bank and serves as an adviser to the ICN and to CADE. She currently is officer of the IBA Antitrust Committee and is a member of the ABA International Developments and Comments Task Force. Ms Araujo holds an LLM from the Georgetown University Law Center.

You have been an antitrust lawyer since 1985, working in industry and private practice, and for nearly 27 years, until your recent retirement you were in-house as the global head of antitrust for a large multinational. What trends have you observed over this time?

An obvious development has been the increased use of electronic and social media. When I started my training contract in a law firm in 1983, we had no computers in the office – the office did not even have a fax but communicated by telex and landline telephone. As an antitrust lawyer, the reliance on computers, iPhones and social media has a very practical side effect, and that is that antitrust investigations have now changed out of all recognition – with very little reliance by investigators on hard-copy documents. Another thing that has changed out of all recognition is the use of the Internet: with relatively little effort it is now possible to keep up with antitrust developments around the world, and as I am a little bit "geeky" about antitrust law, this has given me a lot of personal pleasure, including in my (semi) retirement.

Antitrust is often accused as being overly theoretical. As the retired leader of global antitrust team of a multinational oil company, are there any competition law theories that in your experience you have found are not accurately supported by market realities?

My concerns really do not so much revolve around new theories of harm but rather in the way that some antitrust agencies have applied those theories. For example, it has been good in Europe to have seen a movement back from the characterisation of virtually any exchange of information between competitors as potentially being a "by-object" infringement (as expressed in the *T-Mobile* judgment) to the rather more sensible position now being developed, in Europe at least, that it is vitally important to assess the context in which conduct occurs to see whether it is a by-object infringement or not.

My concern is that overly zealous enforcers (especially perhaps in "newer" antitrust jurisdictions around the world that tend to follow EU case law but without factoring in the caveats that the EU courts have articulated) may incorrectly characterise perfectly legitimate and lawful cooperation between competitors as constituting an illegal arrangement because the collaboration involved the sharing of some competitively sensitive information (CSI). From many years of antitrust practice in business, I think it is important to understand that sharing of CSI is not always indicative of an illegal agreement or a concerted practice. There can be perfectly legitimate and lawful reasons why companies need to cooperate – for example in the context of a joint venture (provided that the information-sharing is objectively needed to ensure the proper operation of the venture). Indeed, in many instances, cooperation between competitors may be procompetitive and efficiency-enhancing. This means not all sharing of information between actual or potential competitors is anticompetitive – so the CSI which is objectively needed to achieve a legitimate end should not be viewed as illegal, but as being ancillary to the primary legitimate behaviour. Indeed, if overenthusiastic enforcers find a concerted practice from a mere sharing of CSI without considering the *context* in which the information is shared, it may chill legitimate and procompetitive collaboration.

As vice-chair of the International Chamber of Commerce (ICC) Competition Commission and chair of the ICC Task Force on Antitrust Compliance and Advocacy you were instrumental in the design of the ICC Antitrust Compliance Toolkit and the ICC's shorter Antitrust Toolkit for SMEs, which complement materials produced by antitrust agencies and other sources of guidance by focusing on practical steps that companies of different sizes can take internally to embed a successful compliance culture. How different are the challenges in building an effective compliance programme today from, let's say, 10 years ago?

Before I answer this question, I would like first to raise an issue of terminology here: in-house compliance specialists are moving away from talking about "compliance programmes" to talking about the need for businesses to act with ethics and integrity. I think less focus on a "programme" to talking about acting with integrity really helps businesses focus on "doing the right thing". It also means that one can "sell" the need for compliance – not by instilling a fear of fines or imprisonment – but rather by encouraging a desire to do business properly. At the end of the day, most people want to do the right thing – they just need to understand what is expected of them. In this way, business people can understand what the benefits of competition are to society, to their own business reputation and to their customers. It also helps shift the discussion, hopefully away from the idea that many antitrust agencies seem to still have that antitrust compliance is merely "window-dressing" or a manual that sits on a shelf somewhere, never to be read. If that is all your antitrust compliance programme is, it can never possibly be effective. If, however, you manage to instil ethical leadership in your organisation, your "programme" will be effective – that is not to say that things will not occasionally go wrong – that is human nature, but you learn from past mistakes and improve by learning. So, I think the challenge is to build ethical leadership, as once you truly have that "Tone at the Top" it will filter through the entire organisation.

In your great article with Daniel Sokol, "Rethinking Compliance", you discuss optimal deterrence and its limits in the context of creating a more effective mechanism for antitrust compliance to take hold in businesses, and propose that antitrust authorities should work with the business community to create a regulatory scheme that rewards good behaviour while punishing bad behaviour. Since you published this article, several antitrust agencies issued compliance guidelines, and some set forth the possibility of giving credit to companies that adopt effective compliance programmes. How have you seen the development of a compliance culture around the world and the role of antitrust authorities in this process?

I think antitrust authorities have a key role in helping spread the compliance/ethical business message, by entering into constructive dialogues with business on what constitutes credible antitrust compliance efforts. As an aside, I would like to make it clear that it has never been the position of the ICC that we were seeking credit for compliance programmes: what the ICC has been doing is engaging in efforts around the world to engage in compliance advocacy. On a personal level, I do think credit for compliance is likely to further boost compliance efforts, although I do understand the position of some agencies. Having said that, I think you only need to look at the huge success of the anti-bribery and corruption enforcers in boosting compliance efforts because of their creative approach to compliance programmes and their willingness to consider some credit for the programme if compliance efforts are genuine. I would therefore like to encourage not only more dialogue with business, but also more dialogue with other enforcement agencies to see how creative use of enforcement tools can support and promote ethical business conduct.

The oil industry has been in the spotlight of many cross-border investigations. Brazil's Petrobras is involved in what is probably the largest corruption probe worldwide. How do you see the role of compliance officers in the implementation of a compliance programme that actually prevents breaches, after a case like Car Wash?

Obviously, I do not wish to comment on the *Car Wash* case specifically, as I only know what has been reported in the compliance and wider press, but going back to two previous answers, I would say that it is in everyone's interests – the agencies, businesses and indeed society at large – to do everything possible to encourage businesses to act with integrity. As I said in the last answer, agencies from different compliance disciplines can usefully learn from each other in how best to encourage and perhaps even reward very genuine compliance efforts. I think it is also important particularly for antitrust agencies to understand that human beings *are* only human, and that mistakes are bound to occur occasionally, but that does not mean that compliance efforts are wholly ineffective. The agencies need to examine carefully the culture and ethos of the organisation. If that is largely a culture of integrity, then some degree of understanding needs to be shown to the enterprise. I would just like to commend the excellent work of the Canadian Competition Bureau in helping businesses understand what in their view constitutes an effective compliance programme (or as I would like to call it, working credibly to achieve an ethical business culture).

The ICC represents several million companies worldwide with the goal to "make business work for everyone, every day, everywhere". How does that translate into your work within the Task Force on Antitrust Compliance and Advocacy?

As you mentioned in a previous question, I am honoured currently to be the chair of the ICC's Task Force on Antitrust Compliance and Advocacy. The work is very much a collective effort of the entire Task Force, and since the first toolkit was first published in 2013, we have worked tirelessly with antitrust agencies and businesses both large and small to promote the importance of ethical and compliance business practices. We have held dozens of workshops around the world (approaching around 100, I think) to explain the importance of competition law to business and society at large, and thus to encourage ethical competition on the merits. At the same time, we have encouraged agencies to enter a more open dialogue with business about the merits of compliance programmes, and have spoken at a large number of agency-organised events. At the same time, while we absolutely condemn cartels and other egregious violations of antitrust law, we encourage agencies to think carefully about the dangers of condemning all collaboration amongst business, since over-enforcement can chill perfectly legitimate and efficiency-enhancing competition.

Global companies have to deal with regulatory frameworks in different countries that can include complex and multi-layered systems of controls, and antitrust and anti-corruption laws that have extraterritorial jurisdiction and thus apply to virtually every company trading internationally. Also, on top of ensuring compliance at national and global levels, they need to be vigilant with partners – vendors and providers must undergo the same checks and controls applied internally. In other words, a combination of high risks on the one hand, and "compliance stress disorder" on the other. What are, in your view, the measures to effectively disseminate a culture of compliance on a global level, taking into account the specificities of each jurisdiction?

I think the starting point absolutely has to be the culture of the corporation. If leaders within the organisation are committed to conducting business ethically and with integrity, then – by and large – most people working within the organisation will also want to "do the right thing". However, you do make an excellent point about the danger of what I term "compliance fatigue". There are now a vast range of laws that multinationals (and even small companies) are expected to comply with. The list seems endless and ever-growing: not just antitrust, but anti-bribery and corruption, anti-money laundering, data protection, trade controls and sanctions compliance, insider dealing compliance, and for listed companies also securities law compliance. This can make busy business people feel that they are been bombarded with requirements and legal advice. I think the solution is to try to avoid compliance fatigue by trying to integrate compliance training on various topics so that the businesses understand compliance requirements in a more holistic way.

I also think it is important to make compliance training accessible to busy business folks who may have many pressing business travel commitments and cannot necessarily give up half a day or whatever time it is to sit in compliance lectures: so my advice is to use the many tools now available: while face-to-face training is of course desirable when it can be achieved, online training is better than no training. Also, make compliance learning a fun experience and not an imposition: some companies use fun tools like gamification and compliance-bots to help avoid compliance fatigue and to instil perhaps a little bit of "competition" into the compliance efforts.

A Court of Appeal decision from September 2018 established that documents, including interview notes and forensic accounting reports generated by mining company ENRC during an internal corruption investigation were protected by privilege and therefore did not have to be disclosed to the Serious Fraud Office. Do you believe the discussion over privilege has been settled after this ruling? Do you see areas where there is still legal uncertainty regarding privilege in the UK?

Of course, privilege laws differ all over the world, so I do not think we can say that the laws on privilege are even close to being settled. Under the *Akzo* doctrine in the EU, for example, in-house counsel (and indeed external counsel who are not qualified to practise in an EU country) have no privilege whatsoever in the context of an EU antitrust investigation, whereas in-house counsel do have legal privilege when it comes to purely UK investigations. I do think this unsettled state of privilege under the *Akzo* doctrine is unfortunate in the extreme, as it is predicated on the (completely erroneous) prejudice that in-house counsel, as "employed" lawyers, cannot give independent antitrust advice. This is clearly an outdated notion and indeed in my experience in-house antitrust counsel can (and do) give very robust antitrust advice. Also, the failure to allow in-house antitrust counsel in EU investigations to benefit from privilege for their advice is seriously counter-productive, as it risks antitrust compliance advice being given in the most effective way which would ensure greater compliance and more ethical business behaviour.

Due process problems have received more attention as fines in competition cases have increased greatly in recent years. The ICN's *Framework for Competition Agency Procedures* seems to be an indication of that, as well as an important step towards fairness and consistency around the globe. Are there procedural fairness issues where you see there is still room for improvement?

First, I must say that I welcome the ICN's *Framework*, and I am very pleased that at the ICN's annual meeting (in Cartegena in Colombia in 2019) there was a fruitful dialogue on procedural fairness. Of course, the topic is a sensitive one to some agencies, as they feel slightly under attack when due process and procedural fairness are being discussed: but the topic is absolutely vital for the fair and proportionate enforcement of antitrust laws, and this can ultimately not only benefit businesses, but the agencies themselves. Without wishing to name any specific countries, there are a number of jurisdictions where even the most basic rights of defence are compromised: for example, I have heard it said that in some countries, even external counsel are not allowed to represent the company on site during an on-the-spot investigation, which clearly compromises the company's right of defence. So I am glad the ICN is now approaching this topic seriously, and I believe this is probably the best place to do this, as more "soft convergence" can be achieved through ICN than perhaps in any other forum.

In your view, how will Brexit impact public and private enforcement in the UK? What do you see as the key challenges ahead for the government, for companies and practitioners?

Well, my personal views on Brexit are well known to my friends. I am a Europhile and wanted the UK to stay in the EU – not only because it is the right thing for the country, but also because I am honoured to be a non-governmental adviser to DG COMP for the work of the ICN (I am grateful to have this position through my Irish nationality). On a practical level, I think there may be a decline in follow-on claims in the English courts post-Brexit and a corresponding increase in civil litigation for antitrust claims in other EU Member States. I do see a likely increase in UK merger control, as the EU Merger Regulation will not apply in the

UK, so there would have to be more UK filings. But at the end of the day, all this can be sorted out. Antitrust enforcement is the smallest of worries for the UK post-Brexit.

From your professional experience at Shell, which do you see as the most important elements of good leadership?

"Tone from the Top." By which I mean a genuine commitment to undertake business ethically and to "do the right thing". But while the culture of the company comes from the top, it is not just the responsibility of the board. Business integrity involves tone at and from the top, tone in the middle and tone right down the organisation.

What do you think is the most pressing topic competition issue today?

Well, I am not sure it is necessarily the most pressing, but I do think that the debate on artificial intelligence/algorithmic collusion is probably one of the most interesting topics. There are now many very interesting articles on the topic, including a 2017 BIAC (the Business and Industry Advisory Committee to the OECD) paper for the OECD. In summary, BIAC concludes that, although the concept of algorithmic collusion seems novel, the legal tests which will have to be applied to establish a violation (for the moment at least, until and unless the law is changed) will still be whether an "agreement" or a "concerted practice" is in place.

Could you tell us about your experience working with other distinguished women in competition over the course of your career?

There have been so many truly inspirational female antitrust lawyers that I have been honoured and privileged to work with (or even work on the other side from) throughout my career that the list is almost too long to cite, but two women antitrust lawyers I have always admired both happen to be British (although there are a large number of inspirational women in other countries, including many very dedicated woman in antitrust agencies and universities around the world), but the two I would note as being particularly inspiring for me personally are Lynda Martin Alegi and Rachel Brandenburger.

Do you believe there are still challenges to be overcome and/or myths to be dispelled regarding female professionals' presence in the marketplace?

I have never seen it (speaking for myself) to be a real challenge to work as a female antitrust lawyer, but I guess that is because I was really fortunate that my husband gave up his career to care for our children. I can see that trying to balance a career and a family can be a challenge, but I think if employers are prepared to be flexible, this is entirely possible. Speaking personally, when I led the antitrust team in Shell, I always tried to be very understanding and flexible about balancing work and family commitments, but I did not just apply this principle to women in the team, I applied it to my male colleagues too.

Suzanne Wachsstock
Walmart

Lauren Stiroh

Suzanne Wachsstock is global chief antitrust counsel at Walmart. In addition to day-to-day advice on a wide range of issues, her responsibilities include managing regulatory inquiries, leading all antitrust aspects of M&A, joint ventures and other transactions, and close engagement on antitrust policy and strategy. She is a member of the ABA Antitrust Law Section Leadership Council, and previously held leadership roles in the Section's Corporate Counseling, International, Insurance and Financial Services and Distribution and Franchising Committees. She also sits on the Antitrust Council of the US Chamber of Commerce and on the board of Women@Competition Americas. Before joining Walmart in 2019, Suzanne spent 11 years as chief antitrust counsel at American Express after a career in private practice, beginning at Davis Polk & Wardwell and ultimately as a partner at Wiggin and Dana LLP, where she co-led the firm's antitrust and consumer protection group.

Lauren Stiroh is chair of NERA's global antitrust and competition practice. She specialises in the economics of antitrust, intellectual property and commercial damages. Dr Stiroh conducts research, prepares expert reports and testifies on issues arising from antitrust allegations such as monopolisation, exclusionary conduct, tying, vertical restrictions, price-fixing, predation, price discrimination and abuse of standard-setting. She works on class certification matters, assessing whether impact and damages from alleged wrongdoing are common to a class, and has performed or critiqued damage calculations in more than a dozen industrial settings. Much of her work focuses on the intersection of antitrust and IP litigation, where she has analysed market power in technology markets, evaluated licensing arrangements, and testified on IP value and valuation.

You have spent a considerable part of your career focusing on competition law. When and how did you first become interested in competition law?

I'm open about the fact that I did not take antitrust in law school because I thought, at the most superficial level, that it sounded boring. At the time, I was focused on constitutional law and thought that I would become a disabilities rights lawyer after a short stint in big law. Instead, I was introduced to antitrust as a first year (probably a first-monther) at Davis Polk and Wardwell, where I sat near a number of the young partners and senior associates in the antitrust group. They initially brought me in to some Hart-Scott-Rodino questions, which I found surprisingly fascinating – I suspect it was the Talmudic nature of the analysis, reminding me of my year studying Jewish texts in Jerusalem. From there I moved to more substantive antitrust issues and litigation matters. I still have fond memories of spending the week between Christmas and New Year that first year holed up in my in-laws' attic, working on a long antitrust memo on lawyer advertising for the New York State Bar Association. I don't recall the specifics of the substantive issue, but I know that after that I was hooked.

Over the next five or so years, as I moved to a small boutique firm and then to Wiggin and Dana, I deepened my antitrust focus as I continued to work on other civil litigation, white collar and appellate matters. Around my sixth year, my mentors at the firm – to whom I remain deeply grateful and appreciative – each independently sat me down and suggested that it would be good both for me and for the firm if I committed to antitrust. I took their guidance, and that decision has driven each of my career moves since that time.

What factors drove you to move from private practice to an in-house position?

I enjoyed private practice and had truly wonderful partners and colleagues at Wiggin and Dana, and I valued the challenges and opportunities of co-leading the firm's antitrust and consumer protection team. So I wasn't actively looking to move in house, but I was intrigued by a headhunter call about an opportunity to move to American Express to build their antitrust function. The more I learned about the company and the role, the more it felt like the right next step to expand my horizons as an antitrust lawyer. I was particularly excited about the opportunity to learn a business from the inside and to see how my advice directly informed the company's strategy and decision-making.

Since this was a new role for Amex, there was some scepticism that antitrust warranted a full-time inside counsel, and I was also asked from the start to take on a commercial lawyer role, managing legal support for a segment of merchant relationships as well as serving as legal adviser to the merchant pricing team. None of us could have predicted at the time how important antitrust would become to the company. But a few months later we received the initial Civil Investigative Demands in the case that would become the *United States v American Express* litigation (later renamed *Ohio v American Express*) that ultimately culminated 10 years later in a hard-fought win in the US Supreme Court. The case brought antitrust to the forefront for the company, and allowed me a front-row seat in the development of antitrust law.

What are some of the challenges that you think in-house lawyers like yourself face when it comes to dealing with antitrust laws, both in regulation and litigation, that private practitioners do not face?

I used to joke that as a young partner in a mid-sized firm, life was about rainmaking; when I came in house, it was about finding an umbrella big enough to protect against the rain that poured in from all sides. In house, very little is abstract or hypothetical – we have to give real-time, real-life, risk-based advice every day, most often by meeting, phone call or email. We don't have the luxury of teams of associates to do research or the ability to draft 20+-page CYA memos. Instead, it is all about building relationships of trust across our business clients so that they seek and value our guidance.

The hardest transition I've seen with young antitrust lawyers moving from outside firms to in-house roles is learning how to communicate advice to business people in a way that is both clear and understandable, and at the same time respectful of the complexity of business decision-making. We need to recognise that, except in rare occasions where the proposed conduct would be criminal or *per se* unlawful, it is the business's role to make business judgments, taking into account the sound and risk-based legal advice that we provide.

What has been the most challenging antitrust matter that you have been involved in and why?

I would have to say the *Ohio v Amex* case, for any number of reasons – including the sheer scope and scale of a case that spanned government and private class and individual actions over a period of 10 years; the substantive complexity, novelty and significance of the antitrust theories at issue; and the challenges of providing practical ongoing legal advice in the face of an extended period of inherent uncertainty.

Working for American Express and now Walmart, both global companies, how do you manage the differences in antitrust policy and enforcement in various jurisdictions across the globe in a way that allows for consistency in business operations?

The short answer is that there is enough commonality across competition law regimes – criminalising horizontal collusion, restricting certain horizontal restraints and prohibiting abuses of monopoly power/dominance – to build the base of a global programme that addresses the most important risks. Beyond that, the programme must be flexible enough to allow for local variations where appropriate. And, most importantly, competition law principles and advice (like all legal guidance) must be communicated in a manner that is sensitive to linguistic, cultural and historic realities across the company and the globe, which means that it is critical to have local teams empowered to train, flag issues and advise, whether in-house or outside.

Have you witnessed changes for the role of women in the profession over your career? Where do you notice changes for women in the profession, particularly with respect to in-house advisers?

I have been truly fortunate to have had wonderful female role models and peers within the antitrust bar from early in my career, including Janet McDavid, Ilene Gotts, Sharis Pozen, Lisa Phelan and Renata Hesse, just to name a few. And I have been uniquely privileged to serve under exclusively female general counsels and chief legal officers since I went in house over 12 years ago. Over the years I have seen significant growth in the numbers of women at the highest levels of leadership within the agencies, in house and even in law firms. But that is not to say by any means that our work is done: we need to keep pressing for true diversity both inside and from our outside firms, and work hard to ensure that all voices, at every level, are heard and respected.

Over the course of your career you have had a major involvement in several professional organisations, including as chair of various committees within ABA Antitrust Section and now the leadership council, as a member of the Antitrust Council of the US Chamber of Commerce, and as a non-governmental adviser for the Federal Trade Commission and Department of Justice to the International Competition Network. What benefits do you think you have gained because of your involvement in these organisations and what advice or guidance would you give others who might be considering involvement in a professional organisation?

I don't think I could overstate the value that these professional associations have had over the course of my career. They have provided opportunities to build strong relationships with antitrust practitioners across the spectrum and at all stages of their careers – government regulators, defence and plaintiffs' bar, in house counsel – and, equally importantly, to develop leadership, presentation and collaboration skills outside the pressures of my day job. They have also allowed me to participate in real-time dialogue and debates around substantive antitrust policy issues.

My advice to young or even later-career lawyers who are considering getting involved in professional organisations is do it: go to a conference and actively network, write an article, organise or speak on a panel, volunteer to update a regulatory comment or casebook – and see where the opportunities lead.

During your tenure at American Express you were a key adviser to the litigation team overseeing civil enforcement actions brought by antitrust authorities, as well as civil litigation brought by private plaintiffs. In your experience, what characteristics do you believe make for an effective outside antitrust counsel and expert team when it comes to tackling competition issues?

One of the most important attributes of a successful outside antitrust team, whether on a bet-the-company litigation or an everyday counselling matter, is the willingness to truly listen to and learn from the business – to take the time to understand the challenges and opportunities facing management, the pressures driving salespeople and the nuances of competition in the industry. Without that deep understanding (and the humility to seek it), outside advisers risk proposing legal strategies that are misguided, ineffective or even ignored. By contrast, outside counsel and experts who have taken the time to truly understand the business can quickly become invaluable partners and advocates, both inside the company and to the outside world.

As in-house antitrust counsel, what would you identify as the most pressing question or topic in antitrust today and why?

In today's political and social environment, antitrust is no longer the exclusive province of obscure, nerdy lawyers and economists – the topic is regularly on the news, and everyone from presidential candidates to my young adult kids seems to have an opinion about what antitrust law is and ought to be. For actual practitioners, the most pressing question is how best to advise in a world of inherent uncertainty – trying to anticipate whether, how and how quickly antitrust enforcement and even legislation may change over the short- and medium-term. More immediately, as leadership of US and international agencies and state Attorney Generals have made clear, we need to be prepared for continued focus on the tech (and tech platform) space; heightened emphasis on the competitive aspects of data acquisition, ownership and usage; and renewed attention to competitive effects outside of price (quality, output, innovation).

Part III
Lawyers

Rachel Brandenburger

Hogan Lovells / University of Oxford

Kelig Bloret-Dupuis

Rachel Brandenburger is recognised globally as a leader in her field. With over 30 years' experience in private practice and government, she provides strategic advice to the boards and senior executives of major US, European and global companies on international antitrust and competition law, foreign investment and trade issues. She is currently a senior adviser and foreign legal consultant to Hogan Lovells US LLP, based in New York. She was Special Adviser, International to the US Department of Justice's Antitrust Division, based in Washington, DC from 2010 to 2013 and a partner in Freshfields Bruckhaus Deringer based in Brussels and London from 1988 to 2009. She is also a visiting research fellow at the University of Oxford's Institute of European & Comparative Law where she has created and teaches seminars on the global dimension of competition law.

Kelig Bloret-Dupuis is the head of competition and consumers legal department for Essilor International. Having joined in 2015 to set up and lead the competition legal department, she dedicated over 18 months to the merger review process of the combination between Essilor and Luxottica and is still involved in major merger reviews at European and international levels. She started her career in 2000 as competition legal counsel at Thales. She joined Orange Competition and Telecommunications Legal Department in 2005, where she was appointed head of legal competition matters on retail markets in 2010. She is also associate professor of competition law at the University of Rennes 1.

How did you come to competition law? What attracted you at the beginning?

When I am asked that question, I think people expect me to say something like, "I have always wanted to be a competition lawyer and when I joined Freshfields as a trainee, my plan was to become a competition lawyer". Nothing could be further from the truth in my case. I joined Freshfields as a trainee (or articled clerk as we were called then) because I wanted to learn to be a practising lawyer in one of the very best firms in London. I was delighted to qualify into the corporate department because it was one of the firm's main departments. (The firm did not have a standalone competition law group then.) My first competition law project came along about two years after I qualified. The firm was handling a large UK and European competition law case in the sugar industry. More resources were needed, and I was asked to join the team as a junior associate in the London office. Freshfields did not have an office in Brussels in those days. Fast-forward three years, the case had concluded successfully, and I had learned a lot about practising competition law in front of the UK and European agencies and courts – and also about the sugar industry. So it was an unexpected opportunity that took me into practising competition law, and it has brought me more opportunities throughout my career than I could have ever imagined and absolutely no regrets.

I think this illustrates how important it is to seize opportunities – even if you feel unprepared for them – because you never know what they will lead to. I took a similar decision when, as a junior partner in Freshfields in London in the mid-1990s, I agreed to move to Brussels with the aim of expanding the firm's then-new office there. That move felt very risky to me at the time – I had just about established myself as a junior partner in the firm's main office – in London – and I was being asked to move to help to develop what was in effect a start-up operation in Brussels. If I am honest – although I, of course, wanted to support the firm's strategy – I was reluctant to move. In fact, that move turned out to be a great opportunity – it opened up possibilities for the firm and for me. I was heavily involved in developing the Brussels office from a very small practice when I first arrived into one of the leading competition law practices in Brussels when I left the firm 14 years later to move to Washington DC. My practice and client base became truly global and I gained insights into how the European Commission and other European institutions work that I would never have had if I had remained in London.

Compared with Europe, it is more frequent in the US to see private practitioners spending a few years working for the Department of Justice (DoJ) or the Federal Trade Commission (FTC). You had the chance to have such opportunity. Has it changed or impacted the way you address a case or advise clients?

Continuing the theme of seizing opportunities, I moved to Washington DC at the start of 2010 to take up an opportunity that I never would have dreamed would have come my way. This was when I was asked by President Obama's newly appointed Assistant Attorney General for Antitrust at the US DoJ, Christine Varney, to become Special Adviser, International to the Antitrust Division (DoJ Special Advisor, International). That time, although the move was much bigger in many ways than my move to Brussels had been, I said yes much more quickly.

Being DoJ Special Adviser, International was a true highlight of my career. I advised on many Antitrust Division investigations that involved extensive cooperation between the Antitrust Division and other antitrust agencies around the world that were investigating the same matters. Among the investigations where the international cooperation has been publicly recognised are the *Deutsche Boerse/NYSE* transaction, the *United Technologies Corporation/Goodrich Corporation* merger, and the *Apple e-books* case. The latter was particularly interesting as it was a civil conduct case and demonstrated that international cooperation can be effective in that enforcement area as well as in the mergers and cartels areas. I also advised the Antitrust Division on other aspects of its work, including revised best practices on cooperation in merger investigations between the DoJ, FTC, and the European Commission that were issued in 2011 on the 20th anniversary of the cooperation agreement between the US antitrust agencies and the European Commission, a Memorandum of Understanding (MOU) that the DoJ, FTC and the (then) three Chinese antimonopoly agencies signed in 2011, and an MOU that the DoJ, FTC, the Indian Ministry of Corporate Affairs and the Competition Commission of India signed in 2012. The Antitrust Division is also involved in multinational organisations like the Organisation for Economic Co-operation and Development (OECD) and the International Competition Network (ICN), including, during the period I was DoJ Special Adviser, International, an OECD project on procedural fairness and a joint OECD/ICN project on international enforcement cooperation. It was a great privilege and honour to advise the Antitrust Division on such wide-ranging aspects of its cooperation initiatives with counterparts around the world.

As to what I learned or how my time as DoJ Special Adviser, International has impacted how I now practise competition law, the answer is a great deal. Indeed, I sometimes think that I learned more in the three and a half years I spent in that role than I did in 30 years with Freshfields. That cannot be right, but it does illustrate how much I learned while I was in Washington DC. It is very valuable to understand the perspectives from both sides of the table. That does not mean that you are automatically supportive of the corporations that are being investigated when you are an agency or government official or that you are automatically supportive of the agency or government when you return to the private sector. But it does mean that you have a broader and deeper understanding of how investigations are carried out and how to conduct your cases most effectively.

In my case, there is also a direct connection between what I learned while I was DoJ Special Adviser, International and the seminars on the global dimension of competition law that I have created and now teach at Oxford University, where I am a visiting research fellow at the Institute of European and Comparative Law and a visiting law fellow at St Hilda's College. Spending time teaching the students, who come from all around the world, and helping them launch their careers in competition law – whether as an academic, a government official or in the private sector – is very stimulating and enjoyable.

What are the two or three cases of special importance in your career?

That is a completely impossible question for me to answer. I do not even know how many cases I have done over my career to date, whether in private practice or as DoJ Special Adviser, International. My cases have involved many different corporations and business sectors. They have included mergers, cartels and conduct/abuse of dominance cases. And they have brought me opportunities to work with many highly professional and skilled people.

Also, I cannot talk about many of my cases – both those I have done while in the private sector and those on which I advised when I was DoJ Special Adviser, International because many of them – especially the non-merger cases – are not public.

Having said all that, here is my answer to your question. Three of the investigations where I advised on international cooperation when I was DoJ Special Adviser, International are public, as is my involvement in them. I have named them in reply to one of your earlier questions. They are the *Deutsche Boerse/NYSE* transaction, the *United Technologies Corporation/ Goodrich Corporation* merger, and the *Apple e-books* case. As I have already explained, the *Apple e-books* case was particularly interesting as it was a civil conduct case and demonstrated that international cooperation can be effective in that enforcement area as well as in the mergers and cartels areas. The *United Technologies/Goodrich Corporation* merger involved the same aerospace sector as the *GE/Honeywell* merger – but, unlike in the *GE/Honeywell* case, the DoJ and European Commission worked closely together throughout their investigations and came to very similar outcomes and settlements that were announced almost simultaneously on both sides of the Atlantic. The Canadian Competition Bureau was also closely involved in that international cooperation. The *Deutsche Boerse/NYSE* transaction shows that, even with close international cooperation, antitrust agencies may not always reach the same conclusions. In that case, the DoJ was prepared to approve the transaction with a small divestment requirement whereas the European Commission prohibited the transaction. This was because the market structures and the regulatory environments in the USA and Europe were significantly different.

With regard to the many cases I have advised on in the private sector, both as a partner in Freshfields Bruckhaus Deringer for over 20 years and more recently as a senior adviser and foreign legal consultant to Hogan Lovells US LLP, I am going to mention IBM's acquisition of Red Hat not necessarily as a favourite case but because it is a recent (merger) case where I worked with the Hogan Lovells global antitrust team. The acquisition was signed on 28 October 2018 and closed barely eight and a half months later on 9 July 2019. IBM believes that its landmark acquisition of Red Hat will redefine the cloud business by offering a next-generation hybrid multi-cloud platform to clients. The antitrust team and I worked together to secure unconditional approvals from the DoJ, the European Commission and several other agencies around the world to enable IBM to close the acquisition on a very challenging timeline.

What would you recommend today to a student asking for an advice to become a competition lawyer: should they enrich their skills with computer coding? Or should they first try in-house practice before becoming a lawyer in private practice?

The legal field has changed greatly since I began my career. As I have said, I spent over 30 years in one firm. I joined Freshfields as a trainee and, when I left to move to Washington, DC, I was one of the most senior partners in the firm's competition practice. Thirty years is a long time. Such a single firm focus is not usually the pattern for lawyers' careers these days – or indeed for anyone's career. Today, there are very many different opportunities for lawyers, including competition lawyers, both within and beyond the field of law. Like the rest of the world, lawyers increasingly have a number of different jobs during their careers.

A lawyer may begin their career in private practice and then move in-house to work for a company or into government or elsewhere in the public sector. They may also return to the private sector later in their careers – or vice-versa. There are also opportunities for secondments from private practice to a corporate position or, in some jurisdictions, to a government agency for a period of time. There are also opportunities to work abroad outside one's home jurisdiction. These different opportunities help us to grow and learn and make us better able to advise our clients, whoever or wherever our clients are.

Lawyers can also decide to leave the legal sector and do something entirely different. A legal training gives you skills for analysing and discussing issues and communicating effectively – and these are essential whatever field you end up in.

There is one more aspect that I will tack on to this answer although you have not specifically asked me about it. That is the importance of having good mentors and sponsors during your career. You need to have people you can trust as sounding boards, people who will give you (constructive) advice and feedback, and people who will help you to promote yourself effectively. Building a career over the years is not a one-person operation, especially at critical stages in a career. Nor are careers without their challenges and setbacks – mine certainly has not been. In the good and the more difficult times, I have been very fortunate to have had a number of wonderful mentors and sponsors, men and women, inside and outside the legal profession. If appropriate mentors and sponsors do not automatically come your way, I advise you to go out and find some and ask them if they are willing to take on the roles. These days, seeing the people I mentor or sponsor develop, flourish, gain in confidence and establish their own satisfying and fulfilling careers is one of the best aspects of what I do.

On international cooperation between authorities, many multilateral and bilateral initiatives exist. What should the focus of those discussions be from your perspective: procedure, workshops or digital tools?

As you will have gathered from what I have already said, international cooperation includes everything you have mentioned and much more. As you say, there are very many initiatives on international cooperation. They include bilateral relations between jurisdictions – jurisdictions that have had discussions and worked together for many years such as the US and the European Commission, the US and Canada, and the US and Japan, as well as newer competition law jurisdictions such as China, India and many others. They also include multilateral organisations such as the OECD, the ICN, and UNCTAD (United Nations Conference on Trade and Development). Cooperation also occurs at a regional level. The longest-established regional organisation is, of course, between the Member States of the European Union, including through the European Competition Network. Newer regional organisations include the Common Market for Southern and Eastern Africa (COMESA) and the Association of Southeast Asian Nations (ASEAN), and others that are developing their own cooperation frameworks.

These organisations cover the entire waterfront of competition law, policy and enforcement and focus on substantive as well as procedural issues in relation to mergers, cartels and conduct/abuse of dominance. Of course, within those broad areas, there is also focus on particularly topical issues. Currently those include procedural fairness and transparency issues (a focus of the OECD and ICN in particular) and many aspects of the digital economy and its impact on competition law, policy and enforcement.

If you were asked to identify one fundamental evolution in the practice of European competition law in the last 20 years or so since 2000, what would say?

I think there have been at least two fundamental evolutions in the practice of European competition law in the last 20 years. One is the globalisation of businesses and competition laws and the proliferation of competition regimes and agencies around the world (140 agencies in 129 jurisdictions at this point in time). This has certainly impacted how corporations do business and how they interact with the competition agencies around the world, as well as how the agencies around the world cooperate with each other.

The other fundamental evolution in the practice of European competition law is the impact of, and inter-relationship with, economics. Since European competition commissioner Mario Monto established the position of chief economist in 2003, after the European Commission had seen three of its merger prohibition decisions overturned by the Court, economics has become an increasingly significant factor in European Commission investigations. As a result, it has become increasingly important for European competition lawyers to understand and be conversant with economics as well as law to be truly effective in their field.

You have not asked this question, but let me ask what I expect the future to bring. I expect economics to continue to play an important role in European competition law. As to globalisation, we are told we now live in a post-globalised world. What that means for the practice of European competition law – or indeed competition law around the world – is unclear at this stage. It is a topic I am thinking about and will be discussing with the Oxford University students when I teach my seminars again next year.

Some European countries are examining the possibility, at national or European level, of introducing post-closing merger control when thresholds are not met. If such an evolution is adopted, how could companies get prepared and prepare their management for such a post-closing control?

I would advise competition agencies to think carefully before changing their laws to enable them to "call in" mergers that fall below the thresholds of their merger regimes. Some jurisdictions – including the US – do have such powers, but I would caution against a global burgeoning of such powers. I do so not only with my private sector hat on, but also from the perspective of agency officials. From a business point of view, there may be uncertainty over how considerable the risk of a deal below the thresholds being called in is and over what period of time that risk lasts. At the least, agencies should provide clear guidance on the circumstances in which they would use such powers. From an agency's perspective, resources need to be devoted to the greatest priorities. Because of their (usually) fixed review timelines, investigations of mergers that meet the thresholds tend to have to take precedence over other (especially conduct/abuse of dominance) investigations. So an important question is: how would investigations of "called-in" mergers fit into an agency's deployment of its (also usually) stretched resources?

On a EU/US merger control comparison, when I started to work I had the great opportunity to participate in the *GE/Honeywell* case (approved by the DoJ but prohibited by the European Commission). At that time, many comments pointed out the differences between the two regimes regarding short-term versus long-term competitive assessment, as well as protection of consumers versus protection of competitors. Times have changed, and we now see some efforts of both authorities to work on similar remedies when addressing the same theories of harm. Do you consider that such "alignment" is limited to a few cases and to merger control, or do you have the impression that convergence also exists in relation to anticompetitive practices?

Thank you for this question. It raises a number of important issues. I am not going to go back and dissect how or why the DoJ and the European Commission came to divergent decisions in the *GE/Honeywell* case – or, to add another case, how the FTC and European Commission diverged in their decisions in relation to the *Boeing/McDonnell Douglas* merger. The decisions were taken some 20 years ago, and a lot has changed since then.

I referred earlier to the close cooperation between the DoJ, European Commission and Canadian Competition Bureau in their investigations of the *UTC/Goodrich Corporation* merger and the convergent remedies settlements in that case. As I explained, that merger also occurred in the aerospace sector – and the outcome was very different from the outcome of *GE/Honeywell*.

It is important to keep in mind that convergence and cooperation are not the same thing. There can be very good cooperation between agencies investigating the same matter but the outcomes may be different because the competitive landscapes in the jurisdictions are different. That is why the DoJ and European Commission reached different conclusions in, for example, the *Deutsche Boerse/NYSE* transaction I mentioned earlier.

There can also be differences in the competition laws, policies and enforcement priorities in different jurisdictions. These differences may be the reasons for different outcomes. This is often said to be the reason why there is less international cooperation between agencies investigating conduct/abuse of dominance cases than there is in relation to merger or cartel investigations. I think the explanation is more complicated than that. There are other differences as well as the underlying laws. For example, conduct/abuse of dominance investigations do not have a clear trigger point at the start of the investigation in the way merger and cartel investigations usually do – the merger filing or the dawn raid search – and so the timelines of different agencies' conduct/abuse of dominance investigations may be too far apart for effective cooperation. Also, corporations subject to conduct/abuse of dominance investigations do not necessarily have the same incentives to cooperate with the agencies and, for example, provide confidentiality waivers as parties to merger investigations or leniency applications in cartel investigations may have.

It is difficult to end the interview without talking about the digital economy. In many conferences, public and private practitioners call on economists to find new tools to adjust the assessment of digital market structure and most importantly to assess real and/or potential effects of some practices on the market. But, it sounds like not much has come out of such discussions. Do you think that economics will be what shows the way to better analyse competition practices in the digital markets? Or do you think that the leadership will come from the political arena (like imposing new regulations on GAFA (Google, Amazon, Facebook, Apple))?

This is, of course, a very important question. Indeed, a day does not go by without there being media reports about the issues surrounding the enforcement of competition law in, and the regulation of, the digital economy. These issues brought antitrust to the forefront of the Democratic presidential candidate debates in the US earlier this year in a way that has not occurred since "trust-busting" Theodore Roosevelt's presidential campaign in the early 20th century.

Briefly, I would highlight four aspects of the questions you have posed. First, the concerns that have been raised about the digital economy go well beyond antitrust and competition law issues and how to measure and assess market power. They are very wide-ranging and include privacy, data protection, consumer protection, advertising and taxation issues, as well as concerns about digital addiction, freedom of speech, fake news and the impact on election voting.

Second, where antitrust fits into this spectrum of concerns and whether antitrust should be looked at in isolation from, or in conjunction with, the other issues and remedies is a very important aspect of this debate. That, in my view, is also the context in which to discuss whether there is a role for regulation as well as enforcement.

Third, the political arena, which is already an active player in this debate. Look for, example, at the congressional hearings in the US and the parliamentary select committee hearings in the UK to name only two examples.

Fourth, there have been many reports written, investigations conducted, and task forces set up, by antitrust and competition law agencies and other institutions around the world. In terms of coordination and cooperation between these various initiatives, it is noteworthy that, the report on digital platforms issued by the Australian Competition and Consumer Commission in June 2019, for example, lists several similar initiatives in the UK, USA and the EU and notes that "coordination across national borders is critical to address competition and consumer protection concerns that arise from the conduct of the leading digital platforms, given their global operations". This observation takes us back to one of the themes of this interview – international cooperation. It will be interesting to see how international cooperation develops as the various investigations, hearings and other initiatives in relation to the digital economy multiply and seek to deliver results.

Deborah Feinstein
Arnold & Porter

Leonor Davila

Deborah Feinstein heads Arnold & Porter's global antitrust group. From 2013 to 2017, she was director of the Bureau of Competition. She had previously served at the Federal Trade Commission (FTC) from 1989 to 1991 as Assistant to the Director of the Bureau of Competition and an Attorney Adviser. She attended Harvard Law School and the University of California at Berkeley. After graduation, she was an associate at Arnold & Porter from 1987 to 1989, and from 1991 to 1995. Later, as a partner, she led the firm's US Antitrust group from 2010 to 2013. Throughout her career, Ms Feinstein has focused on merger and acquisition reviews by antitrust enforcement agencies in the United States and globally, as well as civil investigations and litigation. Her industry experience is broad, and includes retail, food, consumer products, healthcare, chemicals and automotive parts, among others. Ms Feinstein has been consistently lauded as a leading practitioner by *Chambers USA* and other ranking publications.

Leonor Davila is an Associate Director in the Ethics and Legal Compliance Group at Intel Corporation. She specialises in antitrust and anticorruption compliance issues. Prior to joining Intel, Leonor spent most of her career at the Federal Trade Commission (FTC) where she investigated mergers and acquisitions and provided technical assistance to competition agencies around the world. She is a non-governmental adviser to the International Competition Network. She has co-authored several antitrust articles, including articles focused on antitrust compliance programs. In 2019, the Women Competition Professionals recognised Leonor as a top-40 competition professional in the Americas. Leonor has a JD/MA from the George Washington University and a BA from UC San Diego.

Describe your career to our readers, including how you became the chair of the global antitrust practice at Arnold & Porter and why you became an antitrust lawyer.

I became an antitrust lawyer by accident. I had taken Professor Areeda's antitrust class in law school, but he was the only professor who insisted on closed-book exams after the first year. So I walked out of that exam pretty sure I wasn't going to be an antitrust lawyer! But somehow I survived that experience and ended up working on a merger as a summer associate at Arnold & Porter and loved it. One thing led to another and I ended up becoming an antitrust lawyer upon my return to the firm after law school.

Bill Baer was the global head of the firm's antitrust practice when he left to become assistant attorney general in 2013. A few years earlier, Bill had asked me to head the US practice, which I did until I left for the FTC later that year. When I came back to the firm, Bill (who had also returned from government) graciously handed me the reins of the global practice.

You have held several prominent positions in your career, including director of the Bureau of Competition at the Federal Trade Commission (FTC) and now chair of the global antitrust practice at Arnold & Porter: what has been your biggest driver? What inspires you?

I'm lucky to just really love the work. I get to interact with businesspeople and economists as much as I do other lawyers. The antitrust bar is incredibly collegial – we work with each other time and again so we all become friends. Every day I am either learning about new industries or building on my experience from matters in the same industries, and it is fascinating. At the FTC, there were so many different cases that I was like a kid in a candy store – I wanted to be involved even a little bit in every case if I could be!

You have an impressive résumé that includes both public and private sector experience. What were some of the challenges you experienced during the transition from private to public and vice versa?

I first moved from private practice to the FTC only two years out of law school and found myself playing a very different role as assistant to the director of the Bureau of Competition than I had been as a new associate. I was no longer the junior lawyer in the weeds on cases, and I missed rolling up my sleeves and being the one expected to know all the facts. So it was easy to transition back to private practice after two years at the FTC.

When I went back as bureau director, I didn't find thinking about being the enforcer instead of the defence lawyer all that different. Most of my time in private practice was spent thinking about what the agency would do and advising my client accordingly. The challenge was figuring out the role, since there's no clear job description. I found I liked working with the case teams day-to-day, especially when we were in litigation. So to the extent possible, I just did that – even taking and defending depositions a few times when the team was short-handed.

You have been an antitrust lawyer for several years, and you have probably observed developments and trends with regards to antitrust hot topics, for example big data, vertical mergers, and reverse payments. What have been some of the most interesting developments you have observed?

Market entry is one example. The shift in where innovation is expected to come from has been fun to watch. I've joked that when I started practicing law, every defence was "the Chinese firms are coming", then it was "the Japanese firms", then "Wal-Mart will enter" (there were a lot of retail details) and now the argument is that FAANG can enter.

The reality is that many of these issues have been around for some time. For instance, some forget that the landmark 1962 Supreme Court decision in *Brown Shoe* involved a vertical merger. Likewise, data has been a factor in many merger cases over the years. The biggest development I have seen has been the proliferation of information. We now produce volumes of documents and data files of a size unimaginable when the first second requests were issued. And the massive amounts of data allows economists to develop new tools and provide increasingly sophisticated analyses.

Labour monopsony issues continue to be a hot topic in the USA through state enforcement, proposed legislation and statements coming out of the Department of Justice's (DOJ's) Antitrust Division, is there a potential this interest will spread to other jurisdictions? Are effects on workers likely to become a relevant factor in antitrust analysis?

They already have in the sense that both agencies are asking questions routinely about the effect of mergers on labour issues. Bruce Hoffman, former director of the FTC Bureau of Competition, testified to Congress last year that he had instructed FTC staff to examine the potential labour market effects of all proposed mergers. Mostly recently, the DOJ testified to Congress that it will require parties to produce documents that shed light on whether proposed transactions will harm workers.

But I think caution is in order. There is clear space between the potential for a true monopsony impact on a specific labour market due to a transaction, which is at best unlikely in virtually all mergers, and determining that a merger may have an adverse impact on employment because the merged firm may terminate employees for efficiency reasons, or may move jobs to another country. Antitrust laws are not well suited for that sort of merger outcome, unrelated to a lessening of competition. As Robert Pitofsky wrote: "Non-economic concerns play no useful role because it is not possible to achieve those goals to any significant extent through antitrust interpretation." Similarly, an FTC/DOJ OECD paper from

October 2015 explained why employment and other non-competition factors do not play a role in the analysis the US antitrust agencies undertake.

With the recent wave of discussions focused on digital platforms, data, and privacy have come expressions of doubt about whether US antitrust laws can "keep up" with industry changes, what are your thoughts?

Antitrust law has continuously evolved as necessary to deal with a multitude of new market realities and business practices. The multi-year fight over the legality of reverse patent settlements is a prime example of how antitrust can deal with the advent of novel business practices caused by a changing regulatory framework. I'm struck by the fact that antitrust lawyers across the aisle almost universally say that the antitrust laws have been and continue to be sufficient to deal with a changing economy.

You represented AT&T in its successful US$85.4 billion acquisition of Time Warner, which was challenged by the DOJ. What does *AT&T/Time Warner* mean for companies considering vertical acquisitions?

The decision in *AT&T* makes clear that facts matter. Can there be a vertical merger that harms competition? There could be. But vertical mergers have an inherent procompetitive impact, as the empirical literature has shown. The economist for the DOJ acknowledged that one impact of the merger would be a downward pressure on prices because of the elimination of double marginalisation. The debate was about whether any upward pressure existed and how it compared with the downward pressure. And in that case, the evidence showed that the transaction would benefit – rather than harm – consumers.

During your most recent four-year tenure at the FTC, the agency experienced several major merger wins, including in the retail space, such as Staples' merger with Office Depot, where market definition is often a critical issue. What advice do you have for companies that may be thinking about acquisitions but are facing a complex market?

One of the big issues I saw was that the business person view of the market was so different from the legal view of product market. Business people think about the "addressable market" – all the customers they could be selling to, whereas antitrust law thinks about the current customers and what they would do in the face of a price increase. It was true that some customers bought from small companies – in the case of Staples – or that some customers bought from regional players in the *Sysco/US Foods* matter. But that did not account for the customers that had specific needs; thus the "market" for them consisted of different players. Having clients consider a merger's impact on the customers it has, rather than on the whole universe of customers, may assist them in making a proper risk assessment of a transaction.

During your time at Arnold & Porter you worked on the Loews Cineplex Entertainment Corporation merger with AMC Entertainment a complex merger that was resolved with the DOJ and various state attorneys general by the divestiture of 10 theatres. What is your advice to companies facing antitrust review from multiple enforcers at the same time? How were you able to arrive at a settlement that all enforcers could agree on?

The key in working with multiple enforcers is to make sure you are communicating consistently with them – where appropriate. It's important to note that not all mergers lend themselves to coordination across agencies. In *Unilever/Alberto Culver*, the case involved the combination of VO5 with Unilever's shampoo products in both Europe and the US. But there was a big difference. In the US VO5 was a value brand, whereas in the UK at the time, it was a premium brand. So the facts were very different and we needed to explain that to both DOJ and the European agencies reviewing the transaction, so that they realised they didn't actually need to coordinate on the facts as they were so different.

In other cases the fact and issues were identical and we went so far as to routinely have joint calls with the FTC and the EC staff investigating the merger. In the *GE/Avio* matter, we had joint videoconferences with both the case teams and lawyers from all parties present to make sure everyone was hearing the facts consistently – and to allow for efficiency in making business people available to both agencies.

It is often easy to make sure the FTC or DOJ is coordinated with state attorney general offices, because federal and state antitrust enforcers talk routinely. Making sure to copy the states on submissions to the FTC or DOJ, rather than making them always ask, is just one way to make sure state antitrust staff are in a position to ask a question early if they depart from the FTC or DOJ.

In October 2018 you taught a course on advanced mergers economics at the ABA Antitrust Master's course. What is "advanced merger economics"? Why is economic analysis important to an effects-based antitrust framework? Do you have any advice for young agencies with limited experience and resources on how best to apply economic analysis in their work?

Well for me, anything more than calculating HHIs can seem advanced at times! But seriously, thinking about how to use bid data, regressions, and other forms of economic modelling to demonstrate harm or the lack thereof has become increasingly important as the data available for economists to work with has grown. For young agencies, I would say that it's critical to have not only lawyers but economists involved in cases. Shortly after I returned to the FTC, the Bureau of Economics moved into the building I worked in – where the lawyers were several blocks away. Having dozens of PhD economists just down the hall was a true luxury – and I took advantage of it, regularly diverting an economist walking down the hall to come into my office for a minute to explain something to me.

What is your perspective on mentoring and how does it fit into your career?

I have been extremely lucky to have great mentors – both men and women – throughout my career. A very important aspect of being a senior lawyer is the opportunity and obligation to help more junior lawyers learn how to do their jobs better and grow as professionals. That kind of day-to-day mentoring is something I benefited from and try to pass on to others. Mentoring includes helping other lawyers figure out how to progress their careers in a fulfilling way – and I am happy to pass on whatever thoughts I have on that score as well.

What advice would you give to junior female attorneys as they think about moving forward in their careers?

The same advice I would give anyone. First, always do your best job on everything. Assume you are the last person who will look at something before it goes to the client, agency or court. Second, take initiative. Step in if something needs to be done. If you want the next opportunity, ask for it. Third, figure out what you like to do *and* are good at. I've seen plenty of good lawyers who are unhappy and you just won't do your best work if you are miserable doing it. But conversely, if you are just not suited to something and that is the message you are getting, maybe it's time to slightly tweak what you want to do and find that thing that comes naturally.

What has been one of your proudest moments in your career?

Playing a small role in the various litigation successes we had at the FTC. The teamwork at the FTC is incredible and everyone works so hard to fulfil the agency's mission every day. Having the opportunity to help lead the Bureau to so many great outcomes for consumers was a true privilege. Most recently, a proud moment was playing a role for AT&T in its defence of its TimeWarner transaction – working with experts, conducing mock cross-examinations and being one of many to help prepare for the appellate argument. AT&T had created a virtual law firm of the lawyers it had chosen from the various law firms with which it works. Everyone checked his or her ego at the door and collaborated as if we had all been working together for years, making it a truly special experience.

Deborah Garza
Covington & Burling
Fiona Schaeffer

Deborah Garza has been a trusted adviser to clients on strategic transactions, civil investigations, criminal investigations and litigation. Currently Senior Counsel at Covington & Burling, she has served as an acting assistant attorney general, deputy assistant attorney general and chief of staff and counsellor to the assistant attorney general in three presidential administrations. She chaired the Antitrust Modernization Commission, a bipartisan blue ribbon commission created by Congress to advise Congress and the president on the state of US antitrust law enforcement, and co-chaired the International Competition Policy Expert Group, which presented recommendations on international competition policy to the in-coming Congress and President in 2016. Ms Garza chaired the Antitrust Section of the American Bar Association 2018–2019 and has served in the leadership of the Corporations, Securities, and Antitrust Committee of the Federalist Society.

Fiona Schaeffer is an international antitrust lawyer with over 25 years of experience practicing on both sides of the Atlantic. Clients entrust Ms. Schaeffer with the defense of "bet-the-company" criminal and civil cases as well as their most complex transactions. She counsels clients in a variety of industries, with a particular depth of experience in healthcare, financial services, energy, media and communications. Ms. Schaeffer regularly represents clients in FTC and DOJ investigations and follow on class actions in the US and internationally. She also counsels clients on optimizing intellectual property rights and licensing, distribution and marketing practices without creating unnecessary legal risks. Ms. Schaeffer began her legal career in the UK, and has appeared before courts and regulators throughout the EU as well as other significant antitrust enforcement agencies around the world.

You have always been a strong advocate for increasing diversity in the profession and giving women and other minorities opportunities to succeed. What more can we be doing to achieve the goal of greater diversity in the antitrust bar and the legal profession more generally? What would success look like to you?

Those are important questions, Fiona. Ultimately, I think individual, one-to-one, personal actions by enough of us will make the difference.

As chair of the Section, in addition to talking about inclusion in leadership meetings, I reached out to members of the Section to come into the leadership, and in two instances reached out to lawyers who were not already Section members. I am confident that this kind of effort within the Section will continue. In addition, my last responsibility as a former Section chair is to chair the Section's Nominating Committee, which recommends candidates to the highest levels of Section leadership. My colleagues on the Nominating Committee share a personal commitment to diversity, and I look forward to proposing an inclusive slate, reflecting the diversity of our membership.

In my private practice, I made a point of assembling inclusive teams on matters, which was very easy to do at Covington. In some cases that meant reaching out to young lawyers with whom I had not previously worked. They revealed themselves to be superstars.

While at Fried Frank, I instigated and helped our terrific attorney development group to develop something we called the Diversity Network, collaborating with Arnold & Porter and other DC firms. The object was to provide networking opportunities for attorneys of colour in the region. These were social networking opportunities at which prominent members of the bar spoke about their experiences. Debra Lee (former chair and CEO of BET) was our inaugural speaker. The last event I attended before re-joining the Justice Department in 2007 was the largest, drawing attorneys from as far away as Delaware and Pennsylvania. At Fried Frank, we also focused on reaching out to high school juniors and seniors of colour, offering internships at the firm and assistance with applying and preparing for college.

The antitrust bar has made a lot of gender progress since I began practicing law in 1981. I can no longer count on one or two hands the number of women practicing antitrust outside of government, and more than half of my in-house counsel clients have been women. I hope we can see an increase across other dimensions of diversity as well.

What will success look like? Representative rooms and fewer exclamations of surprise at all-female or all – of colour teams are a start. But we can never rest. Decades of hard work and progress can backslide overnight. Enduring change will take a broad, cultural change and consensus that I am afraid we don't yet have. Ultimately, each one of us has to make a personal commitment.

You served as chair of the Antitrust Modernization Commission (AMC), a bipartisan body created to study and report to Congress and the president on issues relating to the modernisation of antitrust laws. When the AMC issued its report in 2007, it concluded that no new or different rules were needed to address the so-called "new economy" issues. Do you believe that conclusion still holds today? Is it time to convene another AMC to examine whether antitrust laws remain up to the task of ensuring effective competition in a digital economy?

I think it *is* a good idea to convene another AMC, with a more narrow focus and perhaps for a shorter life (say, two years instead of three, or three years with interim reports). The primary value of the AMC was its bipartisan approach and our success in replacing heat with light in important areas, even where there wasn't complete consensus. I have found the report and recommendations – as well as the separate Commissioner statements – to be as relevant today as they were in 2007. (I have cited to the AMC report extensively in recent testimony to Congress.) But there is definitely room to re-examine and expand on the report as it pertains to issues that policymakers are considering today. I am particularly thinking of pending legislative proposals and calls to try to use antitrust laws to address issues related to labour and social justice. There is a big push right now to turn the clock back to a "big is bad" era and to try to engineer marketplaces. I think that is a big mistake that will only have to be undone later and in the meantime will perversely hurt economic growth and general welfare. Congress has held hearings that are helpful to public discussion, but I think another bipartisan experts' panel with the right composition could add substantial value.

You previously chaired the Antitrust Section of the American Bar Association. You also are a member of and have served in the leadership of the Corporations, Securities, and Antitrust Committee of the Federalist Society. What role do you think organisations such as these play in developing the antitrust bar, particularly for women interested in the area?

Professional organisations like the Federalist Society and the Section of Antitrust Law of the ABA contribute importantly to the quality of the bar and to influencing shaping law and policy.

The Federalist Society has a conservative and libertarian viewpoint with which I agree. In the process of promoting awareness of those principles and seeking to further their application, the Federalist Society does a tremendous job sponsoring high-quality, fair, open and serious debate on important issues, with never just one point of view represented. I highly recommend Federalist Society videos, publications and podcasts (e.g., the Regulatory Transparency Project's Fourth Branch podcast), which among other things do a great job of fairly explaining complex regulatory and antitrust issues to non-antitrust experts.

The Antitrust Section of the ABA does a fantastic job of educating the bar and promoting sound competition policy. The quality of the content is consistently excellent, from comments submitted to competition authorities around the globe on enforcement policy to publications and programmes. Members approach the work of the Section with the same level of dedication they give to their client and academic work, which is really amazing given the demanding nature of antitrust practice today.

These organisations are also great on an individual level for networking and other opportunities. Many of the relationships I have formed over the course of my career come out of participating in the Antitrust Section: of course, that is how you and I met, Fiona. Whether or not we ever get to have that barbecue, having had the chance to work alongside you and other Section members has enriched my life.

Participating in bar associations expands professional and personal relationships and can open doors and lead to opportunities you would not otherwise have known were there. Importantly for younger lawyers, I think participation in a bar association can facilitate owning your career; it can be a source of empowerment. One could argue that networking outside the workplace is still particularly valuable to women. Indeed, according to an ABA study, female members in particular value the networking opportunities, which is not surprising. And, beyond networking, an association like the Antitrust Section of the ABA or the Federalist Society can be the source of publishing and speaking opportunities that provide more exposure and opportunity for women to shine their lights.

What are some of the most interesting matters you have worked on in your career and why do you think they were important?

The most interesting matters in which I have been involved are those focused on policy, including the AMC and the International Competition Policy Expert Group. ICPEG was a bipartisan group of competition and trade policy experts formed at the invitation of the US Chamber of Commerce ahead of the 2016 election, to advise the incoming Congress and president on matters of international competition and trade policy. Our report can be found at <https://www.uschamber.com/sites/default/files/icpeg_recommendations_and_report.pdf>. I co-chaired the group with Andrew Shoyer at Sidley Austin LLP. Other competition law experts in the group were Terry Calvani, Dennis Carlton, Eleanor Fox, Tad Lipsky, Doug Melamed, Jim Rill and Christine Varney. Quite a group, right?

Although efforts like the AMC and ICPEG don't always have a large, immediate impact, I think it is important to make the effort to step back occasionally to define our objectives and consider the best solution with a consensus-driven process outside the political boiler room. Ultimately, of course, a political decision has to be made, but these kinds of efforts can be a significant input.

We understand you are retiring? What have been the most rewarding aspects of your career? What are you looking forward to in the next chapter of your life?

I retired on 1 October, after very nearly 40 years of practice.

When I look back, I literally see the faces of so many remarkable people that have enriched my professional and personal life in many ways – friends, colleagues, mentors and acquaintances from private practice, the Justice Department, and professional organisations. I wish I could name every one of them; they are the unexpected treasure I didn't imagine when I started in the practice of law.

As for what happens post-retirement, I would like to use some of my new found time to engage in some kind of community service. I was never able to fully commit to community service while maintaining a busy law practice. Pre-COVID, I had very preliminary discussions about participating in an effort to promote access to higher education in the Washington DC Hispanic community and about assisting with a possible antitrust fellowship. Lately, I have been thinking about how I might contribute to the development of effective solutions to social justice issues. I am open to suggestions!

On a more personal level, some people know that I was initially planning to move my show to Nevis, where I own an acre of heaven looking out at the Caribbean sea on one side and a volcano on the other. This was not a popular decision with my family, and a few months ago I received an unsolicited offer to buy the land. After a lot of thought, Chris and I have agreed to sell Nevis and buy a farm in Virginia. We will not be as far away from the maddening crowds as I had hoped, but it will be easier to balance doing good deeds with a more restful retirement, and my family is happier.

What advice would you give law students and young lawyers who are interested in practicing in antitrust?

The most important advice is common to whatever area of law you chose. In my view, lawyers who are the most happy with their career are those who took ownership of it from the beginning. What I mean by that is, if you are at a law firm, not just waiting for what assignments you might get but building your expertise through continuing legal education and seeking out relationships with more experienced practitioners, academics and others in the field. Let partners and more senior lawyers know you want to take on an antitrust project, join a bar group, write, teach. There are so many ways that you can build your expertise and enhance the likelihood that you will have an opportunity to take on antitrust.

I got into antitrust after agreeing to work on an intense project while at Jones Day with Don Baker. Don had spent 10 years at the Antitrust Division, starting out as a trial lawyer and ending as the first (and only) career staffer to be named assistant attorney general (AAG). Don infected me with his passion for antitrust. When he left Jones Day for another firm, I moved to the Antitrust Division as a special assistant to then-AAG J Paul McGrath (replacing my friend and former University of Chicago classmate Rick Rule, who eventually himself became AAG).

My time at the Justice Department set me on my path. I have recommended government service, whether at the Federal Trade Commission or Justice Department, to a number of young lawyers with whom I have worked, and several are now thriving at those agencies!

Janet McDavid
Hogan Lovells

Maria Raptis

Janet McDavid is senior counsel in the antitrust practice of Hogan Lovells, Washington, DC. She has advised on many significant antitrust matters, including for IBM in its acquisition of Red Hat, Mobil Corporation in its merger with Exxon, Carnival Corporation in its acquisition of P&O Princess, and General Dynamics in its many defence industry transactions. She was both co-chair of the IBA Antitrust Committee and chair of the ABA Section of Antitrust Law. She is a non-governmental adviser to the ICN. She is the author of many antitrust books and articles. She advised the Obama, Bush, and Clinton transition teams for the Federal Trade Commission. She was a member of two Department of Defense antitrust task forces, which advised on antitrust issues involved in the defence industry.

Maria Raptis concentrates her practice on representing clients before the Federal Trade Commission (FTC) and Department of Justice. She has advised clients in a broad range of strategic transactions across multiple industries, including, health care and pharmaceuticals, technology, consumer products, entertainment and manufacturing. Ms. Raptis' litigation experience includes defending clients in connection with class actions and multidistrict litigations challenging patent settlements, pricing and other business policies, including Actavis in suits brought by the FTC and private plaintiffs relating to «reverse payment» settlements and De Beers in connection with national class actions involving gem diamonds and a criminal matter relating to industrial diamonds. Ms. Raptis holds a J.D. and B.A. from Columbia University.

A hot topic in antitrust law is whether consumer welfare is the right standard for antitrust law, in the face of what some perceive to be the growing influence of large firms. In fact, however, the adoption of the consumer welfare standard was in part motivated by a belief that antitrust policy had become too aggressive and that large companies were being attacked regardless of any impact on market conditions. Do you see a future where antitrust standards revert to early paradigms, or shift to cover other goals – such as workers' interests, privacy, small business, and innovation?

During most of my career, antitrust analysis has been grounded in fundamental principles and focused on consumer welfare. Contrary to the concerns expressed by some, prices are not the only touchstone in a consumer welfare analysis. Many of the matters I have handled also involved issues of innovation and quality that have been just as important as price, although somewhat more difficult to measure. The US antitrust agencies have done an excellent job identifying and addressing those issues. That makes it possible for advisers to tell clients where the antitrust lines are.

I am a progressive Democrat, so you might expect me to applaud populist antitrust theories. But I think that including populist antitrust concepts in antitrust analysis would make this task more difficult for everyone. Instead of well-established principles grounded in consumer welfare and sound economic theory, we would be applying amorphous concepts like "bigness" or "fairness", some of which turn traditional principles on their heads, such as condemning low prices that do not satisfy predatory pricing standards or punishing innovative companies for creating new products or services that enhance consumer welfare. This could return us to the era of *Von's Grocery*, where the dissent lamented that "the Court grounds its conclusion solely on the impressionistic assertion that the Los Angeles retail food industry is becoming 'concentrated' because the number of single-store concerns has declined". This led Justice Stewart to complain that "the sole consistency that I can find [in the antitrust laws] is that the government always wins". But even that is unlikely to be true in the amorphous world of populist antitrust because the antitrust agencies and private plaintiffs bear the burden of proof.

Where there are legitimate concerns about fairness and employment effects, those issues should be addressed under different regimes, as is done with the Committee on Foreign Investment in the US now, unless, as in the no-poach cases, there is a legitimate antitrust concern directly affecting employment. Antitrust is a well-calibrated tool to protect competition and maximise consumer welfare, but it is poorly suited to tackle other societal problems. We need to respect the limitations of antitrust.

Antitrust analysis that includes amorphous concepts of "bigness" and "fairness" also would more easily lend itself to politically motivated enforcement decisions, which we certainly should eschew, especially in the current political climate.

Vertical transactions are often described as more competitively benign than horizontal mergers, at least in the US, and yet one of the most highly publicised merger challenges in recent memory was the Department of Justice's (DOJ's) move to block *AT&T/ Time Warner*, the first vertical merger challenged in court in decades. And *Staples/Essendant*, a purely vertical deal, was only approved by a 3–2 vote at the Federal Trade Commission (FTC), with a minority of commissioners dissenting and expressing concern that vertical merger enforcement is not rigorous enough.

What accounts for the recent scepticism of vertical transactions in the US? Is it warranted?

I don't think there is greater scepticism of vertical transactions generally. Both US agencies recognise that most vertical transactions are either procompetitive or competitively benign. But there has been scepticism, especially at the Antitrust Division, about behavioural remedies in vertical transactions. I think that scepticism is misplaced because in my experience, most of the remedies imposed in vertical transactions with which I am familiar have been successful and can be accomplished without blocking the whole deal, as the Division sought to do in *AT&T*.

Notwithstanding DOJ's recent loss and the result at FTC, should we expect more challenges to vertical transactions in the near future?

The European Commission has also focused on transactions presenting conglomerate issues again recently, whereas US authorities continue to treat conglomerate theories with extreme caution. A recent example typifying the divergent approaches of the world's leading antitrust authorities would be the European Commission's in-depth investigation into *NXP/Qualcomm*, which the US authorities cleared without a second request.

Is there economic analysis supporting the EC's point of view?

I am not sufficiently experienced in EC conglomerate theory to opine on this issue.

What is your advice to clients trying to reconcile the EU and US approaches?

I always advise my clients that some deals or conduct may raise issues outside the US that are not serious issues in the US. For example, whereas we evaluate vertical restraints, including retail price main- tenance, under the rule of reason, that is not true in Europe, where such restraints are "byobject" and effectively per se illegal. One of the enormous advantages of working in a global law firm is that I have knowledgeable antitrust counsel in the EU and established relationships with experienced EU economic consultants, with whom I can consult on these issues.

US antitrust agencies have stepped up their scrutiny of, and standards for, remedies. A few short years after the FTC concluded that its remedies policy was generally successful and effective, Commissioner Simons recently took a more critical view and said, in effect, we should have a "zero tolerance" policy for failed remedies. The DOJ has renounced behavioural remedies and both agencies have sought greater concessions from parties seeking to clear their mergers (e.g. *Bayer/Monsanto* and *Praxair/Linde*). What should parties anticipate will change as they navigate any necessary remedies in their next deal?

Parties should expect strict scrutiny of remedies because the US agencies are appropriately taking the position that remedies must be both sufficient and effective. That is how we advise our clients.

Do you think there is still space for behavioural commitments in certain cases, or has the Antitrust Division drawn a hard line?

As noted above, I think behavioural remedies can be appropriate for vertical transactions, but they are not appropriate for horizontal deals.

The European Commission has suggested that privacy is an important parameter in competition, and some commentators in the US agree. Will the US embrace a similar approach? Should it?

I very much doubt that privacy will become an issue in US antitrust law, although it is a very real issue in the FTC Bureau of Consumer Protection. The US view is that online firms do not compete with respect to their data privacy policies and that in the absence of a competitive issue, privacy is not an antitrust issue.

What in your view are the main competitive concerns surrounding big data?

Big data has generally not been viewed as a major US antitrust issue. In my view, data is an asset, like other assets such as IP, and there can be antitrust issues with respect to an amalgamation of data, just as there can be with other assets. But that circumstance does seem common in the US.

What do you view as the most interesting emerging questions of antitrust law?

The biggest antitrust issues today in the US and globally involve whether we should continue to focus on consumer welfare or shift our focus to a broader set of issues, such as "big is bad". I never expected the rather arcane subject of antitrust law to be a hot button political issue in a presidential campaign. When Barack Obama's campaign included a brief reference to antitrust in 2008, that was regarded as extraordinary. Now, antitrust issues are debated almost every day by people running for president in the US.

Absent a change in US antitrust laws, there is unlikely to be a major change in enforcement as a result of this debate because, in the end, the US agencies (or private plaintiffs) bear the burden of proof in a federal court, and they are unlikely to be able to sustain that burden of proof relying on amorphous concepts like "big is bad".

What do you wish people understood better about antitrust law?

I wish that the general public better understood that competition produces the best, most innovative, lowest-priced products and services for consumers, and that antitrust enforcement is an essential element of the competitive process because it demonstrates to the business community and the public that "the cop is on the beat".

What should antitrust lawyers – both in government and in private practice – understand better about business?

In the US we have a revolving door, so many government antitrust lawyers – especially the most senior government lawyers – have had experience in private practice. As a result, they understand the real-world implications of their decisions. For example, they understand timing imperatives and the tremendous burdens and costs involved in a second request. When senior government lawyers ignore those issues, despite their experience, such as not complying with agreements that their agencies have reached concerning timing, that causes serious concerns among business people and the private bar, and undermines trust in and respect for the agency. Some of the more junior government lawyers do not fully appreciate those issues, so they simply request things from companies that can be very difficult or costly to provide.

What advice would you have for young female attorneys who want to work on antitrust issues?

If you like antitrust, then do it! The challenges women antitrust lawyers face are not really very different from the challenges women corporate lawyers or litigators face. Trying to achieve a work/life balance is an issue in all practices, including corporate, tax or litigation. Women still disproportionately bear the burden of work and family, but it is getting better. It is also increasingly an issue for both men and women because men want to be involved with their families too, and many male lawyers also have working spouses. If you join a firm, be sure that firm takes a team approach that involves everyone pitching in when necessary to cover for one another in ways that allow you to have a challenging career and outside interests at the same time.

Maureen Ohlhausen
Baker Botts
Catriona Hatton

Maureen Ohlhausen chairs the antitrust group at Baker Botts LLP, where she focuses on competition, privacy and regulatory issues and frequently represents clients in the tech, life sciences, energy and retail industries. She served as acting FTC chairman from January 2017 to May 2018 and as a commissioner since 2012. She directed all FTC competition and consumer protection work, with a particular emphasis on privacy and technology issues. Ms Ohlhausen has published dozens of articles on antitrust, privacy, regulation, FTC litigation and telecommunications law issues and has testified over a dozen times before Congress.

Catriona Hatton Catriona Hatton is the partner in charge of Baker Botts' Brussels office and co-chair of the antitrust practice. She is well known for her work in EU and international merger control, representing clients in some of the largest most complex deals in the market, as well as antitrust investigations and compliance. Catriona was named as a "Global Elite Thought Leader" in antitrust by *Who's Who Legal* (2020), ranked as one of the "Top 100 Women in Antitrust Globally", in Global Competition Review's *Women in Antitrust* and "Lawyer of the Year" in EU law by *Best Lawyers* (2018).

How did you become commissioner and chair of the Federal Trade Commission (FTC)? Tell us a bit about your background.

My road to becoming FTC chairman and commissioner began over 20 years ago in law school, when my professors Judge Douglas Ginsburg and Bill Kovacic inspired me to pursue antitrust law. After clerking at the US Court of Appeals for the DC Circuit, I started at the FTC with a plan to get a couple of years of antitrust agency experience. That turned into over a decade at the FTC as I took on roles with increasing responsibility, moving from the general counsel's office, to a commissioner's office, to finally to becoming the director of the Office of Policy Planning, when I became a political appointee. As OPP director, I ran the FTC's advocacy programme, developed scholarly work and test cases in areas such as the state action doctrine and online commerce that lead to several Supreme Court victories, and authored a comprehensive self-assessment of the FTC in anticipation of its 100th anniversary. This combination of antitrust scholarship, hands-on experience, and agency leadership roles laid the foundation for my service as commissioner and acting chairman across two presidential administrations.

Having experienced public and private practice over the course of your career, with a variety of roles at the FTC and now back in private practice, can you give your take on what the most significant trends or changes have been within antitrust over the years? And what was the most significant merger challenge you ever filed while heading up the FTC?

I have devoted much of my career to antitrust, which the US Supreme Court has characterised as "a comprehensive charter of economic liberty", based on the fact that "the unrestrained interaction of competitive forces will yield the best allocation of our economic resources, and lowest prices, the highest quality and the greatest material progress". First, as I have seen through my work on limiting antitrust immunity under the state action doctrine, excessive occupational licensing restraints and limits on employment mobility, there is a growing bipartisan consensus against anticompetitive restraints, whether from government action or private agreement, that burden the ability of everyday people to start businesses or change jobs to improve their opportunities. Such concerns were the driving force behind the FTC's Supreme Court victory in the *NC Dental* case as well as the increasing enforcement focus on broad non-compete agreements for low-wage workers. As chairman, I started an Economic Liberty Task Force to focus on these issues, and I am encouraged by the sustained interest on all sides of the political spectrum.

Second, some are asking whether antitrust can continue to be effective, given changes in our economy brought about by technological inno-vations. For example, the FTC held hearings and created a new unit in its enforcement bureau and the Department of Justice has announced task forces to examine this question. I applaud this work as I have long supported efforts to improve the agencies' abilities to detect and challenge anticompetitive behaviour as markets evolve and to ensure they have the necessary tools and resources to carry out this work.

These trends also underlie my response to your query about the most significant merger challenge I brought while heading the FTC. Recall that during my tenure as chair we had only one Republican and one Democrat member, but we still pursued a historic number of cases, many of which were far from run-of-the-mill. For example, in the *CDK/Automate* case we blocked an acquisition of a nascent competitor and in *Ottobock/Freedom Innovations* we challenged a consummated merger that was under the IISR threshold. We took bold but bipartisan actions, and succeeded in them, because of the shared belief in the value of competition to provide the best outcomes for consumers and a willingness to bring cases where the evidence and law warranted it.

Given this experience, I am concerned about attempts to push antitrust away from its current focus on how competition benefits consumers, towards using it to pursue other, often conflicting political goals. Some want to turn antitrust into a tool to protect non-competition interests or to punish companies who are disfavoured for a variety of reasons, including for being simply "too big". Creating a political balancing test for antitrust will undermine the ability to reach the kind of successful bipartisan outcomes that we achieved during my tenure as chairman.

When you were sworn in to the FTC in April 2012, politically, you were in the minority as a Republican. But also, as a woman, did you ever feel that there was a double uphill struggle not just as commissioner but also as chairman, to carry out your agenda?

Women have come a long way in antitrust and I was proud to serve on the first all-female led FTC. It's not that we came to different enforcement decisions because we were women, but rather it demonstrated that female leadership was no longer a rarity. As chairman, I had the strong support of FTC staff and much of the enforcement community, who knew me well from my long history at the FTC. This was crucial to navigating successfully a time of change and uncertainty for the first year and a half of the new administration. I did face some unique challenges as a female chairman, however, with some male practitioners predicting that I wouldn't be tough enough to challenge their big mergers as an acting chairman. Any leader faces criticism, however, and my active and successful enforcement agenda, including stopping those mergers, speaks for itself.

Under your leadership at the FTC you oversaw the agency and its involvement in several high-profile privacy and data security probes. Now being back in private practice, how has your advice and counsel changed when dealing with your own clients?

Data has become a highly valuable asset for many companies, driving innovation and competition through more accurate insights into consumer behaviour, customer needs and market outcomes. One of my key discussion points with clients is explaining how these changes have supercharged regulatory scrutiny in both antitrust and privacy and, increasingly, where they intersect. For example, antitrust authorities now subject mergers combining consumer data to more searching review, and they are also examining how large online players use data to gain a competitive advantage. In private practice, I have also been deeply involved with accelerating legislative efforts to create a detailed federal privacy law, recently testifying before the Senate on the issue. If enacted, this legislation will impose a host of new obligations on companies big and small in every industry, and equip the FTC with a variety of new powers. I'm helping my clients to see over the horizon and to be prepared for this new regulatory landscape.

In private practice you headed the FTC practice group at a leading telecoms firm representing and advising tech and telecoms clients. How do the US and Europe compare in their approach to regulating global tech platforms? And with ongoing/increased scrutiny by enforcement agencies into big tech and their practices, do you have any advice for in-house counsel dealing with these issues?

Although there is a fair amount of convergence between the US and the EU in merger review, there has always been more divergence in single-firm conduct liability standards, stemming from differing economic histories, such as Europe's history of state-owned enterprises. This likely underlies the European view that competition means that no single firm should dominate and that antitrust law should disperse economic power as an end in itself. By contrast, the US has had little state ownership of business. Thus, under US antitrust law, simply being big is not suspect unless accompanied by conduct that excludes rivals to the detriment of consumers.

These doctrinal differences long predated online platforms, but the rise of Internet-enabled commerce has made them quite stark. Although the US tech companies do not make up a single antitrust market, large online platforms share common characteristics. They have strong scale efficiencies and network effects that are economically efficient but lead to high concentration, at least in the short term. The EU approach seeks to disperse this economic power through remedies that give rivals access to the dominant platform. The US antitrust enforcement in the tech space thus far has not pursued competitor access based on market structure or network effects, instead asking whether there has been exclusionary conduct. This goes back to the US faith in free markets to produce the best outcomes over time and scepticism of the benefits of forced sharing.

As for my advice to in-house counsel, I provide this context, which is often missing from the simple framing that the US enforcers are beholden to the tech industry, while Europe is not. Understanding the differing goals in the US and Europe improves the ability to predict outcomes more accurately and to address these concerns head on.

If you could go back in time and give your younger self advice, what would you say to her? And what advice would you give a young lawyer driven to make a change within the legal industry having spent your career in public and private practice?

My advice to my earlier self and to any young lawyer is that you can't lead from a crowd. You need to get your ideas out into the marketplace, ask for opportunities, and make things happen. Women are often modest about claiming credit for their ideas and achievements, but you can't just sit back and hope your efforts are noticed and rewarded. Instead, build your reputation by working on publications and committees through professional organisations, like the ABA Antitrust Section. My work as a senior editor on the *ABA Antitrust Law Journal*, event chair, and frequent author and speaker helped me to expand my connections and become well known in the field.

Lisa Phelan
Morrison & Foerster

Elaine Johnston

Lisa Phelan, former chief of the National Criminal Enforcement Section of the Antitrust Division of the US Department of Justice (DOJ), is a partner in Morrison & Foerster's Global Antitrust Law Practice and White Collar Group. With more than 25 years' service at the DOJ as one of the leading authorities in criminal antitrust matters, Lisa draws upon her unmatched investigations, litigation, and enforcement experience to guide clients through high-stakes matters pertaining to international cartel and white-collar investigations. She is Chambers-recognised as at the top in her field to rapidly assess, address and defend corporations and executives for potential claims of collusion and other antitrust violations.

Elaine Johnston is head of Allen & Overy LLP's US antitrust practice and co-head of the global antitrust practice. Her practice covers mergers and acquisitions, antitrust litigation and antitrust advice. She handles matters in a wide range of industries, including banking and financial services, pharmaceuticals, healthcare, oil and gas, chemicals, food products and vitamins. She has been featured in *Chambers USA*, *BTI Client Service All-Stars*, and *Global Competition Review: Women in Antitrust 2016*. Elaine received her LLM from the University of Michigan law school, where she was a Fulbright scholar, and her BA (Hons) and MA from Clare College, Cambridge.

You spent most of your career as an antitrust lawyer at the US Department of Justice Antitrust Division (DOJ), focusing on criminal cartel enforcement. What inspired you to become an antitrust lawyer and spend most of your career in public service?

Like most young law students, I wanted to use my new legal skills to do something that mattered in the world – to make a difference in people's lives. I grew up in an family with very modest economic means, where the price of things made a real difference. The mission of the antitrust laws – to ensure a level playing field for buyers and sellers, and to protect consumers from abuse of power, really appealed to me. At the DOJ I found my work to ensure fair competition, on a local, national and international scale, to be endlessly rewarding.

Who were your most significant career mentors?

My mentors were many and few at the same time. No one person ever really took me under their wing with a very conscious intent to aid me in planning a career, but I learned so much about what to do – and what not to do – by watching and absorbing best practices and integrity in action from many colleagues and supervisors. As a brand new honours programme attorney at the DOJ, fresh out of law school, I was fortunate to be assigned to work with a senior female prosecutor on a national price-fixing investigation. She showed me how to navigate a very male-dominated specialism, pushed me to take on more responsibility than I thought I could handle, and gave me real-time feedback on what I did well, and what I needed to work harder to improve. When I went to work in the Antitrust Division's front office, Joe Widmar and John Clark, the top career officials responsible for civil and criminal enforcement, taught me invaluable lessons about how to be a true leader – giving all credit for good work to the staff attorneys, and taking responsibility with agency leaders for any mistakes made by those they supervised. Throughout my career,

I have learned from those above, below and beside me, how to handle myself in a way that will advance the mission and always leave me feeling proud of how I conducted myself, and I find if you do those things, you will naturally advance in your career.

What do you view as the most important developments in criminal antitrust enforcement in the US and globally during your tenure at the DOJ?

The most important developments in criminal antitrust enforcement during my tenure at DOJ would be: the development of the Leniency programme and its spread around the world; the *United States v Nippon Paper* decision; ACPERA legislation, and the advance of coordination among antitrust authorities globally. The leniency programme, in its 1993 iteration, changed the game in terms of the ability to break into ongoing criminal cartels and gather a level of evidence from an insider that was previously almost impossible for cartel prosecutors to obtain. As antitrust authorities around the world saw the size and breadth of the cartels in significant industries that the DOJ was able to uncover using leniency, dozens wanted to adopt and use this powerful tool as well. This was both a blessing and a curse for the DOJ, as there was tremendous power and effect in having many jurisdictions investigating global conduct simultaneously, yet coordination among countries with significantly different legal systems was a challenge. The *Nippon Paper* decision by the 1st Circuit was critical to establish the DOJ's standing to bring Sherman Act criminal prosecutions against cartels who acted outside the US, but with an effect on US consumers. ACPERA legislation, bringing the opportunity for single vs treble damages in follow-on civil actions to leniency applicants, was critical to lessen the discouraging effect that early leniency applicants felt when they obtained relief from criminal charges but then realised they had admitted liability that would be used in the inevitable civil cases. Finally, the increase in coordination and assistance that jurisdictions around the world can and will provide to each other has been critical to effective cartel enforcement. From MLATs (mutual legal assistance treaties) to extradition to coordinated dawn raids, the world community has come together to send the message that a cartelist can run but not hide from responsibility for cartel conduct.

One of your former colleagues said of you: "If there were a Hall of Fame for antitrust prosecutors, [Lisa] would be a first-round inductee." While this may require some translation for a non-US audience, it clearly indicates that you were viewed as a formidable prosecutor while at the DOJ! What are you most proud of during your time at DOJ?

Wow, I am proud of a lot of things I was able to do at the DOJ. I am proud of the impact my teams and I made in cleaning up many significant industries that were corrupted by cartel conduct, including airlines, shipping, paper, chemicals, auto parts, pharmaceuticals and government contracting. I am proud of the relationships I built with enforcers all over the globe, that enabled us to trust and support one another in accomplishing our missions. I am proud to say I worked hard to hire, train and mentor outstanding attorneys and infuse them with a dedication to public service. I am proud to have been a role model to less experienced female lawyers who otherwise would not have seen many women in the leadership of criminal enforcement at DOJ. And I am proud to say that if you violated the criminal antitrust laws you knew my team and I would be coming at you aggressively, but likewise I was always open and willing to hear that the facts or circumstances might be different then they appeared at first blush and, while I prosecuted more than 300 criminal cases, I walked away from at least triple that many, because the evidence wasn't there and bringing charges would not have been the just thing to do.

Speaking with the benefit of your public sector experience, what advice would you give to private practitioners handling cartel cases in front of the DOJ? What are the keys to being an effective advocate?

As a prosecutor, it always surprised me that there are some defence attorneys that seem to have only one approach – resist and oppose the government on all things, all the time, regardless of the client or facts. While they may think that is an effective approach, in my observation it is often not in the client's long-term interest. Approaching the investigating team with a respectful attitude, acknowledging indisputable facts and making arguments that are likely to resonate with enforcers and their stated goals can go a really long way to having your client viewed favourably. At some point in the years-long investigation and litigation, you may want to call on a record of good faith and mutual respect, and it can make the difference in how much you are heard when it really matters, and whether a close call goes for or against your client. Instead of claiming the government has "no case", point out policy reasons why this might not be the ideal case to bring, or facts that will make it challenging for the government to convince 12 jurors that your client is a criminal. Since the cartel bar tends to feature lots of repeat players, think about the reputation you want to carve with DOJ prosecutors from matter to matter.

Related to that, what were your "pet peeves" as a prosecutor?

Prosecutors are people too, and thus arrogance is never a good look when interacting with public servants, who are likely overworked, under-resourced and underpaid. Also, advising the antitrust prosecutor that he or she likely just doesn't understand the industry or how business works (even if true) is not likely to win friends or influence a tired, stressed prosecutor. Name-dropping who a defence counsel knows in a position of power in the DOJ, or repeatedly threatening to go over staff's heads to their boss anytime you don't like an answer to a request is never appreciated.

After more than 25 years at the DOJ, you have now moved into private practice at Morrison & Foerster. How have you found the transition from "gamekeeper to poacher" after so many years as a prosecutor? Has moving to private practice changed your views on antitrust enforcement? Do you think antitrust regulators are too willing to see conspiracies? Or too sceptical about procompetitive justifications advanced by companies?

To a lot of people's surprise (and maybe mine too), I have actually really enjoyed the transition from enforcer to private practitioner at Morrison & Foerster. As an enforcer, you have to view the world as very black and white, good and evil, if you will, and of course the world is not that way. Most situations have a lot of grey. Good people can intentionally or unwittingly make poor choices. What I do now – and what I enjoy very much and find very rewarding – is to help companies and executives understand what is happening when they get caught up in an investigation by DOJ. I help them understand the process, step by step, and what the prosecutors are thinking and trying to accomplish with each action. I can "translate" prosecutor-speak and explain the goals and options for each side. I help them make very informed decisions about cooperation, and help explain to investigators that they may be missing some crucial facts that may change the analysis when put in context. The change of sides has helped me see that most busy executives just don't fully appreciate all of the types of conduct that could be considered criminal violations, and when they do understand, they are more than willing to change their behaviour. The fact that Sherman Act offences are per se is challenging, because no intent to violate the law is required. While I liked that status as a prosecutor, I can see now that it can seem harsh in the context of well-meaning executives with a lot on their plate. I think lifelong prosecutors, like I was, may be too quick sometimes to see conduct that they think is worthy of that heaviest of sanctions, criminal liability.

There has been a lot of recent discussion about leniency programmes, in particular, whether their use is declining. What are your views on that topic? Have amnesty programmes, weighed down by stringent requirements imposed by regulators to qualify, had their heyday? Has the global proliferation of such programmes hurt their efficacy? What factors do you consider when advising a company whether to seek leniency?

I think companies, rightly, are pausing a little longer in considering whether to seek type A leniency than they might have 10 or 15 years ago. While the tremendous value of avoiding criminal liability for the company and its executives has not declined, companies and their legal advisers now pause to consider the full scope of implications to self-reporting cartel conduct. If the conduct is global, a company faces the prospect of needing to seek leniency simultaneously in a dozen or more jurisdictions around the world, each of which has its own cartel laws, legal system, leniency programme process, and confidentiality and privilege rules. Each will want to be the company's first priority in providing information and documents and witnesses. Moreover, state attorneys general may file their own civil damage actions. Additionally, the company must think through the civil damage liability it will potentially face in the US and increasingly in Europe and elsewhere. This can include dozens of lawsuits, filed by direct and indirect purchasers, some likely to be joined into class actions, others not. The cumulative impact of this proliferation of leniency programmes and others seeking recompense for cartel conduct even from a successful leniency applicant has no doubt had a chilling effect on potential leniency applicants. Added to that has been the tweaking of leniency requirements by enforcers, particularly the DOJ, that provide less complete certainty that executives will all be covered by the immunity provisions of a leniency grant (and those are often the individuals who need to make the decision about whether to seek leniency). Consequently, when I advise a company on the possibility of seeking leniency, we consider all of these factors, along with the timing, effect and scope of any suspicious conduct, before making a determination. Of course, how much time is taken must still be balanced against the time pressure to be first if the conclusion is that self-reporting is the best option.

During the DOJ investigations into price-fixing and other antitrust violations in the financial services industry, a number of banks were allowed to enter into deferred prosecution agreements (DPAs) with prosecutors rather than enter a traditional guilty plea. We have just seen the first case where a company outside the financial services industry – Heritage Pharmaceuticals – entered into a DPA with antitrust prosecutors. Do you expect to see more DPAs being used by antitrust prosecutors or were these "special" situations that should not be read too broadly?

The Antitrust Division was historically very reluctant to offer DPAs as an option to companies engaged in cartel conduct, due to concern that this option could weaken the incentive to seek leniency. The Division wanted companies to be motivated to report quickly, out of concern that the only two options available were total amnesty or criminal felony conviction. DPAs offer a middle ground to this stark set of choices, and may be available at a much later point in time, when all facts have been fully developed. The DOJ, perhaps as an acknowledgement that leniency has become less attractive, for all of the reasons we just discussed, or perhaps to provide additional motivation to companies to develop strong antitrust compliance programmes, announced recently that it will now offer DPAs as an option for companies that can demonstrate that they had in place a strong, robust competition compliance programme, even though a violation occurred. I think this change will encourage more companies to invest in strong compliance programmes (and I am developing these "best in show" programmes for companies now), but only time will tell how frequently the DOJ concludes that a company's programme qualifies, and whether this option strengthens or weakens the leniency programme. It could strengthen it, if the increase in compliance programmes leads to greater detection of cartels which are then reported to the Division under the leniency programme. It could weaken it, if companies decide to forego the leniency programme and instead rely on their potential ability to obtain a DPA at a later point in an investigation. In any event, it has changed the advice and range of options to consider when advising clients.

In October 2016, close to the end of the Obama administration, the US antitrust agencies announced that the DOJ would prosecute naked no-poaching and wage-fixing agreements criminally. President Trump's antitrust chief, Makan Delrahim, has reiterated this policy. However, to date we still have not seen an actual criminal prosecution for these types of agreements. Why not? Did the October 2016 announcement change anything?

We have not seen any of these "no-poach" cases prosecuted criminally yet. In part, that may be because the 2016 guidance gave a safe harbour for conduct that occurred before and stopped as of the October 2016 policy change. While the DOJ has announced that it is investigating "many" no-poach matters, perhaps they are finding that much of the conduct at issue preceded the policy change. Matters involving more recent conduct may be in the early stages of investigation, as it is not uncommon for a criminal grand jury investigation of Sherman Act offences to take several years. Since top DOJ officials, now in two administrations, have made clear they consider agreements not to hire or solicit employees from another company to be serious offences, subject to criminal prosecution and jail, companies and executives would be wise to look closely at their practices and contract terms on these issues and take the DOJ at its word that these types of cases, to protect competition for labour, are coming, later if not sooner.

What are your views on the role played by the large technology companies such as Google, Amazon and Facebook in our lives? Are antitrust laws equipped to deal with the concerns these companies raise? Should antitrust regulators be more willing to wield the antitrust laws against them? Do regulators need new tools? Or is this not an area for antitrust at all?

There sure is a lot of talk about antitrust and big tech right now, huh? Everyone from presidential candidates to German cartel enforcers to state attorneys general are calling for use of the antitrust laws to "rein in" big tech. The Federal Trade Commission has established a technology task force, that they just converted to a permanent unit. The DOJ announced it has several open investigations of major tech companies. Some major fines have been levied here and in Europe. Privacy and antitrust laws seem to be crossing lines. I think that given the size and influence of these companies in our lives, they rightly warrant attention from regulators. That said, the antitrust laws are not meant to be limited to a particular industry, or time and place, and for more than a hundred years they have worked to protect competition. I think the US has the tools in place to protect competition, and the agencies will do their usual careful review to assess whether any harm to competition is occurring and act if it is. The companies can assist by working with enforcers to be sure everyone understands the facts to reach the right results.

You have been a strong champion for women in the legal profession throughout your career. How have you seen the profession change for women over the course of your career? What are the principle challenges currently faced by women in the legal profession? What advice would you give to a young female antitrust lawyer starting out today?

When I first started at the DOJ Antitrust Division, antitrust, and particularly criminal antitrust, was a very male-dominated specialism. When I became the chief of national criminal enforcement, I was the only woman among 18 managers in the criminal programme at the DOJ. Women in the cartel defence bar were even fewer and farther between, and if they appeared it was usually only to carry bags and take notes. The first time I travelled to Japan for MLAT assistance, the Japanese prosecutor chastised me because my affidavit to support his request for a search warrant had not discussed my husband's occupation and where he went to school. Luckily, things have improved considerably for women in the space. I have always tried my best to hire, mentor and encourage younger women lawyers, and transmit my zeal for this area of law. I have made sure they had equal opportunity to work on the most complex matters, and had a seat at the table for litigation. I started a group called "Women in Cartels" to bring together women in government, private practice and in-house that focus on cartel and compliance work. This group and others like it provide the networking and informal opportunities to know what options are available that women sometimes miss, but men have prioritised for a long time. The best advice I would give a young female antitrust lawyer starting out today is: 1) Don't worry so much or try to plan every move. I had four children while litigating cases all over the country and rising through the ranks at the DOJ. If I had paused and thought about what I was doing, I probably would have told myself I was crazy – it couldn't be done. But somehow, it could. 2) It's a long life and career. You don't have to achieve anything by a certain deadline. Keep looking for exciting work that you feel motivated to do, don't be afraid to take chances, and ask people you admire, male and female, for advice as you go.

Looking into your crystal ball, what developments do you expect in the cartel area in the US or globally? Are there particular industries or types of conduct that you see as the logical next targets for enforcement?

Looking more at the headlines than my crystal ball, I think there is definitely going to be more focus by this administration on government contracting and cartels that affected taxpayers. When the Division announced the task force to focus on this conduct, the deputy AG participated, signalling how high priority this initiative is going to be for the DOJ as a whole. Thus defence contractors, companies providing IT and cloud support to the government, those providing care to veterans, etc., had better update their compliance programmes and look for red flags of collusion, because the DOJ will be looking for those red flags. The healthcare industry is another place where I suspect there will be more enforcement efforts. Deputy assistant AG Richard Powers announced recently that there will be more prosecutions in the generic drugs industry, and the DOJ is likely to focus some continuing attention on this industry that drives a huge segment of the US economy. And, as we have said, big tech will no doubt be a continuing source of investigations and possibly charges in the next year or more.

Finally, and on a more personal note: What do you enjoy about being an antitrust lawyer? If you were not an antitrust lawyer, what do you think you would be instead?

What I love about being an antitrust lawyer is that you are always learning about new industries and aspects of the economy and worlds that I knew relatively little about before. When you begin a new investigation, you dig in deep and learn everything you can about something that scientists or engineers or business people or doctors are spending their whole life thinking about. I also love the human psyche aspect, figuring out what motivated people in their conduct, and what will motivate them to open up in the context of an investigation. If I hadn't been an antitrust lawyer, I think I would have been an investigative journalist, because you would do many of the same things and be constantly learning and establishing truth.

Elisabetta Righini
Latham & Watkins
Rima Alaily

Elisabetta Righini is a partner in the Brussels office of Latham & Watkins and a member of its Global Antitrust & Competition group. Her practice centres on European law, in particular State aid and EU regulation and litigation. She advises clients in a variety of sectors, including energy, entertainment, digital services, telecommunications, technology and transportation. Prior to joining Latham, Elisabetta spent 15 years at the European Commission, first as member of its Legal Service, and then as legal and policy advisor to the former Competition Commissioner and Vice-President, Joaquin Almunia. She is a visiting professor at the Centre of European Law in the Dickson Poon School of Law at King's College, London, and a member of its Advisory Board. Ms Righini is the local chair of Latham's Women Enriching Business (WEB) committee.

Rima Alaily is vice president and deputy general counsel for the competition law group at Microsoft Corporation. She and her team help the company comply with competition laws around the world, close mergers and acquisitions and respond to investigations. They also engage with regulators, academics and others to consider the role of competition law in the face of our changing economy and the development of new technology. In addition, she is a long-standing advocate for diversity and inclusion and for civil legal aid, working to provide access to justice for those in need.

You have had a varied career with exciting and challenging roles in the private and public sectors. Why did you become a lawyer and how did you find your way into the field of antitrust?

My path to competition law was a winding one that unfolded over time. The summer before I went to university I worked for my mother, who had a fashion business. We have always had a great relationship, but we are two very strong characters. That summer, she fired me twice over six months. It was clear to me that I should not follow in her footsteps! Instead, I picked the law. It appealed to me because I thought it would be a way to have an impact on my community.

At university, I took a course in international economics with Mario Draghi, the former president of the European Central Bank, and discovered that I loved economics as well. So I ended up finishing law school with a degree in international economic law and a thesis on international trade law. After I completed my LLM in London, I joined a law firm at the same time as the World Trade Organization was forming, and became one of the first WTO litigators. Then the European Commission sort of discovered me in the person of the director of the Legal Service in charge of public international law, Allan Rosas, who asked me to go to Brussels and join their WTO team.

I did my first five years at the Commission's Legal Service dealing with WTO and public international law. And, when I had to choose my next job, it was only natural to pick yet another intersection between law and economics, and so I ended up in the State aid team.

How about you? Why did you decide to become a lawyer and to deal with antitrust?

It's interesting because in some ways my drivers for becoming a lawyer were similar to yours. Like you, I wanted to have an impact on my community, in particular in terms of delivering justice. What excited and energized me at law school was the opportunity to act for marginalised groups and to give a voice to people who were disenfranchised, to drive change to help people, and make a real difference in their lives. As a law student and as a junior lawyer in a law firm in Seattle, I spent a lot of time doing pro bono work.

My initial plan was to stay just two to three years in a law firm, pay off my student debts, and then move into the non-profit sector.

In the end, though, I chose not to leave the private sector. I really enjoyed the work in the private sector and found that it provided an excellent platform to make an impact in my community. I found that from the private sector I was able to contribute in ways that I might not have been able to in the non-profit sector. The private sector also needs people who are civic-minded and who can harness the power of its tools, resources, money and influence for the public good. What I would call "for the right good and just aims". This public-good goal has always been part of my practice. Early on, I focused on direct representation for people in need, but in the last 10 years I have spent a lot of time on the boards of pro bono organisations to help them with fundraising, and to guide their development and strategic thinking.

In my current role at Microsoft, I am extremely proud to be part of a company that is in many ways so civic-minded. For example, Microsoft employees have donated US$2 billion to charitable organisations. Because Microsoft is extremely conscious of the communities in which it operates, I feel extremely good about working for them as an antitrust lawyer.

I have not had the opportunity or privilege to work directly in the public sector. I would be interested to know from you, with experience in both the public and private sectors, what this experience brings to the table. In particular, I know that you served 10 years in the legal service of the European Commission. How does the insight gained from your time at the Commission enriched/improved your skills/instincts as a competition lawyer, and what is the impact that this experience has on expectations of clients and colleagues?

As a member of the Legal Service of the European Commission, my clients were the other Director Generals. So I learned first-hand about the responsibility that goes with creating the law and enforcing it, and the limits that can have. And even more importantly, I learned about how the law evolves as part and parcel of policymaking.

The whole European project is about evolution. It is exciting to see how it all started just by putting together the coal and steel markets of six Member States, to prevent them from using these commodities to make weapons once again. It now comprises 27 Member States, with over 500 million citizens, and regulates a very broad set of areas and aspects of life, creating this unique architecture that is the EU.

The various branches of European law follow the same path. Piece after piece, EU law evolves to tackle new challenges every day. I wrote a piece a few years ago with my colleague at King's College, Prof Andrea Biondi, on the evolutionary nature of state aid control. State aid law originates in only two articles in the Treaty on the Functioning of the EU, that have never changed since they were written by the Founding Fathers in 1957. Yet, the breadth and depth of State aid control has evolved exponentially to follow the developments of the European economy and the needs of its people.

So as a lawyer in private practice, I feel I am uniquely placed to help my clients understand the law *and* how to shape it going forward. I have this sense of where it is legal rules come from, their origin, their philosophy, their scope, *and* where they are going and how they will help shape society. This is something that has really remained with me and makes my daily work so interesting.

You have extensive experience in policymaking. You were at the core of it during your last post at the European Commission, while in office with

Commission Vice President and Competition Commissioner Almunia. Do you believe that competition decisions and enforcement actions are making a difference?

Having been at the core of policymaking for a few years, I felt we could use antitrust order to create a fairer environment, in which the citizens of Europe could all thrive and grow. It may be because I come at antitrust from the State aid angle, which is typically European, that this feeling was so strong. Vice President Almunia took office as Competition Commissioner in early 2010, when the economic and financial crisis was still very acute. It was clear that his policy objective was to steer Member States' public spending towards better goals of growth, inclusion, a greener economy, and to encourage all companies to contribute to these goals.

In State aid, we thus embarked on a reform of the whole rulebook, the so-called tate aid modernisation. We reviewed and readopted more than a dozen State aid legal instruments. And we continued to control State aid in the European market through a plethora of decisions in all fields of the economy: from postal services, to air and land transport, to banks, to the opening of the now-famous investigations into the tax arrangements of multinationals.

Our philosophy of antitrust enforcement, at least in the State aid field, was more about fairness and solidarity, than not pure consumer protection as it seems to be now. We wished to protect the unique model of social economy that has made Europe unique. As I mentioned earlier, European integration started with the creation of an internal market, whose two pillars are antitrust and competition on one side, and regulation on the other. It is this internal market that has then pulled countries and people together to share democratic institutions, a common currency and now even a Charter of Human Rights.

So in this sense, I see the social value of antitrust very strongly. The integration of the economy, through the use of regulation to open up markets and antitrust to ensure their correct operation, has been the furnace that has forged all the other rights. I believe this is unique about Europe.

You are also at the core of competition enforcement, working for one of the largest multinationals in the world. What do you see as the main role of this policy?

Ultimately, I believe in the core premise of antitrust law, i.e., competition leads to better outcomes for consumers, whether it is lower prices, better quality goods or more innovation. In that sense, antitrust drives us towards better social outcomes. Antitrust enforcement is a powerful tool, but it can be a blunt and limited instrument. It necessarily operates case by case: doing it right takes time, and effective remedies can be difficult to craft. And, while it can optimise for consumer welfare as an economic concept, it does not provide an effective or appropriate forum to make decisions that involve trade-offs between competing social or political values. That is not a reason to abandon the enterprise altogether but simply a recognition that building a just and fair society requires more.

Moving onto the tech sector in which we both advise. This is undoubtedly a sector in the spotlight of global regulators. The clients and the issues are global, but do you see discrepancies in the way the various authorities handle matters? Could this be a field where closer intergovernmental coordination and streamlined regulation should occur? Do private practitioners have a role to play in guiding authorities accordingly? What would be your holistic view on this?

Tech regulation is definitely an area where regulators around the world need to become more joined up. It is a critical moment for the sector, with the European Commission and other regulators around the world considering what new tools they will use to deal with digital issues. The European Commission is currently considering a three-pillar approach (a new competition tool, *ex ante* regulation of digital platforms and vigorous enforcement of existing antitrust rules), but the final approach taken need to be consistent across the globe.

Private practitioners have a key role in guiding the authorities. We play a vital role in explaining business models and the incentives driving competition. We understand our clients' business well but also how the regulators think, and we are in a unique position to be a bridge between them at this critical time.

What do you think are the biggest challenges multinational firms face in the antitrust landscape today? Since more and more law firms promise expertise on the complex issues their clients face, what differentiates a practitioner and makes them a trusted adviser? What are your tips for business development as a woman attorney – do we all need to learn golf?

One of the largest challenges that companies face in the antitrust landscape is dealing with a broad range of regulators with growing regulatory powers across the globe. Large global firms are uniquely placed to service this need seamlessly.

To become a truly trusted adviser, not only do you need to be a great lawyer, you also need to have built the experience and relationships with the regulators, and also have a supreme in-depth knowledge of your client's business.

A key for business development as a female attorney is recognising that you already have the key skillset to be extremely successful: listening, overcoming obstacles, etc. Women lawyers generally focus on service and client experience more than just the resulting outcome, and this holistic approach can be very powerful for retaining and attracting new business. Taking the time to network is also important, although this can be challenging for women who may have greater family commitments than their male counterparts.

During your time with Vice President Almunia, the cabinet was composed in large part of women. How was the working culture at the Commission? Did you feel you had to prove yourself double in order to gain the same results as your male colleagues? Were there any stereotypes that you were able to smash, and how advanced do you think the legal world is in the Commission in promoting female empowerment in particular and diversity overall?

My experience in the cabinet of Vice President Almunia was great. He made diversity a fact. The core cabinet was composed of seven members: four women and three men, and all of us had kids. This diversity made our daily work pleasant. And even more importantly, Almunia was a family man himself. It would be rare that he would assume that you wouldn't go and have dinner with your family, or you know, have weekends to spend with the family. This said, the rhythms of the competition cabinet were just crazy because of the sheer amount of work that you had to manage. But there was still a lot of solidarity and support for one another. We worked together to ensure that we could be engaged with our families and yet perform in high-powered roles that required a lot of time and attention.

Did we have to prove more than men? Not in our group. But the Commission more broadly was not nearly as diverse. It has changed a lot since then and made progress. Earlier this month we had the first State of the Union speech by a female president; that is quite an historical moment. And President von der Leyen has prioritised having a diverse College of Commissioners. So that college is now almost 50% women. But the progress has taken time and positive action. Diversity has not happened by itself.

In my personal view, the main point is really to have the leaders set the example, and create space for women or gender diverse persons to thrive and to grow. In this sense, I must admit that coming back to private practice was quite a shock because I found the legal profession to be as male dominated as when I had left it 16 years earlier. When I graduated from law school, there were probably more women than men. And when we entered as first year associates or trainees, there were lots of women. But when I came back at the top of the profession, I found a void. The lack of women is particularly pronounced in competition law.

What has been your experience of gender balance in the workplace?

When I started in private practice doing antitrust work, it was incredibly male dominated. Often, I would be the only woman in the room. I had wonderful male colleagues who accepted and supported me, but I certainly had this sense that I had to show up in a particular way; I had to be "one of the guys" and there were parts of myself that I could not bring into the workplace.

At Microsoft, I had the opportunity to step away from antitrust law and spend three years on the legal team that supported our marketing and consumer business. That legal team was much more diverse, women made up more than half of the team. It was such a change; the dynamics on the team were different. There was much more of a focus on relationships and engagement across a broader range of personal and professional topics at team meetings – by both men and women. I realised how much more relaxed I felt in that environment and how much easier it was to show up authentically in that environment.

One of the great things that has happened at Microsoft over the last 12 years has been the growing diversity. Half of the Microsoft corporate, external and legal affairs department, where I work, is female. And among the senior ranks, the department is over 40% female.

The other day, I had the experience of presenting at a committee meeting for the board of directors. As I wrapped up my presentation, I was struck by the fact that my presentation was sandwiched between those of two other senior women executives, the committee chair was a woman, and half the committee members were women. It just felt so very different, like women belonged there, not that we were kind of lucky to get in.

I credit the progress at Microsoft to our leadership, particularly our CEO Satya Nadella and our president and chief legal officer Brad Smith. There have been many others who have played a role as well, but it is essential that the correct tone, expectations and policies are set at the top. Organisations must work intentionally to create a space where women and all the challenges that we have to deal with are invited, welcomed, accepted, supported and normalised. Ironically, welcoming women changes the dynamic for men too, making it more acceptable to bring more of themselves into the workplace and free themselves of the need to fit a particular predefined stereotype.

I believe that as a female leader I bring a different set of skills from my male counterparts. I approach problems differently, and probably at times have a more holistic approach to issues, including the emotions driving decision-making, and how to navigate these. For example, the way that I approach trying to build positive working relationships with regulators and outside counsel may be somewhat different to the approach of a male leader.

I am a strong believer in the power of network support for a woman's successful career, be this family, peers, mentoring. Have you had specific persons that have supported you throughout your professional choices or have influenced the way you have progressed through your profession?

I fully agree with you on the power of network support for women. That is what has really allowed me to progress in my career and that has made it so enjoyable as well. I have also been very fortunate to have had a number of different mentors both in my public and private sector roles. These have been both men and women. At Latham, we have a very developed mentoring programme for our associates, and I am very proud to be part of this very effective programme at the firm.

It's interesting that you mention your firm's internal mentoring programme. I believe that there is also scope to open up greater links between female associates at law firms and their clients. I personally don't mind hearing from different voices at the law firms we deal with. I enjoy working with junior associates, and really do not mind if they email directly with questions on matters that they are working on. There is not necessarily the need for all questions to be funnelled through one person. I believe that it is essential for relationships to build between associates and clients. These kinds of relationships can be very important for young associates, particularly female associates. They can be an additional source of validation, engagement and confidence-building that can keep women in the profession.

Is there a female way to be a lawyer and an antitrust lawyer? Are there particular skills that you feel female attorneys should focus on developing if striving to obtain leadership positions?

I am convinced that there is a dimension to practicing law as a woman. How can I say this right? I have a lot of respect for my male colleagues. I work with them very closely. But, in general, I think women are more multidimensional; we perceive a more nuanced reality and bring together more parts than men do.

As a result, I find that women are more creative in their approach to work. And they create a different working environment, one that is less competitive and more welcoming. Because women are often juggling competing demands on our time, we rely more on others. I am a single mother with two daughters. So, I need to rely more on our associates and find a different way to work with them than do my male colleagues, who have more time. And I find that client relationships are different. Women tend to network with clients in a broader manner than men. For me, I can weave a lot of the soft knowledge that I pick up into my legal analysis and client relationships.

Much has been written in the press about women "having it all". What is your experience and how would you define "having it all"?

To be honest, it is not a question that I ask myself anymore. In large part, it is because answering the question means buying into unrealistic and strictly defined societal expectations about their roles as a mother, as a spouse or as a professional. If we are lucky, our lives are long and what matters, what opportunities we have and the demands on our time shift from year to year. Early in my career, as a single woman, I was able to focus 100% of my attention and time on myself and my professional success. Later, when I got married and had kids, I made deliberate choices in my career and professional commitments so that I had more time and space for them. Now that my kids are older, I again have more time to contribute more at work and in my community.

I think it is so important that, as women, we step back from time to time and look at our lives with perspective. We need to be patient with ourselves and, most of all, we need to give ourselves and each other grace. If you are not firing on all cylinders at every moment in your life, that is okay. As my mom used to say (oddly borrowed from business guru Stephen Covey) when I was a kid: focus on putting the big rocks in your bucket first and worry about the pebbles later.

And what about you? What is your notion of "having it all"?

The notion of "having it all" is a difficult one for me personally, because I have sacrificed a lot in my personal life for the sake of my profession, starting with living very far away from my beloved Tuscany. Even so, I would not do anything differently if I could. In fact, I have also gained a lot in terms of experience, knowledge, human relationships and just awareness of what makes our world turn. And I love my profession and the career that I have built, I have two wonderful daughters who are becoming strong and independent young women, a very close family, a lot of friends around the globe and more interests than my time allows. So, if I do as you say, and step back and look at my life in perspective, maybe I actually have it all…

Deirdre Trapp
Freshfields Bruckhaus Deringer
Josephine Mackintosh

Deirdre Trapp is an award-winning antitrust practitioner dealing with both contentious and non-contentious antitrust matters. She has considerable experience of appearing before the EC Commission, UK Competition and Markets Authority and other agencies worldwide. She has been involved in a wide range of economic sectors, particularly technology, financial services, consumer goods, energy and transport. She also has extensive experience in the liberalisation and regulation of these sectors under both EU and UK law. Deirdre is highly ranked as a global thought leader in the legal directories and is a frequent speaker on antitrust issues and policy.

Josephine Mackintosh is an assistant legal director at the Competition and Markets Authority, providing legal advice across the range of CMA work, particularly on antitrust and cartels cases and concerning EU Exit. Before joining the CMA in 2017, Josephine trained and worked as an associate in the competition team at Freshfields Bruckhaus Deringer in London for four years, practising mainly in investigations and mergers. Josephine is a member of the W@Competition committee in the UK and is a founder of the CMA's women's network.

You became a partner at Freshfields in 1995 and held the position of global head of the competition group for six years. How have you seen the practice change over the time you have been a partner? Over the course of your career to date, what have been the biggest changes you have seen across the competition law industry, both in terms of changes within law firms and the broader framework within which competition lawyers work?

When I started practicing in the late 1980s, competition law was barely regarded as a distinct specialism in the UK and there were just a handful of specialists within Freshfields buried deep within the corporate department. Today, our competition and trade group is regarded as one of the most important groups in the firm. So the rate and pace of change in the practice of competition law has been pretty significant over my 30 year career.

One of the most important catalysts for change was the introduction of the EU Merger Regulation with its structured approach to the "work sharing" on mergers between the EU Commission and national competition authorities.[1] Many useful policy developments flowed from this in terms of the cooperation between agencies and the wider development of internationally recognised best practices that we now take for granted. Alongside this, many more countries introduced competition laws, often modelled on the EU approach, or, like the UK, started to modernise their existing frameworks. These developments also tended to include a starring role for cartel enforcement efforts – and increased cross-border cooperation in that arena – and a much bigger role for private antitrust proceedings, both following on from agency involvement and standalone private enforcement.

At Freshfields, we figured out the changing landscape early on and established antitrust capabilities, both agency-facing and contentious teams, in all of the jurisdictions where we have offices. We opened our

---

1 Council Regulation (EC) 139/2004 on the control of concentrations between undertakings (EC Merger Regulation) [2004] OJ L24/1.

Brussels office in the late 1980s and had a major fillip from the mergers with Bruckhaus and Deringer in 2000 which added substantially to our capabilities in Brussels, Germany, Moscow and elsewhere. I had the great honour to be appointed global practice leader at the time of the mergers, together with my partner Frank Montag. We were tasked with integrating the three predecessor firms and were also given licence to grow the practice globally. We started an antitrust team in DC led by Paul Yde and bolstered in recent times by my excellent colleagues Mary Lehner and Julie Elmer. We also created a team in Japan, now led by the highly talented Kaori Yamada. It was only on the occasion of the mergers that created Freshfields Bruckhaus Deringer LLP that antitrust law became a fully-fledged standalone practice group in our firm, but I think we have repaid the faith shown in us at that stage.

And we have not stood still. The practice has continued to expand: the contentious work in the US, London and elsewhere has been an important growth factor; and we have added capabilities in Hong Kong and in China, now led by partners Ninette Dodoo, Hazel Yin and Alastair Mordant. For many years we have fostered and maintained close and deep links with our partner firms in places where we don't have offices, through our StrongerTogether network, and this has been highly rewarding, bringing me into contact with some fantastic lawyers globally.

The agencies have also reacted to globalisation with increased international co-operation and dialogue and increased specialism. They are highly professional and sophisticated, and the revolving door between public enforcement agencies and private practice continues to twirl around to the great benefit of both constituencies. There are many wonderful Freshfields colleagues who have enjoyed storied careers in public service and many alumnae to be found in the agencies around the world.

Within the business community, antitrust enforcement, compliance and developing trends are now particularly hot topics. We have seen the very welcome rise of specialist antitrust counsel in-house and the general counsel with whom I deal would typically regard antitrust compliance amongst their top "stay awake" issues. It's a real privilege to be able to work with senior figures in our clients and their internal experts to help deliver on their opportunities and plans and to establish the right systems and controls to protect their businesses.

You have been extremely successful in your career as a competition lawyer. What are the skills that you think make a good competition lawyer, and how do you manage to stay at the top of your game for so long?

What an interesting question! I suspect that the answer lies somewhere in abiding curiosity, high energy, resilience and a good sense of humour.

As I said earlier, the great privilege of working in this field is really learning about your clients business and getting "under the hood" about how they go about doing what they do, why they do it that way and how things might change in the future. People love to talk about what they do and what they want to do, and I do think listening to people is a core skill. Listening skills create a flow of information and ideas; reflective listening assures a common understanding; active listening creates momentum and problem-solving; and empathetic listening helps accept of compromise and new perspectives. I'm often dealing with clients in crisis or facing an existential threat to their business model and the first step is always really to appreciate and understand their concerns.

In my experience, clients seek to understand the antitrust rules and want to abide by them. But along with the beneficial international developments mentioned earlier has also come an increasing complexity of analysis, more burdensome processes – both for the agencies and those subject to them – and increased compliance costs.

It is a truism that business dislikes uncertainty and that has certainly been my experience in practice. Most business people readily recognise and seek to avoid demonstrably harmful behaviour, such a hard-core cartels, but in other areas of antitrust enforcement there are many shades of grey and not necessarily a consensus in the business world that a given practice might be harmful. And of course for clients in business in other jurisdictions the gaps in appreciation can at times be wide. There's many an agreement drafted in the US or for the US market that I've had to turn into something compliant with antitrust norms in the rest of the world. So quite a bit of my job is trying to bridge the communications gap between the agencies and the business community. Being able to explain in a straightforward and commercially relevant way what the antitrust policy drivers are, how they play out in practice, and what this all means for the problem at hand, is key to becoming a trusted adviser.

And it does take a lot of energy and organisational ability to stay abreast of developments and to manage cases with vast disclosure exercises and extended and pressured timetables. This is something that everyone is struggling with now. We undertook some research recently of our many EU Merger Regulation phase 2 cases and discovered that over the period 2012–2017 required documentary production averaged fewer than 100,000 documents. Since then, document production has mushroomed; we're currently averaging around 450,000 documents per phase 2 case. So I'd say another important trait for longevity in this field is being open to new ideas about ways of working and embracing the brilliant ideas of legal-tech-savvy colleagues. Taking care of yourself and your team, and managing the wear and tear of dealing with a large caseload effectively and efficiently, are critical skills these days.

What would be your main piece of advice to a young competition lawyer at the start of her career?

I mentor a number of people both within and outside my own firm and, as a result, have observed a number of common issues over time.

Firstly, it's important for young lawyers to focus on giving advice to clients, putting yourself in the client's shoes and thinking through the issues from their perspective. At the end of the day your job is to connect with the client and solve their problem – if you grasp that early on, your personal and professional development will accelerate. Instead, you see a lot of young lawyers very focused on pleasing their immediate boss or partner and sheltering behind legal debates of, frankly, limited interest to the client who just wants someone who can see the wood from the trees to advise them what to do in the circumstances at issue.

Then there are a couple of behavioural traits that I've observed over time that are perhaps more gender-specific. When I started in practice, my experience overwhelmingly was that I was the only woman in the room, and often the youngest person in the room the room at that. It was, at best, uncomfortable. So I had to learn the hard way. I've been in numerous settings where women have stopped speaking when someone interrupts them rudely, and then even say sorry for speaking at all when actually they are not at fault. There's a lot of physical and verbal minimising that women do which can end up marginalising them. Often unless you've seen yourself on video in a group setting you don't even know you're doing it, because it's so culturally ingrained in women to defer. But you do need a bit of personal presence to get noticed in the right way.

I have also observed that women are often embarrassed about praise for good work and seek to deflect it. While of course you shouldn't claim somebody else's achievements, women need to learn to take credit for their own. You should achieve recognition for what you've achieved and the benefits that you've delivered in your organisation and be proud about that.

I think it is incumbent on employers to provide the right kind of support to colleagues to give encouragement and licence to change some of these ingrained habits. This is not just a female thing; many colleagues from diverse cultural backgrounds face similar challenges in the work place.

It's not the case that the prevailing view is hostile or antagonistic these days – and that's a real change for the better over my career – but people can and do behave in ways which they may not appreciate make it difficult for colleagues from other backgrounds to shine in the work environment. I'm delighted to say that at Freshfields, more than 2,000 colleagues so far have signed up to an Every Day Gender Equality pledge to promote equality by confronting and transforming the problems that still persist for inclusion. The focus is on day-to-day working life and individual actions that can create incremental and tangible changes towards fostering equality. None of it is rocket science but it has had profound results. The kinds of things that are in focus include a recognition that diversity is fundamental to business success followed by an awareness of what inclusive behaviour looks like so that everyone can participate fully and be heard without unwarranted interruption. There is active nurturing, sponsorship and mentoring of diverse talent including diverse client teams, gender-neutral language and diverse client and team events, both by their nature and by their invitees. Of course, there is still a long way to go but, from where I started, there has been tremendous progress.

My top tip for young competition lawyers, therefore, would be to work in the right place for you: one that will actively support your talents and goals and where inclusion and diversity are actively supported in tangible ways.

There has been a lot of attention recently across the legal industry on wellbeing and balance in the workplace. How do you manage to balance a successful career at the highest level with a family life, and what do you think firms should do to support such a balance? Do you have any advice in this respect?

I was made a partner in 1995, when I was eight years qualified, the year after my second child was born. I was the first woman in the history of the firm – founded in 1743 – to be made a partner who had already had two children. And I went on to have a third!

Improving the work/life balance remains a very important topic for me. When I was an associate, the approach was very *ad hoc* because policies were being made up on the run to address my specific circumstances. I was very lucky that the partner I worked for himself had four children and was very family-minded; he gave me a lot of room for manoeuvre and was very supportive when the children were small. He did not care where I was so long as I got things done, which was a radical notion in those days. It will be fascinating to see the new ways of working that emerge sustainably as a result of our COVID-19 experiences, but I suspect that the days of commuting to the office 5 days a week – for both men and women – have now gone for good.

When I started, the expression work/life balance hadn't even been invented, and nobody was attempting to understand the issue. The whole debate about work/life balance and diversity is now mainstream. We've got ourselves to the point where we're discussing unconscious bias – when I first started the bias was conscious!

There have been other encouraging signs, including people taking longer parental leave, and both parents adjusting their working hours to share childcare responsibilities. But there is still a long way to go while the burden of childcare still falls disproportionately on women, an issue now very much discussed again as a result of home schooling and the like during the pandemic. Technology is a great enabler, of course, but can also increase the pressure to be always "on" for work-related matters rather than "in the moment" for whatever else is going on in your life.

I think good communication and expectation-setting is key here. On my big cases where I know the team is going to be engaged for up to a year, we try to have early and frequent discussions about personal commitments to ensure that, so far as possible, family and social life and other non-work-related considerations are respected.

In my experience, lawyers often turn out to be the most reliable, dependable and sensible members of their families or in their social setting and, as a consequence, are often shouldering additional personal responsibilities not necessarily evident in the workplace. It's better if we can talk more openly about these things – and the stresses and strains people find themselves under as a result – to support a more inclusive and diverse workplace.

Do you think the nature of antitrust enforcement is changing? Have you seen this over the course of your career, and do you anticipate changes in the next few years? Are you currently seeing political trends coming through in or having an impact on antitrust enforcement, and do you think we will see more regulators taking into considerations factors outside purely competition concerns (such as the public interest – type considerations, employment or environmental concerns, or an increasing role for "fairness")? Have you seen this manifest itself in projects in which you have been involved? In your role advising companies, how does this affect how you work?

There is definitely a strong wind of change blowing in relation to the role and purpose of antitrust and this is causing a fair degree of intro-spection and soul-searching currently. To my mind, this has been driven predominantly by two trends – first the financial crisis (and the ongoing fall out of the economic impact of the COVID pandemic) and second, the rise of the digital economy.

Following the financial crisis of 2008–2009 there is, and continues to be, much less public trust in the market model and with "experts". There's a strong perception that the application of the regulatory and enforcement framework at that time did not curb the risk of systemic failure in the financial sector and that had ramifications in the wider economy where austerity, particularly as regards the public sector and government spending, continues to this day. The rise of various populist political forces can be found in this period, with politicians now questioning whether antitrust enforcement responds promptly and assertively enough to popular and political concerns.

The consumer welfare standard against which antitrust intervention is routinely measured has served us reasonably well since the 1970s. It is based on a theoretical concept of rational economic actors working within the market seeking to maximise profit by combining inputs in an efficient manner with failure punished by the competitive forces of the market. On this basis, industrial structure reflects the outcome of market forces rather than dictating the way in which those dynamics play out. The concepts have become codified in guidance from a number of competition agencies worldwide focusing on market power defined as the ability of a firm profitably to maintain prices above competitive levels or to restrict output to below competitive levels. This in turn has led to a focus on narrowly defined markets and to the deployment of much economist processing power, modelling impacts on price, output and efficiency. This is a strength: the concepts have, at least until now, enjoyed broad acceptance and are reasonably predictable, which business appreciates.

But it is also potentially a weakness. There is now less agency confidence in, and less political consensus around, the ability of consumers, or at least a large proportion of them, to exercise economic power. The traditional focus of price effects makes less sense when services are offered apparently free to the user and supported by advertising. Likewise, there is increasing concern that enhanced market power can cause other harms – less easy to measure, perhaps, but no less serious for all that. This has led some scholars to hark back to the days before the Chicago school consumer welfare orthodoxy and to resurrect a standalone focus on market concentration per se. The intuition here is that markets with a small number of large companies are likely to be less competitive than a market with many small and medium-sized enterprises. This is because tacit coordination is easier to achieve in concentrated markets; foreclosure of new entrants is more feasible; and large firms have greater bargaining power against consumers, suppliers and labour which exacerbates the distributional inequalities already made more acute as a result of the financial crisis and laid bare again during the current economic crisis.

So we are already in the throes of a fundamental debate. We have all been brought up on "big is not bad but big behaving badly is bad" but that consensus is beginning to fracture.

The reason for that is the rise of the new digital economy and more specifically those large platforms with first mover advantage, substantial network effects and a tendency to "winner takes all" outcomes. The recent OECD 230-page paper *Rethinking Antitrust Tools for Multi-Sided Platforms* shows the difficulty in analysing markets with first and second order network effects and magnifying feedback loops.[2] But it is necessary to embrace this kind of analysis to identify properly both when an early market lead might turn into long-term dominance – and when it might not.

To restore confidence in the market economy, we need both strong competition law enforcement and effective consumer protection, so that competition can take place on the merits. The current debates about updating of existing frameworks to deal with the new technology driven economy is desirable but it is worth remembering that there is still much that is good and useful in what we already have.

And what of the wider debate – issues such as the protection of electoral integrity, media plurality and unbiased news journalism; privacy and data ownership; the ownership of critical national infrastructure; environmental factors; maintaining employment; international reciprocity in market opening and opportunities; or the catch-all of the "public interest"?

---

2   OECD, *Rethinking Antitrust Tools for Multi-Sided Platforms* (OECD 2018).

I'm old enough to have practised in the UK when merger control was determined by the "black box" of the public interest test with the agency making recommendations to government on the case and the minister determining the outcome in a two-line decision with no reasons. I would not like to go back to that regime. That said, these broader public policy issues are important and have salience for consumers (and, as importantly, voters) so adequate mechanisms need to be devised for these matters to be addressed. Otherwise there is a perceived "democratic deficit" which calls the legitimacy of the antitrust system into question or, at the very least, diminishes its importance. I appreciate that this is a debate which causes the agencies profound discomfort, but a resilient and relevant antitrust regime for the next generation will need to tackle these concerns. My plea though, would be to avoid the "black box" and to have the politicians set transparent criteria and proper accountability for the consideration of these issues by those with relevant expertise.

Against this background, do you think there are specific sectors or types of business that will likely face challenges or opportunities? Have you seen particular changes over the course of your career that have been particularly illustrative?

Undoubtedly companies operating in the tech space, and particularly tech platforms, will attract greater scrutiny in the coming years. In fact my team has identified at least 22 antitrust authorities that are investigating online platforms at present. And some agencies are already taking steps to propose changes to the law or evidential standards in relation to cases in these markets.

The report published in the UK in March 2019 by an expert panel led by Jason Furman, President Obama's economic adviser, demonstrates the current direction of travel. This report made far-reaching recommendations, including the establishment of a Digital Markets Unit to support greater competition and consumer choice in digital markets. The task list for this new unit includes the development of a principles-based code of competitive conduct to be applied to companies with "strategic market status", including the provision of platform access on "a fair, consistent and transparent basis". Alongside this *ex ante* regulatory approach, there is also a focus on greater personal data mobility and open system standards to increase consumer switching and competition.

This new policy purpose is to be supported with procedural changes to merger control rules to ensure that merger enforcement is more forward-looking and better able to assess technological developments to preserve competition "for the market". This includes mandatory merger control of all intended transactions by companies with "strategic market status" and a "balance of harm" merger standard which weighs up the potential harm from losing a rival or potential rival (including foregone benefits such as innovation, greater privacy protection and the like) against the magnitude and likelihood of potential benefits to consumers (including enhancements to valuable innovation or the increased speed to market of innovative products and services). The report also calls out the need for a market study into digital advertising focusing on the extent to which digital platforms grant preferential treatment to their own business across the value chain and/or act in other ways that are likely to disadvantage competitors.

Many of these themes are also addressed in the expert report for Commissioner Vestager published in April 2019, exploring how competition policy should evolve to "promote pro-consumer innovation" in the digital age. Likewise, the US Federal Trade Commission's hearings on Competition and Consumer Protection in the 21st Century considered collusive, exclusionary and predatory conduct by digital and technology-based platform businesses; and the impact of big data and privacy on competition. Most of theses agencies are still considering what further powers, if any, they will need to equip themselves adequately for the digital age, a debate accelerated by our increasing dependence on online platforms evident during the present pandemic.

A related development is the recognition that industrial leadership increasingly means technological leadership. The complicating factor is that in the past this kind of innovation was typically paid for from defence budgets and for overwhelmingly military applications. Technological leadership in the future will relate to sectors like cloud computing, artificial intelligence, quantum technology, cybersecurity, robotics, semiconductors, the 5G network and data hosting. These technologies have both civil and military application and are largely developed outside the realm of traditional defence procurement. A number of governments are reacting to that change with enhanced merger control reviews in sensitive sectors as well as additional controls on ownership to protect national security.

This debate is also overlaid with the impact of geopolitical fragmentation. My Washington DC partner, Aimen Mir, previously the most senior official in the Committee on Foreign Investment in the United States for nearly a decade, speaks persuasively of the emergence of China as a significant economic actor at the same time as the rise in economic nationalism. The latter phenomenon arises in reaction to a combination of the economic crisis and the perceived detrimental effects of globalism for domestic economies. So one observes increasingly the "national security" criteria eliding with "economic security" with the attendant difficulty of finding the bright line for open investment while simultaneously protecting security and economic interests.

This debate has ignited recently in the EU following the Commission's decision to block the *Siemens/Alstom* transaction. I don't want to get into the specifics of the case as my firm was heavily involved for one of the parties, but there is a debate to be had about how to assess competition on the merits when an important competitor is sheltered from international competitive pressures in a country with no market access for foreign players, including a lack of international access to public procurement opportunities. The Commission concluded on traditional merger control lines on this occasion and would not support the emergence of a single European champion. But the debate rumbles on at the political level as to whether an override is needed to safeguard international industrial competitiveness.

There will certainly be plenty for the agencies to sink their teeth into. Freshfields' recent M&A report showed that digital investment rose to a new high of US$258 billion in 2017 and technology companies counted for nearly half of all deal targets by volume. So it is unsurprising that politicians and competition agencies are keen to ensure that digital merger-related activity should attract detailed scrutiny and critical technologies do not fall into the wrong hands.

As I work at the CMA, I'm particularly interested in how you expect the direction of the CMA's work to change after Brexit. Do you think the focus of the CMA's work and its priorities might change? In your work advising companies, how do you think this might have an impact on your work as well?

I was waiting for a Brexit question! The post-Brexit focus of the CMA can be most easily discerned from the trenchant letter from the former CMA Chairman, Andrew Tyrie, to the Secretary of State in which he states "the central challenge is that… the UK has an analogue system of competition and consumer law in a digital age".[3]

In the short term, the concern has been the impact of the UK's departure from the EU at the end of this year on the continued smooth running of the UK merger control regime, with a substantial and substantive up-tick in cases expected post-Brexit. The CMA has suggested that transactions notifiable elsewhere internationally should be notified to the CMA on a

3   Letter from the Rt Hon Lord Tyrie to the Secretary of State for Business, Energy and Industrial Strategy dated 21 February 2019.

mandatory basis instead of our traditional voluntary approach. Otherwise the "real" work will be done in other jurisdictions, with the CMA not at the negotiation table.

In the somewhat longer term, Lord Tyrie's proposals aimed to refocus the work of the CMA more directly on protecting the interests of consumers and include an overriding statutory duty to treat customer interests as paramount. This was intended to sit alongside augmented tools to allow the CMA to carry out its duties more quickly and effectively and the surrendering of other functions, including criminal cartel enforcement, to concentrate on core responsibilities.

Overall, the proposals were intended to "mark a decisive shift in favour of the consumer and of businesses that behave fairly and competitively and against those businesses that, among other things, take advantage of consumer vulnerability". In so doing, it may very well be the case that the CMA might depart from other agencies internationally. Even if willing to do so, those agencies that do not also have consumer protection powers, may not be in a position to emulate the CMA. Obviously, Lord Tyrie's departure from the CMA has thrown doubt on the extent and timing of these changes but I would expect to see far reaching proposals in the coming months as the government seeks to deliver Brexit and to extricate us from the economic impact of the pandemic.

Vertical restraints, specifically in online markets, have been a focus of regulatory scrutiny over the past few years, and you have led fascinating work in some of these cases on online travel agencies in particular. How have you enjoyed being involved in an area where the market is changing rapidly and the law requires careful assessment? How does this present challenges?

The online travel agency cases across Europe really bring home the need, as stated in *Cartes Bancaires*, to have regard to "the real conditions of the functioning and structure of the markets – of the economic and legal context".[4] Vertical antitrust cases give rise necessarily to a detailed effects-based analysis which has fallen out of fashion in some jurisdictions when compared to the relatively low-hanging fruit of object infringement cases. In the online travel agency cases, it took a number of agencies a long while to work out who had market power in the industry, how competition across distribution channels played out and who was free-riding on whom. It fell to the legislature in a number of countries to step in where the competition authorities declined to tread and we have been left with an unsatisfactory European patchwork of outcomes. I think that the whole affair was salutary for the agencies and I'm keen to see where the consultation on the Vertical Restraints Block Exemption will take us. This is a fascinating area and one to watch.

The UK competition law framework has a market investigations regime. From your work representing SSE on the energy market investigation, do you think this is a useful tool for taking a broad view assessment of the functioning of competition in a particular market?

I don't want to discuss the energy market investigation in particular but I have been involved in a good number of market investigations since the current regime was conceived and can see its attraction to the CMA as it can impose remedies across a sector without having to resort to protracted enforcement action that captures only the protagonists. Also since the individual companies subject to the market investigation are not "in the dock" and remedies are only rarely specifically targeted at particular firms, there has been relatively little legal challenge to the outcomes. It is also noteworthy that the EC Commission is consulting on the need for a similar regime at EU level, which underscores how powerful a tool it can be.

However, the margin of appreciation on substantive matters afforded to the CMA in the Competition Appeals Tribunal does need to be mirrored

---

4   Case T-491/07 *Groupement des cartes bancaires v European Commission* EU:T:2016:379.

by procedural safeguards to ensure a fair hearing, in the broad sense, for those under investigation. I'm increasingly concerned that those safeguards are being eroded by the political need to complete very quickly what are very often complex and often multi-faceted inquiries. Many of the remedies in the energy investigation were directed at unwinding the effects of the no doubt well-intentioned, but in practice misconceived and distortive, measures put in place by the industry regulator in the preceding years; this should be a cautionary tale. In particular, remedies directed at changing consumer behaviour need very careful design and testing (ideally by behavioural economists and psychologists) before being unleashed on the unsuspecting public who may not react at all as an agency might foresee. So there is a fine balance here in getting to the correct diagnosis of the market shortcomings quickly, dealing fairly with the companies under investigation and being seen to do so.

The last few years has seen an explosion in the number of "disruptor" businesses with new and innovative business models. Do you think the antitrust enforcement toolkit is equipped to consider the business challenges these bring?

We live in such interesting times right now, really a new industrial revolution. Many of the businesses we rely on for daily essential services in search, social and other media, holiday bookings, online retailing and the like were not even in existence a couple of decades ago. Turbulent periods of change always bring calls for more government intervention and that's the inflection point we have reached now, the situation brought into sharp relief by the pandemic. We may need to reshape some "analogue" elements for the digital age, and as part of that to have regard to newer considerations such as big data and privacy, but I'm sure that we will all adapt to the challenges that this will bring.

Christine Varney
Cravath, Swaine & Moore
Bojana Ignjatovic

Christine Varney is a partner at Cravath, Swaine & Moore LLP and chairs the firm's antitrust practice. She is the only person to have served as both the US assistant attorney general for antitrust and as a commissioner of the Federal Trade Commission. Ms Varney formulates global antitrust strategy for clients in connection with joint ventures, mergers, acquisitions, dispositions and other business transactions, including advising on business conduct or potential investments to ensure compliance with antitrust laws, securing regulatory approvals and handling antitrust investigations. Her clients span diverse industries, including cable, financial services, manufacturing, pharmaceuticals, retail, transportation, technology and telecommunications.

Bojana Ignjatovic is a partner at RBB Economics, based in London and Brussels. With close to 20 years' experience in competition economics and described in Who's Who Legal as "outstanding" and possessing "superb analytical skills", Bojana has led RBB Economics teams in some of the largest competition law investigations across Europe. Prior to joining RBB in 2007, Bojana worked at the UK Office of Fair Trading (now the Competition and Markets Authority). Bojana has particular expertise in EU merger control: her recent cases include *Alstom/Bombardier*, *Siemens/ Alstom*, *Spirit AeroSystems/Asco*, *Nidec/Embraco* and *Comcast/Sky*. She also has extensive experience on competition law investigations, including on many recent landmark cases, including on MFN clauses in online hotel agents (acting for Booking.com), excessive pricing (advising Pfizer) and loyalty rebates (advising Unilever, MSD).

Should we continue to rely on the consumer welfare standard, which has long underpinned our approach to antitrust?

More and more, news sources, politicians, antitrust enforcers and antitrust legal scholars express concern over the decline in competition in the United States. Some blame the prevailing framework in antitrust since the 1970s – the consumer welfare standard – with failing to adequately protect consumers, resulting in widespread problems caused by increased concentration and dominant firms. However, there is broad consensus among antitrust scholars and practitioners in favour of the consumer welfare standard and, in practice, antitrust enforcement agencies and courts have continued to apply the consumer welfare standard.

The goal of antitrust is to promote competition and, since the 1970s, the consumer welfare standard has been the controlling lens through which antitrust enforcement agencies and courts have gauged the effect of potential anticompetitive behaviour. Consumer welfare is measured through effects on price and output among a variety of other factors, and the standard's goal is to determine whether trading parties on the other side of a market are harmed.

When rivals merge, there is a concern that in a concentrated market, common ownership will diminish competition and facilitate coordination, leading to higher prices, lower product quality or other harms to customers. When rivals have the ability to coordinate price (conscious parallelism), there is a concern that such coordination will lead to higher pricing and other forms of harm to consumers. When dominant firms engage in behaviour that excludes or discriminates against rivals in a way that entrenches their dominance, there is a concern that such behaviour is driven by anticompetitive conduct rather than competition. In each of these forms of conduct – a merger, a cartel or exclusionary conduct – the consumer welfare standard offers a concrete way to measure harm to competition by focusing on the harm to consumers.

Critics of the consumer welfare standard claim that it is narrowly focused on price to the exclusion of other factors, and that this has led to antitrust under-enforcement in the United States. Some critics also claim that the standard is ill-positioned to handle the actions of dominant firms seeking to capture market share where profits are not the primary near-term goal; Google is often named as an example. However, the consumer welfare standard includes a range of factors that benefit consumers besides price, including a focus on the variety and quality of products and the advancement of innovation. The consumer welfare standard offers predictability as well. In this way, the consumer welfare standard has the tools to allow for more aggressive antitrust enforcement to keep markets competitive. Broader problems tied to large corporations such as excessive political power, data misuse, media diversity or other public policy issues are not the concern of antitrust. Whether antitrust enforcers use all the tools at their disposal is a different question.

As an example, focusing on one increasingly concentrated sector – the healthcare system – both antitrust enforcement actions and other regulatory regimes have operated to enhance competition and benefit consumers. Earlier this year, the 8th Circuit agreed with the Federal Trade Commission (FTC) that the merger of the largest healthcare system in the Bismarck – Mandan area of North Dakota, Sanford, with the largest independent multispecialty physician practice in the area, Mid Dakota Clinic, violated Section 7 of the Clayton Act. The court found convincing evidence that the proposed acquisition was likely to cause price increases and to increase significantly Sanford's leverage with insurers, the root cause of price increases, as well as to reduce the incentive to improve quality.

Meanwhile, the National Health Service introduced a policy in 2006 that increased competition among hospitals. When recommending hospital care, it required general practitioners to provide patients with five options, as well as quality data for each. Because hospital payments are fixed

– whichever hospital a patient chooses gets the payment for care provided to that patient – hospitals ended up competing on quality. This resulted in shorter hospital stays and lower mortality.

Critics of the consumer welfare standard also believe that the standard ignores effects on innovation, but between 2004 and 2014 the FTC alleged harm to innovation in almost one-third of challenged mergers. Evaluating the impact of the transaction on innovation, along with price and product quality, is not new. Indeed, the Department of Justice (DOJ) and FTC's 2010 *Horizontal Merger Guidelines* provide that the agencies consider whether a merger is "likely to diminish innovation competition by encouraging the merged firm to curtail its innovative efforts below the level that would prevail in the absence of the merger". Authorities analyse harm to innovation on a case-by-case basis and consider, among other factors, industry-specific elements, such as market concentration, R&D output and innovation efforts, from merging parties and competitors.

For example, the FTC challenged the Nielsen/Arbitron merger on the grounds of harm to innovation. Nielsen offered a leading TV audience measurement service, while Arbitron offered similar services for radio. The FTC claimed that the merger could harm innovation since both companies were developing a cross-platform audience measurement service. The FTC required a divestiture of competitive assets to protect future competition in the market for cross-platform audience measurement, even though the service itself was still in development. The FTC also examined NXP Semiconductors' acquisition of Freescale Semiconductor and the impact it would have on innovation, ultimately requiring divestitures to remedy the anticompetitive effects of the transaction.

The FTC's review of pharmaceutical mergers also highlights a concern with maintaining innovation. In its challenge to Sanofi's acquisition of Aventis in 2004, the FTC acted to protect potential competition for drugs used to treat excessive blood clot formation. Aventis's Lovenox product had a 90% market share. Sanofi marketed the competing drug, Arixtra, but was also pursuing FDA approval for new indications, which were expected to increase the drug's competitive significance. The FTC challenged the transaction and negotiated a remedy that required Sanofi to divest Arixtra in order to preserve the potential benefits of the new indications. The FTC has recently challenged or required divestitures in several mergers alleging harm to innovation.[1]

Another criticism of the consumer welfare standard is that it ignores buyer power and monopsony concerns since the standard is based on the assumption that lower consumer prices are the goal to be achieved. Some also argue that "consumer" welfare only protects consumers. A labour monopsonist will, by definition, reduce its costs by paying less for labour, often resulting in lower prices for consumers. Some critics claim that focusing on market output (or quantity) might be a better fit for analysing labour monopsony. However, applying the consumer welfare standard means that a merger is judged to be anticompetitive if it disrupts the competitive process and harms trading parties on the other side of the market. The FTC staff investigating Staples's acquisition of Essendant considered whether the combined firm would be able to exercise monopsony power against office supply product manufacturers, concluding it would not.

Calls to abandon the consumer welfare standard in antitrust, while well-intentioned, have not offered a concrete alternative approach that

---

1 For example, on 2 January 2020, Illumina and Pacific Biosciences (PacBio) terminated their planned merger after the FTC said it would block the deal, alleging that Illumina was unlawfully seeking to maintain its monopoly in the US market for next-generation DNA sequencing systems by eliminating potential competition from PacBio. The FTC's action came two months after the UK's Competition and Markets Authority, on 24 October 2019 issued provisional findings concluding that the merger will result in a significant loss of competition between Illumina and PacBio. In addition, Bristol Myers Squibb (BMS) completed its acquisition of Celgene in November 2019 after the FTC required that Celgene divest its psoriasis treatment in order to preserve BMS's incentive to continue developing its own psoriasis product. FTC Chairman Joseph Simons stated that "the antitrust laws protect not only competition today, but competition in the future, especially when it comes to the development of new treatments for chronic conditions." See FTC Press Release, "FTC Requires Bristol-Myers Squibb Company and Celgene Corporation to Divest Psoriasis Drug Otezla as a Condition of Acquisition" (15 November 2019) <https://www.ftc.gov/news-events/press-releases/2019/11/ftc-requires-bristol-myers-squibb-company-celgene-corporation>.

is sustainable within existing law and precedent. I believe that the consumer welfare standard is, for the time being, an appropriate approach to analysing transactions.

Has antitrust enforcement become more politicised? What are your views on how those political pressures can best be resisted?

The modern consumer welfare standard, as described above, is a consistent and reliable framework for antitrust law and enforcement. However, proponents of populist antitrust policies – often called "Neo-Brandeisians" – assert the need to fundamentally reshape how we apply competition laws in order to combat "bigness". The effort to enforce antitrust laws more expansively and to move beyond current precedent contains all the elements of a political debate.

Although the populist position is now prominent in the central discourse, the antitrust agencies largely appear to be resisting changes to the consumer welfare approach and to the economic methods used to assess conduct under that standard. At the FTC's 2018 hearings on antitrust and consumer protection, FTC chairman Joseph Simons cited recent criticism of the consumer welfare standard as one of the primary challenges that the hearings were meant to address. Prior to the hearings, FTC commissioner Rohit Chopra (one of the FTC's two Democratic members) published a comment letter proposing that the FTC use its rule-making authority to bolster antitrust enforcement. More recently, at an antitrust symposium, FTC commissioner Christine Wilson presented her view that the total welfare standard has received too little attention. Total welfare would seek to measure the effect of a practice or transaction on the economic welfare of all participants in a market, including both producers and consumers. The standard also attempts to credit efficiencies to a greater degree.

Despite these statements, the commissioners, including Simons, as well as Makan Delrahim, head of the DOJ's Antitrust Division, have expressed support for an economics-driven approach to enforcement and recognised the importance of the consumer welfare standard. Delrahim publicly remarked on 12 June 2018 at an Open Markets Institute Event that "we don't need to go beyond the consumer welfare standard, because it can get the job done on its own" and that "there are serious risks to democracy in abandoning the consumer welfare standard." More recently, Delrahim stated in an article published by Competition Policy International that "the consumer welfare standard offers several effective features that protect competition despite changing circumstances", noting that the consumer welfare standard is flexible, consistent and predictable, avoids muddling competition with other values, and incentivises innovation.[2]

Legislators, on the other hand, have made proposals that would ease the government's burden when seeking to prohibit a transaction. For example, the Consolidation Prevention and Competition Promotion Act of 2017 introduced by Senator Amy Klobuchar, the ranking Democrat on the Antitrust Subcommittee, would amend Section 7 of the Clayton Act to lower the standard of proof for an agency to block a merger from a "substantial" to a "material" lessening of competition and to require the largest mergers to prove that there is no "material" lessening of competition, shifting the burden of proof from the antitrust agencies. Had the "larger merger" provision been in effect previously, it would have applied to such recent mergers as Amazon/Whole Foods, AT&T/Time Warner and Disney/21st Century Fox. Despite this proposal and others, there does not yet appear to be any consensus for enacting new antitrust standards.

President Trump has often made public statements that echo populist antitrust rhetoric. He has promised to break up companies that he considers

2   "CPI Talks… with Makan Delrahim", *CPI Antitrust Chronicle* (September 2019) <https://www.competitionpolicyinternational.com/wp-content/uploads/2019/09/CPI-Talks-Delrahim.pdf>.

to be too large and to have too much political influence, such as the *AT&T/Time Warner* transaction. Nevertheless, the courts did not agree with the DOJ that the *AT&T/Time Warner* merger would be anticompetitive.

Ultimately, antitrust enforcers should use the existing legal framework to challenge mergers that result in a substantial lessening of competition. While close antitrust scrutiny is appropriate for today's largest and most powerful firms, proper antitrust enforcement should continue to focus on harm to consumers and disruption of the competitive process. It seems unlikely that current leadership at the agencies will veer from enforcing the consumer welfare standard. Antitrust enforcement has a vital role to play in keeping markets competitive, but antitrust law and antitrust institutions are ill-suited to remedying the important concerns associated with the political power of large corporations or other public policy goals, such as income inequality or job creation.

Is competition law in danger of becoming an instrument of trade policy?

There have been increasing claims that competition law is becoming an instrument of trade policy. For example, many blame recent trade tension between the United States and China for causing the demise of Broadcom's bid for Qualcomm in 2018.

In March 2018, President Trump blocked Broadcom's US$117 billion bid for Qualcomm, citing national security concerns. At the time, Broadcom was a Singapore-based manufacturer and supplier of semiconductors and software solutions, but China was the main concern that drove President Trump's decision to block the deal. In a presidential order, President Trump said that "credible evidence" had led him to believe that if Broadcom were to acquire control of Qualcomm, it "might take action that threatens to impair the national security of the United States". At the time, the Committee on Foreign Investment in the United States had advised President Trump that if the deal went through, Huawei and other

Chinese telecommunications companies could displace Qualcomm as leaders in developing 5G cellular network technology. The government's concern seemed to be that Qualcomm would be less innovative under Broadcom's control, since Broadcom was known for buying companies and holding on to only their most profitable units, which likely would not include its costly and time-intensive R&D.

The unusual decision to stop a merger raised questions about the extent to which the Trump administration was willing to intervene in a proposed merger. Although a presidential action against foreign investment in an American company is rare and has reportedly only taken place four times in the past 30 years, I do not view this as an instance of competition law being used as an instrument of trade policy – this was a case of legitimate national security issues determining the US government's response to a proposed transaction.

Recently, China's antitrust regulatory authority (SAMR) has closely monitored Diodes Inc's proposed acquisition of Lite-On Semiconductor Corp. The former is a US manufacturer and supplier of semiconductors, and the latter is Taiwanese with a Shanghai-based affiliate. Concerns have been raised by industrial associations representing Chinese smartphone suppliers that if SAMR does not stop the deal, a Chinese-affiliated semiconductor company will become an American one. This reflects growing scrutiny of American M&A efforts in China, and appears to be a reaction to rejections of Chinese efforts to acquire and do business with US companies, such as ZTE, a Chinese smartphone and telecommunications company that was temporarily banned from purchasing parts from US companies.

How crucial a role do you think market definition should play in merger assessment? Is defining the relevant market a critical step in merger analysis?

Market definition continues to play a crucial role in merger analysis. Defining the relevant market in a merger analysis provides a way to understand a proposed merger's likely competitive effects. In this regard, my views align with those expressed in the 2010 *Horizontal Merger Guidelines*: "The measurement of market shares and market concentration is not an end in itself, but is useful to the extent it illuminates the merger's likely competitive effects." Or, as Herbert Hovenkamp has written more colourfully, "prediction of harmful price increases is the dog, and market definition but the tail".[3]

Market definition is, of course, not the only tool available to evaluate a proposed merger's likely competitive effects. For example, in the initial proposed *Staples/Office Depot* merger, the FTC could show that Staples already charged higher prices in markets where it faced no competition from Office Depot. In that case, market definition was not required to show that the merger would likely increase office supply prices. More recently, economists and antitrust commentators have developed additional tests to evaluate a merger's likely competitive effects without resorting to market definition, such as Joseph Farrell and Carl Shapiro's upward pricing pressure (UPP) test. These approaches, which assess direct effects on competition, are not incompatible with market definition in a merger analysis. As the 2010 *Horizontal Merger Guidelines* acknowledge, such direct evidence can help shape the definition of a relevant market. Even in the *Staples/Office Depot* merger, defining the relevant market was essential for determining what types of retailers might counteract the merger's likely effect on prices. Market definition, unilateral effects tests (like the UPP) and even potential new economic approaches can together provide a more complete understanding of a merger's potential effects on competition.

In contrast, when litigating, defining the relevant market for a proposed merger is still essential. Some commentators have criticised market definition and advocate for only employing approaches that show direct

---

3   Herbert Hovenkamp, "Markets in Merger Analysis" [2012] 57 Antitrust Bull. 887, 914.

competitive effects. Regardless of the truth of these critiques, antitrust lawyers litigating merger cases should continue to rely on market definition for two primary reasons. First, even though new analytical tools are available, lawyers, competition agencies and courts are comfortable and have experience with evaluating mergers based on concentration in the relevant market. Second, and perhaps more importantly, there is no reason to abandon a useful and tested tool for evaluating competitive effects.

Following on from AT&T/Time Warner, what role do you think behavioural remedies can and should play in resolving vertical merger concerns?

I am a firm believer that it would be a mistake for competition regulators to fail to consider behavioural remedies when resolving vertical merger concerns. Current officials at the US competition agencies have a preference for structural remedies in the context of vertical mergers, but they generally do not discard behavioural solutions in tandem with structural solutions to protect against consumer harm. Opting only for structural remedies deprives regulators of a useful tool for addressing potential consumer harm from vertical mergers.

There are reasons for competition agencies to prefer structural remedies, such as the certainty they bring and the speed at which they can be achieved. But it is easy to overstate these benefits, in particular, the lower administrative costs associated with structural remedies. For example, behavioural remedies achieved through arbitration agreements, like the ones from both the *AT&T/Time Warner* merger and the Comcast/NBCU joint venture, demonstrate that such remedies can address competitive concerns without making the agencies responsible for the long-term monitoring of firms' day-to-day business.

While the *Comcast/NBCU* deal raised concerns that the joint venture could reduce competition by charging higher prices to Comcast's video distribution competitors, it also promised to increase innovation and consumer access to video programming on several platforms. By requiring "baseball-style" arbitration to determine content-pricing when video distributors and the joint venture failed to agree, the settlement's behavioural remedy offered a solution tailored to address precisely the potential harms and preserve the benefits.

For the *AT&T/Time Warner* merger, AT&T put in place a similar remedy to address concerns that it would raise prices of Time Warner content to harm rival video distributors. While the DOJ filed suit to block the merger, despite AT&T's self-imposed behavioural remedy, both the US District Court for the District of Columbia and the DC Circuit stressed in their rulings that AT&T's baseball arbitration offer provided a behavioural mechanism that addressed the vertical merger's potential harm. While arbitration agreements will not always provide an appropriate remedy, behavioural remedies, in general, provide competition agencies with an approach that enables them to negotiate flexible and tailored remedies.

Online privacy: what is the right balance between self-regulation, *ex ante* regulation and antitrust?

An increasingly important question is where does antitrust law fit in when consumer privacy is at stake? There have been calls for increased antitrust enforcement of "big data" and associated privacy issues – defined as people's ability to control the terms under which their personal information is acquired and used – and some believe that this area is a major challenge to society and competition law in the United States. Most large US technology companies require consumers to waive all rights to their data with a single consent box and a great deal of fine print. A report from McKinsey Global Institute estimates that big data could generate an additional US$3 trillion in value every year in just seven industries and, of this, US$1.3 trillion would benefit the United States. Data collection has many procompetitive effects, such as producing new goods and services, optimising business processes, producing targeted marketing, improving organisational management and improving innovation. However, there is also a concern that large technology companies will use their dominant position to collect and use data in anticompetitive ways, and that personal data will not be protected in the process.

US regulators tend to view competition and consumer privacy as distinct issues, but regulators abroad are increasingly viewing some privacy abuses as inextricably linked to market power. Although the concern that companies with market power have access to voluminous data is arguably a separate issue, it is also a facet of the same problem as data privacy since much of the data being collected involves sensitive consumer information, such as health and financial data. Antitrust may be concerned with data that is not available to potential entrants in the market and therefore push for data access, data portability and data standardisation. However, consumer protection concerns about the unintended uses of the data may lead to a push for the consumer to have a right to restrict how their data is used, which could impact competition by reducing a potential entrant's access and portability to data.

On the consumer privacy side, there has long been a debate as to whether self-regulation or government regulation is needed. Self-regulation is based on the three traditional components of government – legislation, enforcement and adjudication – and these functions are carried out by the private sector rather than the government. In the 1990s and through the mid-2000s, the FTC adopted a policy that embraced the idea that self-regulation is the least intrusive and most efficient means to ensure fair information practices online. Fast forward to 2019 – the FTC just approved a US$5 billion settlement of its investigation into Facebook's privacy practices in the wake of the Cambridge Analytica controversy, which involved collection of personal information of 50 million Facebook users without their consent as part of a political influence campaign.

Still, many believe that such a levy is insufficient to deter powerful technology companies and that what is needed are strong, clear rules to protect consumers.

Europe has recently taken charge by implementing a comprehensive framework regulating how companies protect EU citizens' personal data with the General Data Protection Regulation (GDPR). There is also country-specific enforcement of privacy laws in Europe. A central element of Europe's new regulations is that companies must clearly explain how data is collected and used. The United States, in contrast, currently has a patchwork of federal, state and industry-specific enforcement, which generates some heterogeneity within the country. Europe's experience is being closely watched by US policymakers, who are considering a new federal privacy law.

In January 2019, the French data protection authority (CNIL) fined Google €50 million for not properly disclosing to users how data is collected across its services – including its search engine, Google Maps and YouTube – to present personalised advertisements. The CNIL said that Google's practices obscured how its services "can reveal important parts of [users'] private life since they are based on a huge amount of data, a wide variety of services and almost unlimited possible combinations". The penalty was the largest to date under the GDPR.

In February 2019, Germany's Federal Cartel Office – the Bundeskartellamt – ruled that Facebook was exploitatively and illegally forcing users to agree to the collection of data from third-party sites in order to use Facebook's core service. It is reported that the Bundeskartellamt worked closely with German data protection authorities during its Facebook investigation. This was the first well-known investigation in Europe clearly bridging the topics of antitrust and data protection. However, upon Facebook's appeal, a German court granted Facebook a temporary injunction and ordered the suspensive effect of the Facebook complaint (i.e., Facebook would not need to implement the decision within the 12-month period set by the German agency), expressing criticism of the agency's ruling since granting an injunction requires a finding that an annulment of the decision is predominantly probable.

The European Commission has analysed antitrust implications of large datasets, whether in merger review – e.g., *Facebook/WhatsApp, Microsoft/ LinkedIn* and *Apple/Shazam* – or, more recently, in abuse of dominance review with the opening of a formal investigation into Amazon to assess whether Amazon's use of sensitive data from independent retailers who sell on its marketplace is in breach of EU competition rules.

Since September 2018, the FTC has held a series of public hearings on Competition and Consumer Protection in the 21st Century. There, the former director of the Bureau of Consumer Protection admitted that big data was a growing problem and that there are no laws that really deal with this aggregation of data. However, current antitrust analysis accounts for how firms compete using data. Data markets and sets are highly differentiated, and each investigation looks closely at the specific facts of the case. In October 2018, the attorneys general of a dozen states submitted comments in response to the FTC raising concerns about possible long-term anticompetitive harms arising from the aggregation of big data by a small number of dominant platforms, including data that implicates consumers' privacy interests. The AGs stated their support for the consumer welfare standard to protect competition in the context of big data and data privacy. In July 2019, the DOJ announced its review into whether and how market-leading online platforms have achieved market power and are engaging in practices that have reduced competition, stifled innovation or otherwise harmed consumers. It has been reported that Amazon, Apple, Facebook and Google are all potential targets of the DOJ's review. In remarks given by US Deputy Attorney General Jeffrey Rosen at the American Bar Association's 2019 Antitrust Fall Forum on 18 November 2019, Rosen discussed the DOJ's review, stating that "in a relatively short amount of time, [online platforms] have disrupted industries, amassed substantial economic power, and developed business models that monetise potentially sensitive consumer information that they control." However, he noted that "we do not view antitrust laws as a panacea for every problem in the digital world. Indeed, we will not ignore any harms caused by online platforms that partially or completely fall outside the antitrust laws. We are keeping in mind other tools in areas such as privacy, consumer protection, and public safety as part of a broader review of online platforms."

Although it is unclear at this point whether the US antitrust framework is equipped to handle or even should handle a privacy – antitrust hybrid approach to big data, such questions are currently being discussed in public discourse. Striking the right balance between regulating both the privacy and competition aspects of data aggregation is important since data aggregation enables competition and innovation, and privacy regulation can either stifle competition if it is too strict or reduce access to consumer data if it is so lax that consumers distrust companies and withhold access. Certain consumer data must be regulated by distinct regulatory systems, such as health and financial information, given the heightened sensitivity of such information. Ultimately, there is a middle ground where the sensitivity of data intersects with the importance of innovation and competition, as well as the concerns about the competitive advance of having access to big data, and it is at that intersection that antitrust authorities might play a greater role in analysing consumer privacy and competition.

Do you think that the regulators have the right balance in the emphasis placed on internal documents, relative to market or economic evidence?

Regulators view the totality of information available in analysing whether conduct is anticompetitive or whether a merger will create an anticompetitive effect. In general, they want to see the three baskets of evidence – documentary, testimonial and economic – pointing in the same direction.

Documentary evidence consists of internal business documents. Testimonial evidence consists of statements from the merging firms as well as statements from customers and competitors. Finally, economic evidence is gathered from the firms and their competitors.

Regulators should only conclude that conduct is anticompetitive if all three baskets of evidence demonstrate that the behaviour in question results in anticompetitive effects. Of course, there are cases where one basket of evidence is stronger than the others. In such cases, the competition agencies should consider the weight of the evidence in order to reach a decision.

For example, in the AT&T/Time Warner merger litigation, the DOJ believed it had presented strong testimonial evidence of the merger's likely competitive harms from competitors. This testimonial evidence, however, could not sway either the district court or court of appeals to block the merger when the DOJ's economic and documentary evidence was found to be lacking.

If you had to pick one case in your illustrious career as being the most rewarding experience, which would you choose and why?

My most rewarding experience was representing Netscape in *United States v Microsoft Corp.*, 253 F.3d 34 (D.C. Cir. 2001). In that case, the government had sued Microsoft pursuant to Sections 1 and 2 of the Sherman Act, alleging monopolisation and anticompetitive conduct – namely that Microsoft was illegally tying their Windows operating system to its web browser, Internet Explorer. At the time, my client, Netscape, offered competing web browsers and we argued that Microsoft's bundling of its operating system with its web browser impermissibly restrained competition. We consequently urged the DOJ to investigate and sue Microsoft for their anticompetitive conduct. We also met with the DOJ and successfully contested Microsoft's claim that its Windows operating system would not work with web browsers other than Internet Explorer.

Since then, *United States v Microsoft Corp.* has been used as precedent by the DOJ for pursuing enforcement of Section 2 of the Sherman Act. Specifically, the case has been used to establish how the DOJ analyses perceived procompetitive and anticompetitive effects from a dominant firm's conduct and determines whether these effects harm competition and consumers.

What are the main insights about private practice you learned from public service and vice versa?

One of the main insights I have acquired through my career in the public sector has been the importance of being straightforward and credible. During my time at the DOJ and the FTC, I often found that I was most receptive to parties' arguments when they were honest and direct with the agency in providing requested information and had reasonable requests. Similarly, now in private practice, I have had significant success by being straightforward and reasonable with regulators. It is incredibly important to always maintain your credibility in your work. Professional relationships rely indispensably on credibility, honesty and consistency, and my advice to clients is always supported by this foundation.

My practice today largely focuses on mergers and acquisitions and, in that context, clients need to have reasonable and realistic information and advice in dealings with the antitrust agencies as well as their stakeholders. I have the benefit of understanding how both agencies think about antitrust markets and economic analysis, and this insight has proven to be invaluable for my clients in private practice when given the right context and risk assessment.

What is the one piece of advice you would give to young women starting out in competition law today?

I would advise young women starting out in competition law to work for good people. Looking back at my career, I have been very lucky to work with people who were invested in my growth and development. As the legal field becomes increasingly competitive, it is important to find mentors and sponsors who will take an interest in your career, provide you with growth opportunities and support you. I also believe strongly in mentoring the young women around me – don't pull the ladder up once you have arrived. Finally, in addition to working with good people, I have also found it important to have an understanding and encouraging life partner. My husband has been incredibly supportive throughout the various stages of my career and has always been my biggest cheerleader. I advise all young women, choose your life partner well. In the end, that matters more than anything else.

Concurrences
Competition Laws Review

Concurrences Review

Concurrences is a print and online quarterly peer reviewed journal dedicated to EU and national competitions laws. It has been launched in 2004 as the flagship of the Institute of Competition Law in order to provide a forum for academics, practitioners and enforcers. Concurrences'influence and expertise has garnered interviews with such figures as Christine Lagarde, Bill Kovacic, Emmanuel Macron and Margarethe Vestager.

CONTENTS

More than 12,000 articles, print and/or online. Quarterly issues provide current coverage with contributions from the EU or national or foreign countries thanks to more than 1,500 authors in Europe and abroad. Approximately 35 % of the contributions are published in English, 65 % in French, as the official language of the General Court of justice of the EU; all contributions have English abstracts.

FORMAT

In order to balance academic contributions with opinions or legal practice notes, Concurrences provides its insight and analysis in a number of formats:

- Forewords: Opinions by leading academics or enforcers
- Interviews: Interviews of antitrust experts
- On-Topics: 4 to 6 short papers on hot issues
- Law & Economics: Short papers written by economists for a legal audience
- Articles: Long academic papers
- Case Summaries: Case commentary on EU and French case law
- Legal Practice: Short papers for in-house counsels
- International: Medium size papers on international policies
- Books Review: Summaries of recent antitrust books
- Articles Review: Summaries of leading articles published in 45 antitrust journals

BOARDS

The Scientific Committee is headed by Laurence Idot, Professor at Panthéon Assas University. The International Committee is headed by Frederic Jenny, OECD Competition Comitteee Chairman. Boards members include Bruno Lasserre, Mario Monti, Howard Shelanski, Richard Whish, Wouter Wils, etc.

ONLINE VERSION

Concurrences website provides all articles published since its inception, in addition to selected articles published online only in the electronic supplement.

WRITE FOR CONCURRENCES

Concurrences welcome spontaneous contributions. Except in rare circumstances, the journal accepts only unpublished articles, whatever the form and nature of the contribution. The Editorial Board checks the form of the proposals, and then submits these to the Scientific Committee. Selection of the papers is conditional to a peer review by at least two members of the Committee. Within a month, the Committee assesses whether the draft article can be published and notifies the author.

e-Competitions Bulletin

CASE LAW DATABASE

e-Competitions is the only online resource that provides consistent coverage of antitrust cases from 55 jurisdictions, organized into a searchable database structure. e-Competitions concentrates on cases summaries taking into account that in the context of a continuing growing number of sources there is a need for factual information, i.e., case law.

- 15,000 case summaries
- 3,000 authors
- 85 countries covered
- 30,000 subscribers

SOPHISTICATED EDITORIAL AND IT ENRICHMENT

e-Competitions is structured as a database. The editors make a sophisticated technical and legal work on all articles by tagging these with key words, drafting abstracts and writing html code to increase Google ranking. There is a team of antitrust lawyers – PhD and judges clerks - and a team of IT experts. e-Competitions makes comparative law possible. Thanks to this expert editorial work, it is possible to search and compare cases by jurisdiction, legal topics or business sectors.

PRESTIGIOUS BOARDS

e-Competitions draws upon highly distinguished editors, all leading experts in national or international antitrust. Advisory Board Members include: Sir Christopher Bellamy, Ioanis Lianos (UCL), Eleanor Fox (NYU), Damien Géradin (Tilburg University), Fred Jenny (OECD), Jacqueline Riffault-Silk (Cour de cassation), Wouter Wils (DG COMP / King's College London), etc.

LEADING PARTNERS

- Association of European Competition Law Judges: The AECLJ is a forum for judges of national Courts specializing in antitrust case law. Members timely feed e-Competitions with just released cases.

- Academics partners: Antitrust research centres from leading universities write regularly in e-Competitions: University College London, King's College London, Queen Mary University, etc.

- Law firms: Global law firms and antitrust niche firms write detailed cases summaries specifically for e-Competitions: Allen & Overy, Baker McKenzie, Cleary Gottlieb Steen & Hamilton, Jones Day, Norton Rose Fulbright, Skadden, White & Case, etc.

The Institute of Competition Law

The Institute of Competition Law is a publishing company, founded in 2004 by Dr. Nicolas Charbit, based in Paris, London and NewYork. The Institute cultivates scholarship and discussion about antitrust issues though publications and conferences. Each publication and event is supervised by editorial boards and scientific or steering committees to ensure independence, objectivity, and academic rigor. Thanks to this management, the Institute has become one of the few think tanks in Europe to have significant influence on antitrust policies.

AIM

The Institute focuses government, business and academic attention on a broad range of subjects which concern competition laws, regulations and related economics.

BOARDS

To maintain its unique focus, the Institute relies upon highly distinguished editors, all leading experts in national or international antitrust: Bill Kovacic, Mario Monti, Eleanor Fox, Laurence Idot, Fred Jenny, Ioannis Lianos, Richard Whish, etc.

AUTHORS

3,800 authors, from 55 jurisdictions.

PARTNERS

- Universities: University College London, King's College London, Queen Mary University, Paris Sorbonne Panthéon-Assas, etc.

- Law firms: Allen & Overy, Cleary Gottlieb Steen & Hamilton, Baker McKenzie, Hogan Lovells, Jones Day, Norton Rose Fulbright, Skadden Arps, White & Case, etc.

EVENTS

More than 350 events since 2004 in Brussels, London, New York, Paris, Singapore and Washington, DC.

ONLINE VERSION

Concurrences website provides all articles published since its inception.

PUBLICATIONS

The Institute publishes Concurrences Review, a print and online quarterly peer-reviewed journal dedicated to EU and national competitions laws. e-Competitions is a bi-monthly antitrust news bulletin covering 85 countries. The e-Competitions database contains over 15,000 case summaries from 3,000 authors.

15 years of archives
27,000 articles

4 DATABASES

Concurrences Review
Access to latest issue and archives

- 12,000 articles from 2004 to the present
- European and national doctrine and case law

e-Competitions Bulletin
Access to latest issue and archives

- 15,000 case summaries from 1911 to the present
- Case law of 85 jurisdictions

Conferences
**Access to the documentation
of all Concurrences events**

- 350 conferences (Brussels, Hong Kong, London, New York, Paris, Washington DC)
- 250 PowerPoint presentations, proceedings and syntheses
- 450 videos
- Verbatim reports

e-Books
Access to all Concurrences books

- 34 e-Books available
- PDF version

NEW

New search engine
Optimized results to save time

- Search results sorted by date, jurisdiction, keyword, economic sector, author, etc.

New modes of access
IP address recognition

- No need to enter codes: immediate access
- No need to change codes when your team changes: offers increased security and saves time

Mobility

- Responsive design: site optimized for tablets and smartphones

See also: Women & Antitrust - Voices from the Field, Vol. I

In this first volume of Women & Antitrust, leading competition professionals from around the world present reflections and forecasts on topical issues in antitrust and competition law and policy. Nestled among the exchanges are insights into the professional paths of the women interviewed. Through personal anecdotes, they share perspectives on their chosen roles, if and how gender has informed their career choices, and offer advice to young practitioners interested in joining this field.

This volume has been published in cooperation with W@Competition.

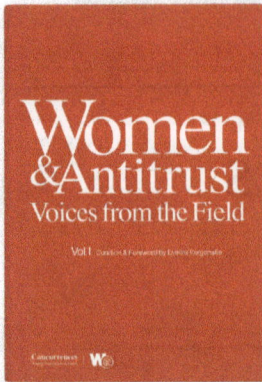

Foreword by Evelina Kurgonaite

Curation & Foreword by **Evelina Kurgonaite**

Evelina Kurgonaite is the founder and chair of "Women At" (W@) – a platform that connects and promotes women professionals around the world. She also leads W@ Competition – a W@ branch dedicated to women in antitrust.

> ❝ *Congratulations on the important initiative and presentation of Women & Antitrust: Voices from the Field. Indeed, over the past years, we have seen the "glass ceiling" breaking with the increasing role of women in the global competition bar. This is noticeable not only in law firms, but also at the enforcement level, whether in Europe, the United States or in Asia. Some competition authorities are led by women – in the US, the EC, and France, among others. Many important agency positions are held by highly experienced women. In companies, competition departments of legal divisions have seen an increasing number of women taking leading roles. Similarly, at both the partner and associate levels of European, Asian and US law firms, a significant number of women are now practicing competition law. Concurrences, in partnership with W@Competition, is taking an initiative by sharing the reflections and forecasts of the reality of this world. Again, congratulations.* ❞

Jacques Buhart, Partner, McDermott Will & Emery

DETAILS

Pages : 306
Price : 35 € - 40 $ - 30 £
ISBN : 978-1-939007-89-6

Send your order to

Institut de droit de la concurrence
19 avenue Jean Aicard
75011 Paris

Institute of Competition Law
61 - 63 Rochester Place
NW1 9JU - London

Institute of Competition Law
106 W 32nd St - Suite 144
10001 - New York

ORDER

Full Name: ⊔⊔⊔⊔⊔⊔⊔⊔⊔⊔⊔⊔⊔⊔⊔⊔⊔⊔⊔⊔⊔⊔⊔
e-mail: ⊔⊔⊔⊔⊔⊔⊔⊔⊔⊔⊔⊔⊔⊔⊔⊔⊔⊔⊔⊔⊔⊔⊔⊔
Institution: ⊔⊔⊔⊔⊔⊔⊔⊔⊔⊔⊔⊔⊔⊔⊔⊔⊔⊔⊔⊔⊔
Street: ⊔⊔⊔⊔⊔⊔⊔⊔⊔⊔⊔⊔⊔⊔⊔⊔⊔⊔⊔⊔⊔⊔⊔
City: ⊔⊔⊔⊔⊔⊔⊔⊔⊔⊔⊔⊔⊔⊔⊔⊔⊔⊔⊔⊔⊔⊔⊔
Zip Code: ⊔⊔⊔⊔⊔⊔⊔⊔⊔⊔⊔⊔⊔⊔⊔⊔⊔⊔⊔⊔
Country: ⊔⊔⊔⊔⊔⊔⊔⊔⊔⊔⊔⊔⊔⊔⊔⊔⊔⊔⊔⊔⊔⊔

www.concurrences.com
book@concurrences.com

Concurrences
Antitrust Publications & Events